Enter other Correction Symbols in this column as your instructor may direct	
	ab = 11
	ad = 4
	agr = 6
	ap = 15
	ca = 5
	cap = 9 Capitals
	coh = 25 Coherence in general
	cs == 3 Comma Splice
	d=19-22 Diction
	e = 20 Exactness
	ef=23-30 Effectiveness in the Sentence
	emp = 29 Emphasis
	frag = 2 Fragment
	g = 19 Good Use ~ Glossary
	gr = 1-7 Grammar
	grt = 1 Grammatical Terms
	ital = 10 Italics
	k == Awkward. Recast
	let = 34 Letters
	lib = 33 Library and Term Paper
	m = 8-11 Mechanics
	ms = 8 Manuscript Form and Revision
	o = 13 Superfluous Commas
	p = 12-17 Punctuation
	plan=32 Planning the Whole Composition
	pv = 27 Point of View
	ref = 28 Reference of Pronouns
	sp = 18 Spelling
	sub=24 Subordination
	t == 7 Tense
	u == 23 Unity and Logical Thinking
	var = 30 Variety
	w = 21 Wordiness
	x == Obvious Error. Correct it.
	∧ = 22 Omission of Words
	// = 26 Parallelism
	¶ = 31 Paragraph
	no ¶ == No Paragraph
	,/ = 12 Comma
	;/ = 14 Semicolon
	ʺ⁄ = 16 Quotation Marks
	./ ?/ !/ :/ -/ ()/ []/= 17 Period and Other Marks

Harbrace Handbook of English

JOHN C. HODGES
The University of Tennessee

The English Workshop Series

HARCOURT, BRACE AND COMPANY

NEW YORK   1951   CHICAGO

ENGLISH WORKSHOP SERIES

WARRINER'S HANDBOOK OF ENGLISH
(Grades Nine and Ten)

HARBRACE HANDBOOK OF ENGLISH
(Grades Eleven and Twelve)

ENGLISH WORKSHOP: GRADE NINE

ENGLISH WORKSHOP: GRADE TEN

ENGLISH WORKSHOP: GRADE ELEVEN

ENGLISH WORKSHOP: GRADE TWELVE

TO THE STUDENT

Numbers or Symbols. A number (or a symbol) written in the margin of your theme calls for a correction. If a number is used, turn directly to the boldface number at the top of the page. If a symbol is used, first consult the alphabetical list of symbols on the inside cover to find the number to which you should turn.

Ordinary References. The ordinary reference will be to one of the thirty-four boldface numbers (or symbols) standing at the head of the thirty-four sections of the handbook. Study the section to which you are referred — the whole of the section if necessary — until you understand thoroughly the correction that should be made. The rule in large boldface at the beginning of each section covers the section as a whole. Usually you will need to search further, to find the rule in smaller boldface that treats more specifically the error you have made, and then to master the method of correction there explained. An *ex* written by your instructor after a number calls also for the writing out of the appropriate exercise.

Specific References. Whenever your instructor wishes to refer you to a specific part of a section, he will add the appropriate letter to the boldface number (or symbol).

EXAMPLES 2a (*or* frag–a), 18b (*or* sp–b), 28d (*or* ref–d), etc.

General References. Sometimes your instructor may give you a very general reference from which you are to determine and correct your error. For example, the symbol **gr** will refer you to the whole division on GRAMMAR, including sections **1–7**; the symbol **m** to the division on MECHANICS, sections **8–11**; the symbol **p** to the division on

PUNCTUATION, sections 12–17; and so forth. An obvious error may be called to your attention by the symbol **x**, and general awkwardness by the symbol **k**.

Supplementary Help. Some of the principles treated in English handbooks can be mastered only by students who understand the fundamentals of the sentence. A well-developed sentence sense is especially helpful in the mastery of sections 2 (Sentence Fragment), 3 (Comma Splice), 4 (Adjectives and Adverbs), 6 (Agreement), 12 (The Comma), 14 (The Semicolon), 24 (Subordination), 25 (Coherence), 26 (Parallelism), and 30 (Variety). If you have difficulty in understanding these sections, you should first master the fundamentals of the sentence treated in section 2e (Sentence Sense), and then turn again to the principle immediately involved. If you fail to understand any term of grammar used in the handbook, consult the alphabetical list in section 1 (Grammatical Terms).

Revision. After you have mastered the principle under-lying the correction of each error, you should make careful revision in the manner prescribed by your instructor. One method of revision is explained in section 8 (Manuscript Form and Revision).

CONTENTS

GRAMMAR

CONTENTS

CONTENTS

CONTENTS

MECHANICS

CONTENTS

CONTENTS

xiii

CONTENTS

SPELLING

DICTION

CONTENTS

CONTENTS

CONTENTS

CONTENTS

GRAMMAR

GRAMMATICAL TERMS

1. Consult the following list as needed for explanations of grammatical terms.

Absolute. An absolute expression is one that is grammatically independent of the rest of the sentence. Usually it consists of a noun or pronoun followed by a participle, a construction often called the **nominative absolute.**

> *The game having ended,* the crowd went home.
> He did not lock the door, *the key having been stolen.*

Abstract noun. See **Noun.**

Active voice. See **Voice.**

Adjective. A word (one of the eight parts of speech) used to modify (*i.e.,* describe or limit) a noun or pronoun.

Descriptive adjective: *honest* man, *white* pony, *blue* sky, *waving* flag.

Limiting adjective: *my* book, *its* nest, *his, her, our, your, their* property (possessive); *that, this* house, *these, those* apples (demonstrative); *whose* cap? *which* coat? *what* dress? (interrogative); the boy *whose* dog was lost (relative); *one* pear, *three* plums, *first* robin, *third* sparrow (numerical); *a* street, *an* avenue, *the* park (article).

(See also section **4, Adjectives and Adverbs.**)

Adjective clause. A subordinate clause used as an adjective.

The man *who is honest* will succeed.

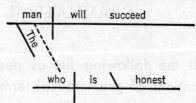

[The clause, equivalent to the adjective *honest*, modifies the noun *man*.]

Adverb. A word (one of the eight parts of speech) used to modify (*i.e.*, describe or limit) a verb, an adjective, or another adverb. An adverb indicates time (*now, then, today*), place (*here, there, outside*), manner (*calmly, quickly, clearly*), or degree (*very, somewhat, only*).

Stand *here*. [*Here* modifies the verb *stand*.]

Stand beside the *very* old clock. [*Very* modifies the adjective *old*.]

Stand *very quietly*. [*Very* modifies the adverb *quietly*, which modifies the verb *stand*.]

(See also section **4, Adjectives and Adverbs**.)

Adverbial clause. A subordinate clause used as an adverb.

I shall leave the house *after she comes*.

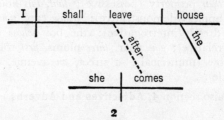

[The adverbial clause *after she comes* modifies the verb *shall leave* and indicates time. Adverbial clauses may also indicate place, manner, cause, purpose, condition, concession, comparison, or result.]

Antecedent. The name given to a word or group of words to which a pronoun refers.

This is the *man who* came to the house. [*Man* is the antecedent of the relative pronoun *who*.]

When *John* and *Mary* came, *they* told us the facts in the case. [*John* and *Mary* are the antecedent of the personal pronoun *they*.]

Appositive. A substantive set beside another substantive and denoting the same person or thing.

Mr. Smith, our *dentist*, is visiting *England*, his native *country*. [*Dentist* is in apposition with *Mr. Smith*, and *country* is in apposition with *England*.]

Article. Articles are classed as adjectives. The definite article is *the*. The indefinite articles are *a* and *an*.

Auxiliary. A verb that helps to form other verbs. *Have, may, can, be, shall, will, must, ought*, and *do* are the common auxiliaries.

I *shall* go.
He *was* sent away.
He *has been* promoted.

Case. The position or change in the form of a substantive to show its use in the sentence. The three cases used in English are the nominative, the possessive, and the objective. (See also section **5, Case.**)

Clause. A group of words that contains a verb and its subject and is used as a part of a sentence. A clause may be main (independent, principal) or subordinate (dependent).

3

(1) A main (independent, principal) clause expresses within itself a complete thought and can stand by itself as a simple sentence.

The moon rose and *the stars came out.* [Two main clauses, either of which can stand by itself as a simple sentence.]

(2) A subordinate (dependent) clause is not complete within itself and cannot stand alone. It is used as a noun, an adjective, or an adverb.

That he will run for office is doubtful. [Noun clause: a subordinate clause used as the subject of the sentence.] (See also section **2e, Sentence Sense.**)

Collective noun. See **Noun.**

Colloquial. Appropriate to spoken or informal rather than to written or formal language.

Common noun. See **Noun.**

Comparison. The change in the form of an adjective or adverb to indicate degrees of superiority in quality, quantity, or manner. There are three degrees: positive, comparative, and superlative.

EXAMPLES	*Positive*	*Comparative*	*Superlative*
	good	better	best
	high	higher	highest
	quickly	more quickly	most quickly

Complement. A word or words used to complete the sense of the verb. The complement may be an object, a predicate noun, or a predicate adjective.

OBJECT: John bought the *book.*

PREDICATE NOUNS:

Samuel was a good *child.* [The predicate noun *child,* referring to the subject *Samuel,* is also called the

4

predicate complement, the subjective complement, or the predicate nominative.]

He called the man a *hero*. [*Man* is the direct object. The noun *hero*, referring to *man*, is called the **objective complement** or the **predicate objective**.]

PREDICATE ADJECTIVES:

The boy is *obedient*. [The predicate adjective *obedient*, referring to the subject *boy*, is also called the **subjective complement** or the **predicate complement**.]

Jack colored the egg *blue*. [*Egg* is the direct object. The predicate adjective *blue*, referring to *egg*, is also called the **objective complement** or the **predicate objective**.]

Complex sentence. See **Sentence.**

Compound sentence. See **Sentence.**

Compound-complex sentence. See **Sentence.**

Concrete noun. See **Noun.**

Conjugation. The inflectional forms of the verbs indicating tense, voice, mood, number, and person.

CONJUGATION OF THE VERB *TO DO*

(Principal Parts: *do, did, done*)

INDICATIVE MOOD

Active Voice		*Passive Voice*	

PRESENT TENSE

Singular	*Plural*	*Singular*	*Plural*
1. I do	we do	I am done	we are done
2. you do	you do	you are done	you are done
3. he does	they do	he is done	they are done

PAST TENSE

1. I did	we did	I was done	we were done
2. you did	you did	you were done	you were done
3. he did	they did	he was done	they were done

FUTURE TENSE

Singular	*Plural*	*Singular*	*Plural*
1. I shall do	we shall do	I shall be done	we shall be done
2. you will do	you will do	you will be done	you will be done
3. he will do	they will do	he will be done	they will be done

PRESENT PERFECT TENSE

1. I have done	we have done	I have been done	we have been done
2. you have done	you have done	you have been done	you have been done
3. he has done	they have done	he has been done	they have been done

PAST PERFECT TENSE

1. I had done	we had done	I had been done	we had been done
2. you had done	you had done	you had been done	you had been done
3. he had done	they had done	he had been done	they had been done

FUTURE PERFECT TENSE (seldom used)

1. I shall have done	we shall have done	I shall have been done	we shall have been done
2. you will have done	you will have done	you will have been done	you will have been done
3. he will have done	they will have done	he will have been done	they will have been done

SUBJUNCTIVE MOOD

Active Voice   *Passive Voice*

PRESENT TENSE

if I, you, he do   if I, you, he be done
if we, you, they do   if we, you, they be done

PAST TENSE

if I, you, he did   if I, you, he were done
if we, you, they did   if we, you, they were done

PRESENT PERFECT

if I, you, he have done   if I, you, he have been done
if we, you, they have done   if we, you, they have been done

IMPERATIVE MOOD

PRESENT TENSE

Do!

Conjunction. A word (one of the eight parts of speech) which connects words, phrases, or clauses. There are

6

two kinds, co-ordinating conjunctions and subordinating conjunctions.

(1) **Co-ordinating conjunctions** connect words, phrases, and clauses of equal rank: *and, or, but, for, either . . . or, neither . . . nor.*

(2) **Subordinating conjunctions** connect subordinate clauses with main clauses: *if, although, since, in order that, as, because, unless, after, before, until, when, whenever, while, wherever,* etc.

Conjunctive adverb. An adverb which connects main clauses and thus forms compound sentences: *however, therefore, nevertheless, hence, then, too, besides, also, so, further, moreover, indeed, still, only, thus, otherwise, consequently, accordingly,* etc.

Construction (Syntax). The grammatical functions of words, phrases, or clauses in the sentence.

Co-ordinate. Of equal rank, as two nouns, two subordinate clauses, or two main clauses.

Copula (Copulative verb, linking verb). A verb used to express the relation between the subject and the predicate noun or adjective. "He *is* merry." The chief copulative verbs are *be, become, seem, appear.*

Declension. See **Inflection.**

Demonstrative adjective. See **Adjective.**

Demonstrative pronoun. A pronoun that points out. "*This* is good; *that* is bad."

Dependent clause. See **Clause.**

Descriptive adjective. See **Adjective.**

Diagramming. An arrangement of words on lines to show relationships within the sentence. Various forms are used. Any form is "correct" if it helps the student to understand the sentence. A diagram is only a means to an end, not an end in itself. One form of diagramming in common use is illustrated below.

The very feeble woman carefully placed the cakes on the shelf.

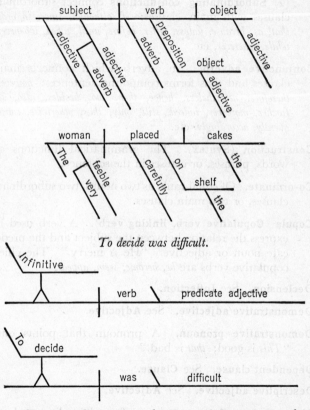

To decide was difficult.

(See other diagrams under **Gerund, Sentence,** and especially under section **2e, Sentence Sense.**)

8

Direct address (Nominative of address, vocative). A noun or pronoun used parenthetically to direct a speech to a definite person.

I hope, *Mary*, that you will go.   *Mary*, close the door.

Direct object. See **Object.**

Ellipsis (Elliptical expression). An expression grammatically incomplete but clear because omitted words can be readily supplied.

Mary is prettier than Helen (is pretty).
Whenever (it is) possible, you should take exercise.

Finite verb. A verb or verb form that makes a complete assertion and may thus serve as a predicate. "The sun *rose*." "The sun *is rising*." Infinitives, participles, and gerunds are not finite verbs.

Gerund. A verbal noun ending in *ing*. The gerund should be carefully distinguished from the verbal adjective (the present participle), which also ends in *ing*.

Swimming is enjoyable.

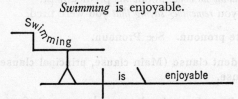

[Gerund — the verbal noun used as subject.]

The *swimming* boy was rescued.

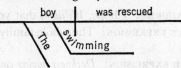

[Present participle — the verbal adjective modifying the noun *boy*.]

9

Since the gerund is a noun, it may function as subject (as in the sentence given above), as object of a verb ("I enjoy *swimming*"), as object of a preposition ("By *swimming* he reached shore"), as a predicate noun ("My chief recreation is *swimming*"), or as an appositive ("My chief recreation, *swimming*, has some disadvantages"). The gerund, like a noun, may be modified by an adjective: "*Skillful* swimming saved his life."

But the gerund shows its verbal origin by its ability to take an object ("Swimming the *horse* across the stream was difficult") or to be modified by an adverb ("By swimming *rapidly* he escaped").

Gerund phrase. See **Phrase.**

Idiom. An expression in good use that is peculiar to a language. (Idioms sometimes violate established rules of grammar, but are nevertheless sanctioned by usage.)

He *made no bones* about his predicament.

Do you *remember saying that* you were tired?

Indefinite pronoun. See **Pronoun.**

Independent clause (Main clause, principal clause). See **Clause.**

Independent element. Any word or group of words that has no grammatical connection with the rest of the sentence.

DIRECT ADDRESS: I hope, *William*, that you can go.

DIRECTIVE EXPRESSION: The whole family, *we hope*, will come.

ABSOLUTE EXPRESSION: *Darkness having come*, he slipped away.

INTERJECTION: *Ah*, this is the sport I enjoy.

Indirect object. See **Object.**

Infinitive. A verbal regularly preceded by *to* and used as a noun, an adjective, or an adverb. After certain verbs the *to* is often omitted: "He helped (*to*) *make* the kite." "He dared not (*to*) *go* away."

USED AS A NOUN:

To walk was a pleasure. [Subject.]
He began *to open the box.* [Object of verb.]
Her wish was *to see him leave.* [Predicate noun.]
He was about *to leave.* [Object of preposition.]

USED AS AN ADJECTIVE:

I have work *to do.* [*To do* modifies the noun *work.*]

USED AS AN ADVERB:

He enlisted *to become an aviator.* [The infinitive modifies the verb *enlisted.*]

The infinitive shows its verbal origin by its ability to take a subject ("I asked *him* to go"), to take an object ("I wanted to pay *him*"), or to be modified by an adverb ("I asked him to drive *slowly*").

Infinitive phrase. See **Phrase.**

Inflection. A change in the form of a word to show a change in meaning or in relationship to some other word or group of words. The inflection of nouns and pronouns is called **declension**: *man, man's, men, men's; I, my, me,* etc. The inflection of verbs is called **conjugation**; that of adjectives and adverbs is called **comparison.**

Intensive pronoun. See **Pronoun.**

Interjection. A word (one of the eight parts of speech) expressing emotion and having no grammatical relation with other words in the sentence.

Oh, I can hardly believe it.
Whew! That was a narrow escape.

1 grt

Interrogative pronoun. See **Pronoun**.

Intransitive. See **Verb**.

Limiting adjective. See **Adjective**.

Linking verb. See **Copula**.

Main clause (Independent clause, principal clause). See **Clause**.

Modifier. Any word or group of words that describes or qualifies another word or group of words. See **Modify**.

Modify. To describe or qualify the meaning of a word or group of words. In a diagram modifiers are attached to the words they modify.

A very old man hobbled slowly along the road.

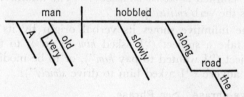

[*A* and *old* modify *man;* *very* modifies *old;* *slowly* and *along the road* modify *hobbled;* *the* modifies *road.*]

Mood (Mode). The form of the verb used to indicate the manner in which the action is conceived. English has indicative, imperative, and subjunctive moods. See **Conjugation**.

The **indicative mood** states a fact or asks a question.

The sun is shining.
Is the sun shining?

The **imperative mood** gives a command or makes a request.

Release the prisoners.
Please open the door.

The **subjunctive mood** expresses a doubt, a condition contrary to fact, a wish or regret, a concession, a supposition.

I wish that mother were here.
If I had my way, you would not go.
If I should be gone, wait for me.

Nominative. See **Case.**

Nominative absolute. See **Absolute.**

Nominative of address. See **Direct address.**

Nonrestrictive modifier. A nonessential modifier. A phrase or clause which could be omitted without changing the essential meaning of the sentence.

The airplane, *which is now being manufactured in large numbers,* is of immense commercial value.

Noun. One of the eight parts of speech, the name of a person, place, or thing.

Nouns are used as:
(1) SUBJECTS OF VERBS: The *dog* barked.
(2) OBJECTS OF VERBS, VERBALS, or PREPOSITIONS: He opened the *door* to let the *dog* into the *house.*
(3) PREDICATE NOUNS: She was his *secretary.*
(4) APPOSITIVES: Mr. Brown, our *neighbor*, is sick.
(5) NOMINATIVES OF ADDRESS: *Mary*, will you help us?
(6) ADJECTIVES: *Spring* rains; *John's* coat.
(7) ADVERBS: He returned *home.*

Nouns are classified as:
(1) COMMON or PROPER.

A **common noun** is the name applied to any one of a class of persons, places, or things: *man, woman, city, state, chair, bed.*

13

A **proper noun** is the name applied to specific individuals, places, or things: *Henry Ford, Jane Addams, New Orleans, Texas,* the *Parthenon, Washington Monument.*

(2) COLLECTIVE.

A **collective noun** is a name applied to a group: *band, flock, jury, army.*

(3) CONCRETE or ABSTRACT.

A **concrete noun** names something that can be perceived by one or more of the senses: *water, trees, man, river.*

An **abstract noun** names a quality or general idea: *love, ambition, hate, pity.* (See also section **2e, Sentence Sense.**)

Noun clause. A subordinate clause used as a noun. It may be used as subject, direct object, appositive, predicate nominative, object of a preposition.

Whoever comes will be welcome. [Subject.]

I hope *that he will recover.* [Object of the verb.]

The hope *that he might win* upheld him. [Appositive.]

This is *what I asked for.* [Predicate nominative.]

I shall spend the money for *whatever seems best.* [Object of the preposition *for.*]

Number. The change in the form of a verb, a noun, or a pronoun to designate one (*singular*) or more than one (*plural*). See **Conjugation.**

Object. A noun or pronoun (or a phrase or clause used as a noun) that receives the action of a transitive verb or completes the meaning of a preposition.

Direct object. Any noun (or its equivalent) that receives the action of a transitive verb.

14

He raked *leaves*. [Noun.]

He supplied *whatever was needed*. [Clause used as a noun.]

Indirect object. A term applied to a noun or pronoun that precedes the direct object.

He gave *me* an apple. [*Apple* is the direct object, *me* the indirect object, of the verb *gave*. Perhaps it would be better to explain *me* as the object of an implied preposition *to*.]

Object of a preposition. Any noun (or its equivalent) used to complete the meaning of a preposition.

He walked into the *house*. [*House* is said to be the object of the preposition *into*.]

Objective complement. See **Complement.**

Participial phrase. See **Phrase.**

Participle. A verbal adjective. "The *rising* sun, a *concealed* weapon, a *lost* opportunity." The present participle, which ends in *ing*, should be carefully distinguished from the gerund (a verbal noun), which also ends in *ing*. (See **Gerund.**) The past participle ends in *ed*, *d*, *t*, *en*, *n*, or makes an internal change.

PRESENT PARTICIPLES: *concealing, losing, rising, selling, singing*.

PAST PARTICIPLES: *concealed, lost, risen, sold, sung*.

Parts of speech. The eight classes into which words are grouped according to their uses in the sentence: *verb, noun, pronoun, adjective, adverb, conjunction, preposition*, and *interjection*.

Passive voice. The form of the verb which shows that the subject is being acted upon. See **Conjugation.**

Person. Changes in the form of verbs and pronouns to indicate whether a person is speaking (first person), is spoken to (second person), or is spoken about (third person). See **Conjugation.**

FIRST PERSON: *I* see the boy.
SECOND PERSON: Can *you* see the boy?
THIRD PERSON: *He* sees the boy.

Personal pronoun. See **Pronoun.**

Phrase. A group of words which has no subject or predicate and is used as a single part of speech.

Prepositional phrase:

The man *with red hair* is my brother. [Adjective.]
My brother lives *in the city.* [Adverb.]

Participial phrase:

The door *leading to the porch* is open. [Adjective.]

Gerund phrase:

Reckless driving along the highways is responsible for many wrecks. [Substantive.]

(See also Section **2e, Sentence Sense.**)

Infinitive phrase:

To err is human. [Substantive.]

Verb phrase:

He *has been employed* for a year. [Verb.]

Predicate. The part of the sentence which tells what is said about the subject.

He *runs.*
She *can sing.*
The baby *has been playing.*

Predicate adjective, predicate complement, predicate nominative, predicate noun, predicate objective. See **Complement.**

Preposition. A word (one of the eight parts of speech) used to show the relation of a noun or pronoun to some other word in the sentence.

He ran *with* the team.
The bird is *in* the tree.

Prepositional phrase. See **Phrase.**

Present tense. See **Tense.**

Principal clause (Main clause, independent clause). See **Clause.**

Principal parts. The forms of any verb from which the various tenses are derived: (1) present infinitive, (2) past tense (first person singular), and (3) the past participle.

EXAMPLES		
see	saw	seen
take	took	taken
love	loved	loved

Pronoun. A word (one of the eight parts of speech) used instead of a noun.

Personal pronouns: *I, you, he, she, it.* (See the declension under section **5, Case.**)

Interrogative pronouns: *who, which, what.*

Relative pronouns: *who, which, that.*

Demonstrative pronouns: *this, that, these, those.*

Indefinite pronouns: *each, either, any, anyone, some, someone, one, no one, few, all, everyone,* etc.

Reciprocal pronouns: *each other, one another.*

Reflexive pronouns: *myself, yourself, himself,* etc.

You hurt *yourself.*
He ruined *himself.*

17

Intensive pronouns: *myself, yourself, himself,* etc.

> I *myself* will go.
> You *yourself* should go.

Proper noun. See **Noun.**

Reciprocal pronoun. See **Pronoun.**

Reflexive pronoun. See **Pronoun.**

Restrictive modifier. An essential modifier. A phrase or clause which cannot be omitted without changing the essential meaning of the sentence.

> Men *who are industrious* will succeed.

Sentence. A group of words containing a verb (predicate) and its subject and expressing a complete thought. Sentences are classified structurally as (1) simple, (2) compound, (3) complex, or (4) compound-complex.

> (1) **Simple sentence.** A sentence containing one main clause but no subordinate clauses.
>
> > Birds fly.
> > Birds and bats fly. [Simple sentence with compound subject.]
> > Birds and bats swoop and fly. [Simple sentence with compound subject and compound predicate.]

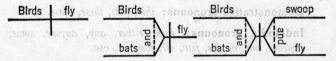

> (2) **Compound sentence.** A sentence containing two or more main clauses but no subordinate clauses.

The moon rose and the stars came out.

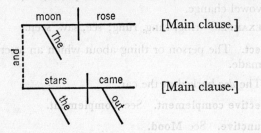

[Main clause.]

[Main clause.]

(3) **Complex sentence.** A sentence containing one main clause and one or more subordinate clauses.

Birds fly when they are startled.

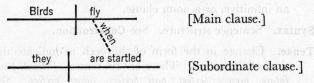

[Main clause.]

[Subordinate clause.]

(4) **Compound-complex sentence.** A sentence containing two or more main clauses and one or more subordinate clauses. *Engines roared overhead and a bomb fell where we had stood.*

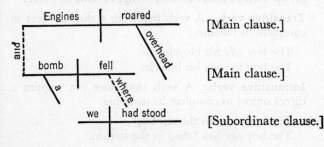

[Main clause.]

[Main clause.]

[Subordinate clause.]

Simple sentence. See **Sentence.**

19

Strong verb. A verb that forms its principal parts by a vowel change.

EXAMPLES ring, rang, rung; see, saw, seen.

Subject. The person or thing about which an assertion is made.

The *dog* barked at the car.

Subjective complement. See **Complement.**

Subjunctive. See **Mood.**

Subordinate clause. A dependent clause. See **Clause.**

Substantive. Any word or group of words used as a noun. A substantive may be a noun, a pronoun, a gerund, an infinitive, or a noun clause.

Syntax. Sentence structure. See **Construction.**

Tense. Change in the form of the verb to indicate the time of the action. There are six tenses: *Present, past, future, present perfect, past perfect, future perfect.* See **Conjugation.**

Transitive. See **Verb.**

Verb. A word (one of the eight parts of speech) or word group used to assert action, being, or state of being.

Transitive verb. A verb requiring a direct object to complete its meaning.

The boy *sold* his bicycle.
The boy *has sold* his bicycle.

Intransitive verb. A verb that does not require a direct object to complete its meaning.

The boy *fished* in the stream.
The boy *has been fishing* in the stream.

(See also section **2e, Sentence Sense.**)

Verb phrase. See **Phrase.**

Verbal. A word derived from a verb but used as a noun or adjective. See **Infinitive, Gerund, Participle.**

Vocative. See **Direct address.**

Voice. Distinction in the form of the verb to indicate whether the subject of the sentence acts (**active voice**) or is acted upon (**passive voice**). See **Conjugation.**

Weak verb (Regular verb). Any verb that forms its principal parts by adding *ed, d,* or *t* to the infinitive: *love, loved, loved; sweep, swept, swept.*

2 frag

SENTENCE FRAGMENT
(PERIOD FAULT)

2. Do not write a sentence fragment — a phrase or a subordinate clause — as if it were a complete sentence.[1]

A fragment cannot stand alone. It must be (1) included in the sentence with the main clause or (2) rewritten to form a sentence by itself.

WRONG He stayed until late in the autumn. Hoping thus to regain his health. [Main clause. Participial phrase.]

RIGHT He stayed until late in the autumn, hoping thus to regain his health. [Participial phrase included with the main clause.]

RIGHT He stayed until late in the autumn. He hoped thus to regain his health. [Participial phrase made into a sentence.]

WRONG He stayed until late in the autumn. Because he hoped thus to regain his health. [Main clause. Subordinate clause.]

RIGHT He stayed until late in the autumn because he hoped thus to regain his health. [Subordinate clause included with the main clause.]

[1] For an explanation of any grammatical term that you do not understand, consult the alphabetical list in section 1, Grammatical Terms.

RIGHT   He stayed until late in the autumn. He hoped
         thus to regain his health. [Subordinate clause
         made into a sentence.]

To determine whether any group of words is a sentence or only a sentence fragment, one must (1) find the subject and predicate and (2) learn whether this subject and predicate are introduced by a subordinating conjunction. If the supposed sentence does not have *both* subject and predicate, it may be dismissed at once as a mere phrase. *Hoping thus to regain his health*, for example, has no predicate. *Hoping* is a participle and *to regain* is an infinitive, but there is no verb to serve as a predicate. Even when there are both subject and predicate, they may be introduced by a subordinating conjunction and thus made into a subordinate clause. *Because he hoped to regain his health* has the subject *he* and the predicate *hoped*. But since these words are introduced by the subordinating conjunction *because*, the group of words is still only a subordinate clause — a sentence fragment.

Make a diagram — at least get a mental picture — of the heart of each sentence: its subject + its predicate. Then if you find that subject and predicate are not introduced by a subordinating conjunction such as *because*, *since*, *if*, or *when*, you may be reasonably sure that the sentence is complete.

He stayed until late in the autumn.

He	stayed

[Subject + predicate.]

The diagram shows subject and predicate, and there is no subordinating conjunction: the sentence is complete.

2 frag

2a. Do not write a participial phrase as a complete sentence.

WRONG   I made little progress. Finally giving up all my efforts. [Main clause. Participial phrase.]

RIGHT   I made little progress, finally giving up all my efforts. [Fragment included with the main clause.]

RIGHT   I made little progress. Finally I gave up all my efforts. [Fragment made into a sentence.]

WRONG   On we went. The sun shining down on us from a clear blue sky. [Main clause. Noun and participial phrase.]

RIGHT   On we went, with the sun shining down on us from a clear blue sky. [Fragment included with the main clause.]

RIGHT   On we went. The sun shone down on us from a clear blue sky. [Fragment made into a sentence.]

EXERCISE. Correct each sentence (1) by making the participial phrase into a separate sentence and (2) by including the participial phrase with the main clause.

1. I sat up late into the night. Doing my homework and listening to the radio.
2. The city is very smoky. This smoke coming from homes, trains, and factories.
3. Large crowds of people stood in line. Waiting to buy their tickets to ride the merry-go-round.
4. They drove along for fifty miles. The guide talking all the time about the ways of animals.
5. The poem is seven stanzas long. Each stanza containing eight lines.

2b. Do not write an appositive as a complete sentence.

WRONG The city has two big markets. The Western Avenue Market and the Wayside Market. [Main clause. Appositives.]

RIGHT The city has two big markets, the Western Avenue Market and the Wayside Market. [Fragment included in the sentence.]

EXERCISE. Either change the punctuation and make the whole into one sentence, or make the appositive into a separate sentence.

1. There were two great singers on the program. Lawrence Tibbett and Grace Moore.
2. As the story opens Emma Woodhouse is in her early twenties. Just the age at which the world looks bright and gay.
3. Civilization is composed of two definite periods. One of realism and one of idealism.
4. This little town seems like another world. Something different from anything else.
5. She is a very precise woman. One of those persons whose visits always seem longer than they actually are.

2c. Do not use a subordinate clause as a complete sentence.

WRONG I enjoyed the book. Probably because it dealt with college life. [Main clause. Subordinate clause.]

RIGHT I enjoyed the book, probably because it dealt with college life. [Fragment included with the main clause.]

25

2 frag

EXERCISE. Include each subordinate clause with a main clause, or make the subordinate clause into a main clause that may stand as a separate sentence.

1. Clym could see the bright days ahead and contemplate his future success. Though his life was not destined to fulfill his hopes.
2. John had never had the privileges of a city boy. Since he had always lived in the country.
3. If one searches diligently for the truth of things because he has a motive. Studying proves profitable and interesting.
4. Therefore the radio and many other modern methods which are now used to help solve our criminal problems.
5. The study of English increases my knowledge. Most of all because it lets me know how ignorant I am.

2d. Do not write as a complete sentence any other fragment, such as a prepositional phrase, an infinitive phrase, a detached item of a series, or a member of a compound predicate.

WRONG Our valley is noted for its heavy rainfall. Especially during the winter months. [Main clause. Prepositional phrase.]

RIGHT Our valley is noted for its heavy rainfall, especially during the winter months. [Fragment included with the main clause.]

WRONG I like to go roaming through the woods. To find strange birds' nests in out-of-the-way places. [Main clause. Infinitive phrase.]

RIGHT I like to go roaming through the woods, to find strange birds' nests in out-of-the-way places. [Fragment included with the main clause.]

26

WRONG The next pocket contained a lock covered with rust. Also a brass chain and a small notebook with most of the pages torn out. [Main clause. Detached items in a series.]

RIGHT The next pocket contained a lock covered with rust, also a brass chain, and a small notebook with most of the pages torn out. [Fragment included with the main clause.]

WRONG She tried to stand up. Struggled for a good footing, and then fell. [Main clause. Members of a compound predicate.]

RIGHT She tried to stand up, struggled for a good footing, and then fell. [Fragment included with the main clause.]

EXERCISE. Point out each sentence fragment, and show why it is a fragment. Make the revision necessary to eliminate the fragment.

1. Slacks are very comfortable for hot summer days. Especially in the mountains of East Tennessee.
2. The huge stalk grew from a small seed. Reached its peak, and began to wither away.
3. The "batman" has a dangerous task. To jump from the plane and glide to earth on batlike wings.
4. Several improvements are needed in the town. For instance, a tennis court, a swimming pool, and a baseball diamond.
5. Football is a fascinating game. Fascinating because of its very simplicity.

At times sentences may be grammatically incomplete and yet clear because omitted words can be readily supplied by the reader. Such elliptical expressions occur in commands, questions, exclamations, and especially in dialogue. But these incomplete sentences are not

real fragments since the completion is unmistakably
implied.

EXAMPLES   Open the door.   How much?   Well done!
"How old are you?"   "Sixteen."

Modern authors sometimes use for special effect fragments that are clearly nothing but fragments.   Experi-
enced writers, however, may take liberties that are
unwise for students learning the fundamentals of English composition.

Note: If you cannot understand the explanations given in
section **2a, b, c, d,** above, or if you continue to write
sentence fragments in your themes, master the fundamentals of the sentence treated in **2e, Sentence Sense,**
below.   Then turn again to section **2a, b, c, d.**

EXERCISE ON THE SENTENCE FRAGMENT

Identify each fragment as a phrase, a subordinate clause,
or a group of phrases and subordinate clauses.   Correct the
error (1) by including the fragment with the main clause,
(2) by making the fragment into a sentence, or (3) by
providing a main clause for the group of phrases and
subordinate clauses.   Use your judgment to determine the
most suitable method of correction.   Identify the two
sentences that are complete and need no revision.

  1. A fitting epitaph for John Brown, one of the most radical
     abolitionists before the Civil War, who was so obsessed
     by his one idea that he died fighting valiantly for it.
  2. The success of an individual depends to a great extent
     upon mental capacity.   The key to success being the
     brain.
  3. Advertising serves two purposes.   A means of display-
     ing merchandise and an opportunity to add to the
     appearance of the building.

4. I have learned from picture shows how stiff and formal operas are. A place where people must wear their very best evening clothes and carry their opera glasses.

5. The main reason being that this man's word can seldom be accepted with the feeling of security.

6. The decorations were very beautiful in the large gymnasium. The halls of which were filled with fortune tellers.

7. Third, the cultured group. There are not many people in this division.

8. Many people had planned to see the game. Thus bringing much money to the city.

9. Some of America's greatest men admitted that they were superstitious, Theodore Roosevelt being one of them.

10. Superstitions were in the world a long time ago. Probably as far back as the Roman Empire, when people worshipped many gods.

11. How to navigate yourself and a woman through a revolving door at the same time.

12. The reason for its deceptiveness being that too much of the plot is revealed.

13. A small round spot approximately one fourth of an inch in diameter.

14. I expect to get ideas. Ideas of other men about the vocation I have chosen.

15. We can learn much about right living by observing the lives of others. Imitating their good habits and avoiding their bad ones.

16. The girls in their best evening gowns and the boys dressed in their black tuxedos with white shirt fronts.

17. The largest lake covering seventy-five acres.

18. Although Molly shows Andy and his brother that their ideas are wrong. They continue to think of things as they had thought of them before.

19. The book deals with changing fashions. Changes that might occur at any time. At the present day or in centuries to come.

20. In the annex, which was a very small room containing bedsteads, chairs, stools, game-boards, and almost everything used by the Egyptians.

21. They were both against marriage and always said that nobody would be good enough for either of them to marry. The result being the marriage of each to the other.

22. Bookworms usually read more fiction than scholars. Scholars being deep in a book about physics or chemistry.

23. It requires a skilled person to write an interesting theme. That is, a theme interesting enough to hold a reader's undivided attention.

24. The situation is another thing that creates interest. The duke and his guest, who has come to arrange a marriage between the duke and the master's daughter.

25. I can always find something new there. Some street that I have not seen or some park.

26. I can form friendships. Friendships that will last all my life.

27. Iron is one of the commonest and cheapest of all metals. Although it has not always been cheap.

28. The purpose of my coming to college is to gain knowledge. Not only the knowledge that can be turned into dollars and cents but the knowledge that gives a cultural background.

29. One will find that nearly all boys can give several reasons for entering college. Some of which are satisfactory and some of which are not.

30. In the first quarter the teams were very evenly matched, neither team getting very close to the other's goal.

2e. Sentence Sense

This supplement to section 2 has been prepared especially for students who have trouble in mastering the principles involved in the following sections of the handbook:

2, Sentence Fragment (Period Fault)
3, Comma Splice (Comma Fault)
4, Adjectives and Adverbs
6, Agreement
12, The Comma
14, The Semicolon
24, Subordination
25, Coherence in General
26, Parallelism
30, Variety

The student who does not have a well-developed "sentence sense" will find it difficult to recognize sentence fragments and will continue to make this most serious error. He may also continue to make comma splices simply because he cannot recognize main clauses; to make errors in agreement because he cannot determine the verbs and associate them with their subjects; to misuse the comma because he lacks the ability to distinguish such parts of the sentence as main and subordinate clauses, adverbial clauses, adjective clauses, compound predicates, and phrases. Any student who does not understand the usual and normal construction of the sentence should develop his sentence sense and then study anew the sections of the handbook which cause difficulty.

(1) Recognizing Verbs

The verb is the heart of the sentence. Any group of words without a verb is only a sentence fragment. A verb asserts something. It is used (1) in making a statement, (2) in asking a question, or (3) in giving a command.

1. The rain *falls* gently.
2. *Are* you happy?
3. *Walk* carefully.

The verb may consist of one word (as in the three sentences above), of two words, of three words, or of four words, depending on its inflectional form.

1. The rain *will fall* gently.
2. The rain *has been falling* gently.
3. The rain *should have been falling* gently.

The words that make up a single verb are often separated.

1. It *is* not *raining*.
2. It *will* almost certainly *rain* tomorrow.

A verb may be combined with *not*, or with a contraction of *not*. In such sentences the *not*, or the contraction, is no part of the verb.

1. He *cannot go*.
2. He *can't go*.
3. It *isn't* cold.
4. He *doesn't know*.

The student who can find the verb (sometimes consisting of several words) and can separate it from other elements has gone a long way toward understanding the sentence.

EXERCISE 1. For each of the following sentences supply an appropriate verb — a word that asserts something.

1. The pitcher —— the ball.
2. —— the money with the order.
3. The rain —— incessantly against the window.
4. —— you confident of his support?
5. Opposition only —— him more persistent.

EXERCISE 2. Underscore the verb (or verbs) in each of the following sentences.

1. Often there were a dozen or more planes at the airport at the same time.
2. Enormous waves were beating against the piers.
3. Have you ever considered taking a trip to Alaska?
4. Can't something be done about the smoke in our city?
5. Since so many people want to attend the big games, wouldn't it be profitable to build a larger stadium?
6. When the Scouts were asked to pitch the tents, they went to work with much enthusiasm.
7. We all like the things that give us a sense of well-being.
8. The population of Los Angeles has increased greatly since the last census.
9. After I returned home, I was pleased to get the news that James had been promoted.
10. The need for adequate defense has been growing more urgent.

EXERCISE 3. Underscore the verb (or verbs) in each of the following sentences.

1. All the woodwork should have been polished before the paper was cleaned.
2. The cow was annoyed by the flies and heat, and kept moving restlessly all night.
3. "How do you manage to do all this work?" I asked.

4. You will find out what the real difficulty is if you go to the bottom of the trouble.
5. Wait a minute until the picture is taken.
6. The children had been seriously trying to add to the family income.
7. The situation had developed to a point where something had to be done immediately.
8. Dishonest men can, of course, be influenced by graft.
9. Jane, tired by her heavy day's work, may have gone to bed.
10. In spite of all that he says, I am not at all sure he will succeed.

Note: Ask a competent person to check the accuracy of your spotting of verbs.

    If you can mark the verbs accurately, you are ready to take up the next exercises. If not, mark verbs in other lists of simple sentences and get assistance in checking the accuracy of your work.

Caution: Do not confuse verbs and verbals.

Infinitives, participles, and gerunds [1] are called verbals. They are derived from verbs, but they are not verbs. Unlike verbs, they cannot make a statement, ask a question, or give a command. In the sentences below, the verbs are in italics and the verbals are in boldface.

INFINITIVES

1. I *hope* **to go.**
2. **To go** *is* easier than **to stay.**

PARTICIPLES (adjectives derived from verbs)

1. The **whistling** wind *died* down.
2. The officer *stopped* the **speeding** car.

[1] If you do not know the meaning of such grammatical terms, consult the alphabetical list in section 1, **Grammatical Terms.**

34

3. The **loaded** wagon *overturned*.
4. **Having completed** the work, the laborer *departed*.

GERUNDS (nouns derived from verbs)

1. **Walking** *is* good exercise.
2. He *enjoys* **walking**.
3. By **walking** home he *saved* money.

EXERCISE 4. Underscore each verb with a straight line, each verbal with a wavy line.

1. Some people are not afraid of trying anything.
2. Her hair, closely cut in the prevailing fashion, was turning gray.
3. My reason for taking the course was to get credit toward the degree.
4. It is possible to drive to the beach and to go out in the sailboat the same afternoon.
5. He had his own methods for repairing the roof.
6. The news left us disturbed.
7. To defend their home from the Indians was an acute problem for the first settlers.
8. The firm decided to open the new store at once.
9. Harvesting grain with the new machines makes farming an interesting occupation.
10. He had the look of having been defeated at every turn.

EXERCISE 5. Underscore each verb with a straight line, each verbal with a wavy line.

1. To show your anger is to admit that you feel she is superior.
2. The little dog seemed to enjoy chasing balls, carrying bits of wood, and tagging along after his master.
3. On the stage one saw a blindfolded man drawing cards from a box.
4. It is a thrilling sight to see a football squad come dashing out onto the field.

5. The sailors, exhausted from rowing the heavy lifeboats and tired from lack of sleep, anxiously awaited the rescue ship.
6. She had a purpose in asking me to come: to ask me to take the office of secretary.
7. It has become an established practice to retire officers at a certain age.
8. We were seeking a quiet vacation — to fish a little, read a little, and rest a great deal of the time.
9. Scattered rows of mill homes, showing signs of wear, dominated the landscape.
10. Buying directly from the wholesale houses eliminated paying high retail prices.

Note: Ask a competent person to check your accuracy in marking verbs and verbals. If necessary, mark verbs and verbals in other lists of sentences. **Do not turn to the next section until you can identify verbs readily and can distinguish them from verbals.**

(2) Finding the Subjects of Verbs

Every verb has its subject, that part of the sentence about which the verb asserts something. This subject may be a noun, a pronoun, or some word or group of words functioning as a noun. In each of the following sentences the verb is italicized, as usual; the subject is in boldface.

1. **Birds** *fly.* [The subject is a noun.]
2. **Airplanes** *are flown.* [The subject is a noun.]
3. **He** *is* old. [The subject is a pronoun.]
4. **Walking** *is* good exercise. [The subject is a gerund.]
5. **To walk** *is* good exercise. [The subject is an infinitive.]
6. **That he was hungry** *was* evident. [The subject is a subordinate clause.]

36

7. The **airplane,** having reached Miami after a long
   flight from South America, *circles* the city before
   landing at the airport.

No matter how long or how involved the sentence,
the subject may readily be found — if the verb has first
been recognized. Simply ask, "Who or what?" In the
sentence listed above, who or what *circles?* The airplane *circles.* It is sometimes helpful to diagram the
subject and verb by placing the two on a horizontal
line and separating them by a vertical line, thus:

airplane	*circles*

Any student who can bring the subject and verb together in this way should have little trouble in making
the two agree.

Caution in regard to subjects: In commands the subject is
   usually not expressed.

1. *Go* into the house.   [The subject **You** is understood.]
2. *Open* the door.   [The subject **You** is understood.]
3. *Mind* your own business.   [The subject **You** is understood.]
4. **You** *mind* your own business.

The subject of an interrogative sentence is usually
clearer when the sentence is recast in the form of a
statement.

Has the **last** of the deserters *surrendered?*
[The **last** of the deserters *has surrendered.*]

last ·	has surrendered

2e frag

EXERCISE 6. Underscore each verb once, each subject twice. Then diagram the subject and predicate of each sentence.

1. The little dogs bark furiously.
2. He found a purse with money.
3. Fishing is good recreation.
4. William enjoyed his school work.
5. The team, after being outplayed for three quarters, won the game.
6. To do your work well is essential for success.
7. The trees sway in the wind.
8. Speaking before a group is good practice.
9. She likes tennis and badminton.
10. To be a successful writer is difficult in this age of competition.

Each sentence in Exercise 6 is a *simple sentence;* that is, it consists of a group of words (not a subordinate clause) containing only one verb and one subject. A simple sentence may have a compound subject (**Mary** and **Jane** *played*), a compound predicate (**Mary** *sang* and *played*), or both compound subject and compound predicate (**Mary** and **Jane** *sang* and *played*).

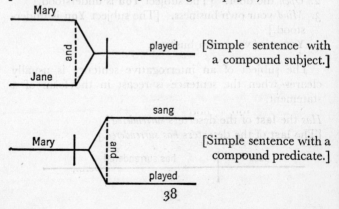

[Simple sentence with a compound subject.]

[Simple sentence with a compound predicate.]

38

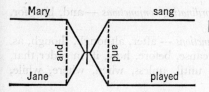

[Simple sentence with a compound subject and a compound predicate.]

EXERCISE 7. Diagram the subject and predicate of the following simple sentences. Note that some of the subjects and predicates are compound.

1. Harry and James entered the School of Commerce.
2. The children laughed and played all the way home.
3. All boys and girls like pets.
4. Bear and deer roam through the forests.
5. He hammered and pounded on the door with all his might.
6. The lightning and thunder terrified the women and children.
7. The winds and waves drove the fishing craft on the rocks.
8. During the game, women and men shouted and yelled.
9. You and I do not like the thought of war.
10. The man and his wife carve trinkets and sell them on the market.

(3) Recognizing All the Parts of Speech

1. VERBS: receive, tell, think, has told, has been told, *etc.*
2 (3). NOUNS (PRONOUNS): man (he), Mary (she), book (it), *etc.*
4. ADJECTIVES: happy, hot, rapid, fast, *etc.*
5. ADVERBS: happily, hotly, rapidly, fast, *etc.*[1]

---

[1] Sometimes a word may be any one of several parts of speech, according to the function of the word in the sentence.

The *fast* train was late. [*Fast* used as an adjective.]
The train moved *fast*. [*Fast* used as an adverb.]
Fast and pray daily. [*Fast* used as a verb.]

39

2e frag

6. CONJUNCTIONS: *Co-ordinating conjunctions* — and, but, for, or, nor.

    Subordinating conjunctions — after, although, though, as, as if, as long as, because, before, how, if, in order that, since, so that, till, until, unless, when, where, while, why, *etc.*

7. PREPOSITIONS: about, above, across, after, against, among, around, as far as, at, before, below, beside, between, by, down, for, from, in, in spite of, into, like, of, on account of, onto, over, since, to, toward, under, until, unto, up, upon, with, within, *etc.* [Note that some prepositions, such as *after*, *before*, and *since*, are used also as conjunctions.]

8. INTERJECTIONS: oh! whew! alas! bah!

1. VERBS. The *verb* — a word or word group that asserts action, being, or state of being — is the most important of all the parts of speech. Since it is the very heart of the sentence, it should be mastered first of all. (See the detailed treatment at the beginning of section **2e**). The verb has but one use in the sentence: it is the simple predicate.

Caution: Make every verb agree in number with its subject.

Birds *fly*.   The man *is* old.

Birds	*fly*

[Subject + verb.]

man	*is*

[Subject + verb.]

2 (3). NOUNS (PRONOUNS). A *noun* is the name of a person, place, or thing. (A *pronoun* is a word used instead of a noun.) Nouns and pronouns have many uses in the sentence. Some of their common uses are

as (a) subjects of verbs, (b) objects of verbs, (c) predicate nominatives, and (d) objects of prepositions.

Caution: Be careful to use the nominative case of pronouns for subjects of verbs and for predicate nominatives, the objective case for objects of verbs and prepositions.

(a) Subjects of verbs.

The *boy* played.   *He* played.

boy	played

[Subject (a noun) + verb.]

He	played

[Subject (a pronoun) + verb.]

(b) Objects of verbs.

The boy ate an *apple*.   He ate *it*.

boy	ate	apple

[Subject + verb + object.]

He	ate	It

[Subject + verb + object.]

(c) Predicate nominatives.

The man is a *beggar*.   It is *he*.

man	is \ beggar

[Subject + verb + predicate nominative.]

It	is \ he

[Subject + verb + predicate nominative.]

41

2e frag

(d) Objects of prepositions.

> The beggar came to the *boy* for *help*.
> He came to *him* for *help*.

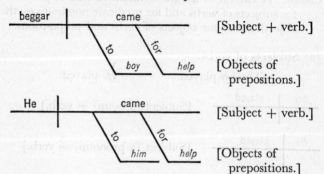

beggar | came	[Subject + verb.]
to *boy* / *for* help	[Objects of prepositions.]
He | came	[Subject + verb.]
to *him* / *for* help	[Objects of prepositions.]

The indirect object may be considered the object of the preposition *to*, usually implied.

The boy gave the *beggar* an apple.   Give *me* an apple.

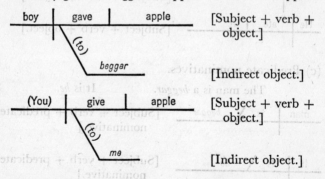

boy | gave | apple	[Subject + verb + object.]
(to) beggar	[Indirect object.]
(You) | give | apple	[Subject + verb + object.]
(to) me	[Indirect object.]

EXERCISE 8.   Underscore all verbs once and all nouns and pronouns twice.   Then diagram the sentences to show the function of each noun or pronoun.

frag 2e

1. The students have completed examinations.
2. They are ready for a vacation.
3. The book on the desk has blue covers.
4. James Smith is the captain of the first team.
5. The new manager readily gave me the money for the ticket.
6. Gently he opened the front door.
7. The merchant sold a bushel of red apples.
8. Cold weather kills the tender plants.
9. The smoke lay over the city like a black cloud.
10. Hungry birds perched very quietly on the branches of the little tree.

4, 5. ADJECTIVES AND ADVERBS. *Adjectives* and *adverbs* are modifiers. That is, they describe or limit other words. Adjectives modify only nouns or pronouns. Adverbs modify only verbs, adjectives, or other adverbs.

Caution: Do not confuse adjectives and adverbs. When necessary consult a good dictionary to determine whether a word is an adjective or an adverb. (Some words may be either.) Do not allow a word listed by the dictionary only as an adjective to modify a verb, an adjective, or an adverb. Do not allow a word listed only as an adverb to modify a noun or a pronoun.

In the following sentences, adjectives are in boldface, adverbs in italic. In the diagrams the modifiers are attached to the words they modify: adjectives only to nouns or pronouns; adverbs only to verbs, adjectives, or other adverbs.

The tall man walked *rapidly*.

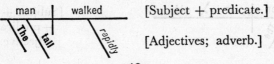

[Subject + predicate.]

[Adjectives; adverb.]

43

The *exceedingly* **tall** man walked *very rapidly*.

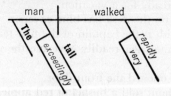

The **third** man *quietly* pushed **the dirty** clothes behind **the wooden** door.

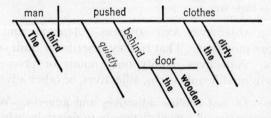

A *predicate adjective* (used especially after *is, was, were*) helps to complete the meaning of the verb at the same time that it refers back to the subject. (In the diagrams such an adjective is not attached to the subject but is placed in the position of the object after a line sloping back toward the subject.)

The clothes were **dirty**.   **The** man is **old**.

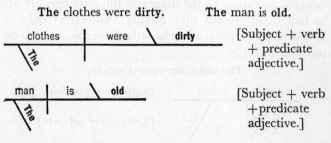

[Subject + verb + predicate adjective.]

[Subject + verb + predicate adjective.]

44

frag 2e

As a rule the predicate adjective (not the adverb) follows *is, was, were, seems, becomes,* and the verbs pertaining to the senses (*feel, look, smell, sound, taste*).

The town seems **deserted.   The** woman looked **young.**

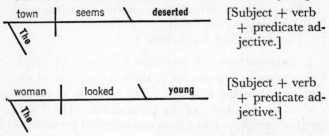

[Subject + verb + predicate adjective.]

[Subject + verb + predicate adjective.]

But the adverb (not the predicate adjective) is used when the modifier refers to the manner of the action of the verb.

The woman looked *angrily* at him.

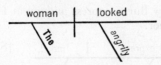

EXERCISE 9.   Diagram the sentences in Exercise 8, attaching each adjective or adverb to the word it modifies.

EXERCISE 10.   In some of the following sentences a word listed by the dictionary only as an adjective is wrongly made to modify a verb, an adjective, or an adverb.   In other sentences a word listed only as an adverb is incorrectly made to modify a noun or pronoun.   Look up each questionable word in the dictionary and supply the correct form.   Then diagram the corrected sentence.

1. The nervous woman moved rapid across the street.
2. I feel badly today.

2e frag

3. The girl was dressed most beautiful.
4. He can swim across the stream easy.
5. The rose smells sweetly.
6. I sure was tired.
7. He ate his meals regular.
8. The engine performed perfect during the whole trip.
9. Many apples taste sourly.
10. That candy sure is delicious.

6. PREPOSITIONS. A *preposition* is a word placed before a noun or a pronoun to show its relation to some other word in the sentence. The noun or pronoun is said to be the object of the preposition. The English language employs fewer than one hundred prepositions, and only half of these are in common use.

Caution: Select prepositions carefully to express the exact relation between the object of the preposition and the word modified by the preposition.

The poems *by* Burns express *with* great force the mood *of* the author.

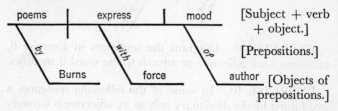

poems	express	mood	[Subject + verb + object.]
by	with	of	[Prepositions.]
Burns	force	author	[Objects of prepositions.]

EXERCISE 11. Determine which of the sentences in Exercise 8 contain prepositions. Diagram each sentence in which a preposition is used.

7. CONJUNCTIONS. A *conjunction* is a word used to connect words, phrases, or clauses. The five *co-ordinating conjunctions* (*and, but, for, or, nor*) connect words,

46

phrases, or clauses of equal rank. The *subordinating conjunctions* (such as *after, because, if, since, till, when, where, while*) connect subordinate clauses with main clauses.

Caution: Select conjunctions carefully to express the exact meaning. Use as conjunctions only the words so designated by a good dictionary.

In diagrams conjunctions are usually placed on broken lines drawn between the parts connected by the conjunction.

Boys *and* girls played on the lawn *and* walks *and* even out in the street.

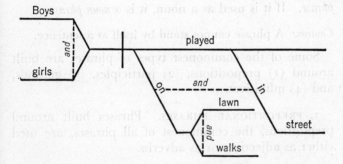

EXERCISE 12. Note all conjunctions in Exercises 6, 7, 8. Diagram each sentence in which a conjunction appears.

8. INTERJECTIONS. An *interjection* is a word expressing emotion; it has no grammatical relation to other words in the sentence. If the emotion is strong, the interjection may be followed by an exclamation point, but it is more commonly followed by a comma. In

diagrams the interjection is usually set off by itself to indicate its independence of the rest of the sentence.[1]

Oh, I can hardly believe it.

$$\underline{\text{Oh}}$$

| I | can believe | [Interjection.] |

[Subject + predicate.]

(4) Recognizing Phrases

A *phrase* is any group of related words which has no subject or predicate and is used as a single part of speech. If the phrase modifies a noun or pronoun, it is an *adjective phrase.* If it modifies a verb, it is an *adverb phrase.* If it is used as a noun, it is a *noun phrase.*

Caution: A phrase cannot stand by itself as a sentence.

Some of the commonest types of phrases are built around (1) prepositions, (2) participles, (3) gerunds, and (4) infinitives.

1. PREPOSITIONAL PHRASES. Phrases built around prepositions, the commonest of all phrases, are used either as adjectives or as adverbs.

---

[1] Other independent sentence elements, such as nouns of address and absolute expressions, may be diagrammed in the same way.

William, we need your assistance.

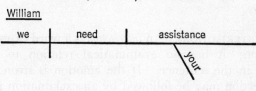

48

The man *with red hair* is my brother.

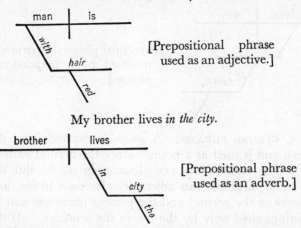

[Prepositional phrase used as an adjective.]

My brother lives *in the city.*

[Prepositional phrase used as an adverb.]

EXERCISE 13. Identify all prepositional phrases in Exercises 6, 7, 8. Determine whether each phrase is used as an adjective or as an adverb. Diagram three sentences containing adjective phrases and three containing adverb phrases.

2. PARTICIPIAL PHRASES. The *participle* is derived from the verb and is used as an adjective. Therefore the participial phrase is always an adjective phrase. Participles are either present (*bringing, hoping, leaving*) or past (*brought, hoped, left*).

A person *bringing good news* is always welcome.

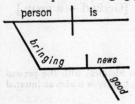

[Participial phrase. *News* is the object of the participle.]

49

2e frag

The good news *brought by the person* was welcome.

[Participial phrase: a participle modified by a prepositional phrase.]

3. GERUND PHRASES. A *gerund* is derived from the verb and is used as a noun. Since the gerund ends in *ing,* it is called "the verbal noun in *ing.*" But the present participle (an adjective) also ends in *ing,* and therefore the gerund and the present participle can be distinguished only by the use in the sentence.[1] If the verbal in *ing* is used as a noun, it is a gerund; if it is used as an adjective (that is, if it modifies a noun or a pronoun) it is a participle.

Running water seldom freezes.

[Participle — an adjective.]

Running is good exercise.

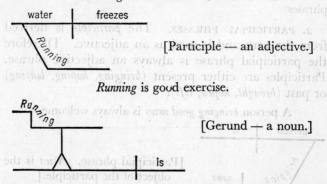

[Gerund — a noun.]

[1] The gerund always ends in *ing;* it is identical with the present participle. The past participle ends in *ed, d, t, en, n,* or makes an internal change.

Since the gerund is a noun, a phrase built around a gerund is used as a noun.

Running a grocery store is sometimes profitable.

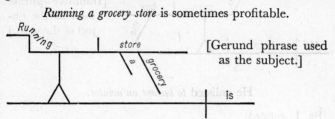

[Gerund phrase used as the subject.]

He was paid well for *running the grocery store*.

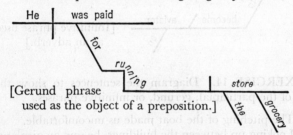

[Gerund phrase used as the object of a preposition.]

4. INFINITIVE PHRASES. The infinitive is the verbal regularly preceded by *to* and used as a noun, an adjective, or an adverb. Phrases built around infinitives have the same uses.

To walk through the town was a pleasure.

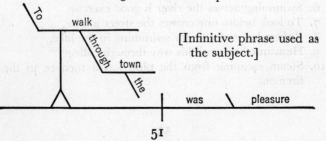

[Infinitive phrase used as the subject.]

51

He began *to open the box.*

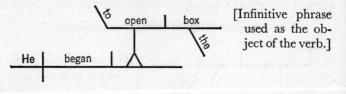

[Infinitive phrase used as the object of the verb.]

He enlisted *to become an aviator.*

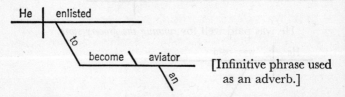

[Infinitive phrase used as an adverb.]

EXERCISE 14. Diagram the sentences to show the uses of the participial, gerund, or infinitive phrases.

1. The pitching of the boat made us uncomfortable.
2. Looking up between the buildings, he saw an airplane.
3. The shouting of happy students rushing down the street announced the victory.
4. Having finished his examinations, the student was ready to go home.
5. Balancing dangerously on the steel beam, the riveter risks his life daily.
6. Swimming across the river is good exercise.
7. To look before one crosses the street is wise.
8. Robert has a dislike for swimming in the lake.
9. He wanted to work his way through college.
10. Steam escaping from the pipe was a menace to the firemen.

frag 2e

(5) Distinguishing between Main Clauses and Subordinate Clauses

Anyone who can point out verbs and their subjects can also point out clauses, for a clause is simply a group of words containing a verb and its subject. There are two kinds of clauses:

1. Subordinate (also called *dependent*) clauses.
2. Main (also called *independent* or *principal*) clauses.

1. SUBORDINATE CLAUSES. A subordinate clause cannot stand alone. It depends upon the rest of the sentence for its meaning.

EXAMPLE *When it rains*, the work stops. [*When it rains* is a subordinate clause preceding the main clause. A sentence containing a main clause and one or more subordinate clauses is called a *complex sentence.*]

Subordinate clauses are used as adverbs (called *adverb clauses*), as adjectives (called *adjective clauses*), or as nouns (called *noun clauses*).

(a) Adverb clauses.

Any clause that modifies a verb is an adverb clause.

EXERCISE 15. Draw a wavy line under the one adverbial clause in each of the following sentences.

1. She left the house when the rain stopped.
2. The physician came as soon as he was called.
3. The car passed while we were talking.
4. The girl left home because she wanted work.
5. The child stopped where he was told.

53

The connecting words (conjunctions) used in these five sentences are *when, as soon as, while, because,* and *where.* Other conjunctions commonly used to introduce adverbial clauses are *after, although, as, before, if, since, than, though, till,* and *unless.* Each subordinate clause modifies the verb of the main clause. In other words, it serves as an adverb. Therefore it is called an *adverb clause.*

EXERCISE 16. Diagram the sentences in Exercise 15, thus:

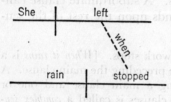

| She | left | [Subject + predicate of main clause.] |

[Connecting word.]

| rain | stopped | [Subject + predicate of subordinate clause.] |

(b) Adjective clauses.

Any clause that modifies a noun or a pronoun is an adjective clause.

EXERCISE 17. Draw a wavy line under the one adjective clause in each of the following sentences.

1. I had a teacher who had once lived in Denmark.
2. The book which he wrote was well received.
3. Mr. Smith, who is my neighbor, is a lawyer.
4. James read the article, which dealt with civic problems.
5. Mr. Wilson recommended a resort that was on the bay.

Each subordinate clause in the preceding exercise modifies a noun. In other words, it serves as an adjective. Therefore it is called an *adjective clause.* Adjective clauses are usually introduced by the relative

frag 2e

pronouns *who*, *which*, or *that*. The relative pronoun also serves as the subject of the subordinate clause.

EXERCISE 18. Diagram the sentences in Exercise 17, thus:

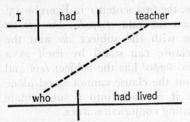

[Subject + predicate of main clause + object of the verb.]

[Line showing the word modified by the subordinate clause.]

[Subject + predicate of subordinate clause.]

(c) Noun clauses.

A clause that functions as subject, as object, or in any other capacity as a noun, is a noun clause.

EXERCISE 19. Draw a wavy line under the one noun clause in each of the following sentences.

1. He says that Jack is an artist.
2. That we can defend our country is certain.
3. I asked what he meant.
4. Bob wonders who told the news.
5. What worried Tom was the loss of his knife.

EXERCISE 20. Diagram the sentences in Exercise 19, thus:

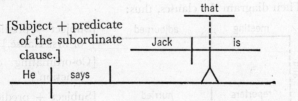

[Subject + predicate of the subordinate clause.]

55

Caution: Each of the sentences in Exercises 15–20 consists of one main clause and one subordinate clause. Each of the main clauses can stand by itself as a sentence. But any one of the subordinate clauses, if allowed to stand by itself, would be merely a sentence fragment. Let us take, for example, the first sentence in Exercise 15: **She** *left* the house when the **rain** *stopped.* *She left the house* is a main clause with the subject *she* and the predicate *left*. The clause can stand by itself as a sentence. *When the rain stopped* has the subject *rain* and the predicate *stopped*, but the clause cannot stand alone as a sentence because it is made into a subordinate clause by the subordinating conjunction *when*.

2. MAIN CLAUSES. A main clause has both subject and predicate and is not introduced by a subordinating conjunction. A main clause modifies nothing. It is independent. It can stand alone as a simple sentence.

EXAMPLE When it rains, *the work stops.* [*The work stops* is a main clause.]

A sentence containing two (or more) main clauses and no subordinate clause is called a *compound sentence.*

EXAMPLE The war was long, but the people kept up their courage.

EXERCISE 21. In the following compound sentences point out the subject and the predicate of each main clause. Then diagram the clauses, thus:

meeting	adjourned	[Subject + predicate of first clause.]
and		[Co-ordinating conjunction.]
reporters	hurried	[Subject + predicate of second clause.]

1. The meeting adjourned promptly at three o'clock, and the reporters hurried away to interview the speaker.
2. Jane likes to play tennis, but Mary prefers to knit and crochet.
3. The building must be completed before the end of the year, or we shall be forced to find other quarters.
4. We halted at the edge of the forest, but our dogs continued the chase.
5. Some of the boys climbed the mountain; others collected wood to make a fire.

Caution: Main clauses are separated by a comma only when joined by one of the co-ordinating conjunctions (*and, but, or, nor, for*), as in the first four sentences in Exercise 21. Otherwise a semicolon must be used, as in the last sentence of Exercise 21. Using only a comma between main clauses not joined by *and, but, or, nor,* or *for* is a serious error known as the *comma splice*. It is still worse to use no punctuation whatever between main clauses.

EXERCISE 22. Point out the subject and the predicate of each main clause. Draw a wavy line under each subordinate clause and classify it as (1) an adverb clause, (2) an adjective clause, or (3) a noun clause.

1. The boy failed in his work because he did not study each assignment in its proper order.
2. The maple that is in the corner of the yard is a mass of red, yellow, and green.
3. The officer said that William, who was driving a new car, was breaking the speed limit.
4. When summer comes the parks are filled with children who play on the grass.
5. That the airplane is becoming safer every day is easily proved by statistics.

6. The new bridge which spans the Mississippi at Baton Rouge is another indication of progress in the South.

7. The first settlers journeyed until they came to a river, and there they pitched their camps for the night.

8. As the nights grew longer and the days correspondingly shorter, the explorers worked unceasingly to provide food and shelter for the long, bitter, cold days ahead, when it would be impossible to venture far from the base.

9. Who could have ransacked the house and found the hidden papers was a question which baffled the detectives.

10. Mr. Smith, who led the way and who knew where wild game might be found, kept a close watch for bears' tracks as we walked; but during two hours of tramping through the underbrush, not a trace of any kind of animal could be found.

11. The boy who lives in the country thinks that it is very easy to earn a living in the city.

12. Crowds of people lined the streets and cheered the soldiers who were on their way to the front.

13. The child called loudly for help, but his mother, who was in the yard, did not hear him.

14. When the rain stopped the sun began to shine, and the caravan moved on.

15. That he is sincere is beyond question, but his actions show a lack of good judgment.

COMMA SPLICE
(COMMA FAULT)

3. Do not write sentences together with only a comma between them (comma splice), or worse still, without any punctuation.

WRONG The current was swift, he could not swim to shore. [Comma splice.]

WRONG (EVEN WORSE) The current was swift he could not swim to shore. [Worse than a comma splice.]

RIGHT The current was swift. He could not swim to shore.

A comma splice can always be corrected by placing a period at the end of the first sentence and beginning the second sentence with a capital letter, as in the example above. But other methods of correction are possible, and frequently preferable.

3a. The comma splice is often best corrected by subordination.[1]

WRONG The current was swift, he could not swim to shore.

RIGHT Since the current was swift, he could not swim to shore. [First statement (a main clause) reduced to a subordinate clause.]

RIGHT The current was so swift that he could not swim to shore. [Second statement (a main clause) reduced to a subordinate clause.]

[1] See also section 24, Subordination.

59

RIGHT   The swiftness of the current prevented his swim-
        ming to shore. [The two main clauses reduced to
        a simple sentence.]

RIGHT   Because of the swift current he could not swim to
        shore. [First main clause reduced to a preposi-
        tional phrase.]

3b. The comma splice may also be corrected by co-ordination.

WRONG   The current was swift, he could not swim to shore.

RIGHT   The current was swift, and he could not swim to
        shore. [The two statements separated by a comma
        + the conjunction *and*.]

RIGHT   The current was swift; he could not swim to shore.
        [The two statements separated by a semicolon.]

RIGHT   The current was swift. He could not swim to
        shore. [The two statements separated by a period.]

Two or more main clauses cannot stand in the same
sentence, separated only by a comma, unless they are
joined by one of the co-ordinating conjunctions: *and,
but, or, nor, for*. Sometimes it is helpful to make a
diagram, at least to form a mental picture, of the subject and predicate of each main clause and the joining
word, as thus for the sentence, *The current was swift, and
he could not swim to shore.*

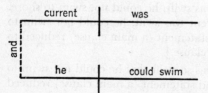

current	was	[Subject + predicate of first clause.]
and		[Co-ordinating con-junction.]
he	could swim	[Subject + predicate of second clause.]

3c. Do not let a conjunctive adverb or a transitional expression trick you into making a comma splice.

When a conjunctive adverb such as *then, thus, so, therefore, however* — or any transitional expression such as *in fact* or *on the other hand* — is used to connect main clauses, a semicolon or a period must be used between the clauses.

WRONG   The two teams line up for the kickoff, then comes the thrill.

RIGHT   The two teams line up for the kickoff; then comes the thrill.

RIGHT   The two teams line up for the kickoff, and then comes the thrill.

WRONG   The story was not true to fact, however, it was interesting.

RIGHT   The story was not true to fact; however, it was interesting.

RIGHT   The story was not true to fact, but it was interesting.

WRONG   Bears in the park are very tame, in fact, they will eat food from one's hands.

RIGHT   Bears in the park are very tame; in fact, they will eat food from one's hands.

3d. Avoid making a comma splice with divided quotations.

WRONG   "Your answer is wrong," he said, "correct it."

RIGHT   "Your answer is wrong," he said. "Correct it."

Exceptions: Short co-ordinate clauses in series, parallel in form and unified in thought, may be separated by commas:

RIGHT   I came, I saw, I conquered.

ALSO RIGHT   I came; I saw; I conquered.

Informal writing furnishes frequent examples of sentences separated by commas. Occasional examples are found in more formal writing. But such liberty is not recommended for the student learning the fundamental principles of English composition. He should make sure that all of his main clauses are separated (1) by a comma + *and, but, or, nor,* or *for,* (2) by a semicolon, or (3) by a period.

Note: If you cannot readily pick out verbs and their subjects and distinguish between phrases, subordinate clauses, and main clauses, you will probably continue to write comma splices. If so, you should first master the fundamentals of the sentence treated in section **2e, Sentence Sense,** and then study again section **3, Comma Splice.**

EXERCISES ON THE COMMA SPLICE

A. Correct each of the following sentences by some method of subordination.

1. I enjoy the spring, I like to see everything come to life.
2. Making a decision takes time, we have to recall past experiences before we can express an opinion.
3. The next morning we got up early and went to Silver Springs, this is a most unusual place.
4. You are only what you make yourself, you must try to put everything into your work.
5. On the paved roads were many cars, some were new and others were fit only for the junk heap.
6. We are always meeting new and interesting people, still we are often lonely.
7. The dog went directly to the fire, then he began to lick himself.
8. I must make this course count, I must work harder than I have been working.

9. The light from the flickering lamp fell on his watch, it was just ten o'clock.

10. The air was hot and stuffy, even the flies were too exhausted to hum.

B. Correct each of the following sentences by some method of co-ordination.

1. She must not be too bold, in fact, I like a timid girl.

2. Society meant little to our grandmothers, their chief interest consisted in making a good home for their children.

3. I knew she would come, in all these years she has never broken a promise.

4. "There is no one at home," he said, "we shall have to find another place."

5. He did not mean to hurt the boy, he only intended to frighten him.

6. Some of us are wise by nature, some of us never become so.

7. The race is in progress, the cars are travelling so fast that they soon become mere specks in the distance.

8. I had just finished packing my trunk when the doorbell rang, it was the expressman who had come for my trunk.

9. The boys have a gymnasium of their own, why not have one for the girls?

10. Jack was a boy with personality, you felt that he would arrive at the top some day.

C. Correct each of the following sentences by the method which seems most appropriate.

1. In his youth he spent many free and thoughtless hours in the forests, he did not worry about anything but having a good time.

2. The only impediment to wider use of electricity for heating has been the cost of current, present rates

encourage the hope that its use for this purpose will increase rapidly.

3. A new play is written by a different author every week, consequently the plays differ greatly in style.

4. The sea took her husband and sons one by one, the bodies of some were never found.

5. "Elizabeth will be down in a few minutes," she said, "have a seat and make yourself at home."

6. The Jews were the first religious martyrs in history, let us hope that they will prove to be the last.

7. The topic should not be very long, just a phrase or even one word tells what the theme is about.

8. The first thing that impressed me was the snow, during the preceding week it had covered all the shrubs.

9. There is a small fee for bathhouse and shower, otherwise no charge is made.

10. I do not know the outcome of the game yet, I only hope our team wins.

11. I like some of my professors, they are really interesting.

12. Drunken people do not arouse the admiration of nearby spectators, as they suppose, the result is quite to the contrary.

13. The car sped down the road, then it suddenly swerved toward the ditch along the road.

14. We talked a few minutes longer about the mystery, then asking those present not to say anything about it, we went home.

15. He has made a map of the roads in the state, it will be valuable to the travelling public.

16. Some hid behind chairs, some hid behind the sofa, I found my way into a dark closet.

17. We approached the house, it was dark and deserted.

18. There are two roads one may take, one turns to the left, the other goes right on.

19. I went out to inquire how much the tickets cost, then I came back and told my friend.

ADJECTIVES AND ADVERBS

4. Distinguish between the adjective and the adverb and use the correct form for each.

You may learn from a good dictionary the correct form for the adjective or the adverb, but only your ability to analyze the sentence will show whether an adjective or an adverb is needed. If you lack this ability, you may find it advisable to study section **2e, Sentence Sense.**

Adjectives modify (qualify) only nouns or pronouns; adverbs modify verbs, adjectives, or other adverbs.

>   *adj.*   *adv.*   *adv.*   *adj. (participle)*   *adv.*
> EXAMPLE The too often neglected child had now become
>   *adv.*   *adv.*   *adj.*
> almost desperately hungry.

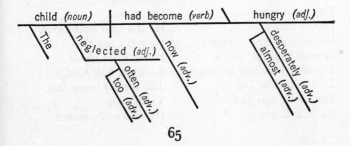

[The predicate adjective *hungry* qualifies the noun *child*. The other adjectives and all the adverbs are attached to the words they modify.]

The ending *ly* is the most common for adverbs: *rapidly*, *smoothly*, *evenly*, etc. But some adjectives have the same ending: *saintly*, *womanly*, *manly*, etc. Other words ending in *ly* may be used as either adjectives or adverbs.

Adjective	*Adverb*
He was an *only* son.	The boy has *only* two apples.
He was a *cowardly* knight.	He acted *cowardly*.
The *early* bird gets the worm.	He rose *early* to go to work.

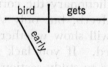
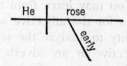

Many of the most commonly used words have the same form for the adjective and the adverb.

Adjective	*Adverb*
He replied in a *high* voice.	Place it *high* on the shelf.
The man is an *early* riser.	Go home *early*.
She was a *quick* worker.	Speak up *quick*.
It was a *slow* bus.	Drive *slow*.
The noise was *loud*.	Speak *loud*.
I have *little* energy.	He is a *little* ambitious.
He lives in a *far* country.	He went too *far*.
Stop at the *right* place.	Please do it *right*.
The fact was *hard* to face.	Kick the ball *hard*.
The train was *late*.	The soldier came *late*.
The clock was *fast*.	Think *fast*.
All is *well* today.	He was *well* pleased.

4a. Avoid making an adjective modify anything other than a noun or pronoun; avoid making an adverb modify anything other than a verb, an adjective, or another adverb.

Especially common is the misuse of the adjective to modify a verb.

WRONG One can drown in a pool as *easy* as in a lake. [The adjective *easy* cannot modify the verb *can drown*.]

RIGHT One can drown in a pool as *easily* as in a lake.

WRONG I drive fast and sometimes *careless*. [The adjective *careless* cannot modify the verb *drive*.]

RIGHT I drive fast and sometimes *carelessly*.

The adjective is frequently misused to modify another adjective.

WRONG *Most* any man would enjoy a vacation. [The adjective *most* cannot modify the adjective *any*.]

RIGHT *Almost* any man would enjoy a vacation. [The adverb *almost* substituted for the adjective *most*.]

WRONG I was *real* tired. [The adjective *real* cannot modify the adjective *tired*.]

RIGHT I was *really* tired.

WRONG I was *sure* glad to go. [The adjective *sure* cannot modify the adjective *glad*.]

RIGHT I was *surely* glad to go.

Usually adverbs are misused only because of gross carelessness.

WRONG The story is told in a *convincingly* manner.

RIGHT The story is told in a *convincing* manner.

67

4 ad

4b. As a rule *is, was, seems, becomes,* and the verbs pertaining to the senses (*feel, look, smell, sound, taste*), are followed by an adjective.

RIGHT   The man is *old*. [*Old* is an adjective modifying *man: old man.*]

RIGHT   The girl was excited. [*Excited girl.*]

RIGHT   The town seems deserted. [*Deserted town.*]

RIGHT   The Indian became hostile. [*Hostile Indian.*]

RIGHT   The boy felt lonesome. [*Lonesome boy.*]

RIGHT   The woman looked young. [*Young woman.*]

RIGHT   The flower smells sweet. [*Sweet flower.*]

RIGHT   The report sounds exaggerated. [*Exaggerated report.*]

RIGHT   The milk tastes sour. [*Sour milk.*]

Exception: The modifier is an adverb when it refers to the manner of the action of the verb.

RIGHT   The blind beggar felt *cautiously* along the wall. [The adverb *cautiously* qualifies the verb *felt*. How did he feel? *Cautiously.*]

RIGHT   The woman looked *angrily* at him. [The adverb *angrily* qualifies the verb *looked.*]

4c. A modifier following a verb and its direct object is an adjective if it refers to the object, an adverb if it refers to the manner of the action of the verb.

RIGHT   The boy held the rope *tight*. [*Tight* is an adjective: *tight rope.*]

RIGHT   The boy held the rope *tightly*. [The adverb *tightly* describes the manner of the holding.]

RIGHT   He held the boat *steady*. [*Steady* is an adjective: *steady boat.*]

RIGHT   He held the boat *steadily* on its course. [The adverb *steadily* describes the manner of the holding.]

4d. Make comparisons accurate and logical.[1]

	Positive	Comparative	Superlative
ADJECTIVES	bad	worse	worst
	good	better	best
	warm	warmer	warmest
	tired	more (less) tired	most (least) tired
ADVERBS	badly	worse	worst
	well	better	best
	warmly	more (less) warmly	most (least) warmly

Some adjectives, such as *good* and *bad*, and some adverbs, such as *well* and *badly*, have an irregular comparison. But these are among our common words and are seldom confused. In general the shorter adjectives (and a few adverbs) form the comparative degree by adding *er* and the superlative by adding *est;* the longer adjectives and most adverbs form the comparative by the use of *more* (*less*) and the superlative by the use of *most* (*least*).

RIGHT Today is *warmer* than yesterday.
RIGHT In fact, today is the *warmest* day of the year.
RIGHT He was the *taller* of the two boys.
RIGHT He was the *tallest* of the three boys.

A few adjectives and adverbs are logically incapable of comparison: *round, square, perfect, equal, entirely, now, then, there,* etc.

WRONG This hoop is *rounder* than that.
RIGHT This hoop is *more nearly round* than that.

[1] For the meaning of *comparison* see section 1, Grammatical Terms.

4 ad

4e. In general avoid the use of a noun as an adjective or an adjective as a noun.

WRONG The English teacher calls for an *autobiography* theme.

RIGHT The English teacher calls for an *autobiographical* theme.

WRONG The frontier was only a short *distant* away. [*Distant* is an adjective.]

RIGHT The frontier was only a short *distance* away.

EXERCISES ON ADJECTIVES AND ADVERBS

A. Correct all errors in the use of adjectives or adverbs. In making the corrections diagram the sentences to show that each adjective modifies a noun or a pronoun; each adverb a verb, an adjective, or another adverb.

1. Sometimes she did not act so good.
2. New York won the World Series very easy.
3. She went to most every dance.
4. Mother does all kinds of work rapid.
5. A good hog has short legs and a reasonable wide body.

B. Correct all errors in the use of adjectives and adverbs.

1. I could not possible avoid a collision.
2. The slow method gives a much smoother job than that of cutting the metal rapid.
3. Basketball is more easy followed than football.
4. She was more livelier than any other person in the group.
5. She was the largest of the two.
6. Most any day will be satisfactory.
7. I think that most everyone would agree with me.
8. Will I be able to walk good when I get up?
9. The author pictures the scenes so vivid that the reader is eager to know what will happen next.

10. It was real kind of you to answer my letter so prompt.
11. The older people do not change greatly; they grumbling accept the inevitable.
12. I felt important and special privileged.
13. The green bowl is rounder than the blue one.
14. Football is a national known sport.
15. It sure did look bad for our team.

C. Select the correct form within the brackets and give your reason. If more than one form is correct, explain why.

1. I like it so well that I [sure, surely] would like to go back.
2. This attracted the attention of [most, mostly] men.
3. It is [surprising, surprisingly] to know that some people who have the most money have the least common sense.
4. We thought [sure, surely] we had acted [quick, quickly] enough.
5. When one has finished college, one will know how to meet [most, almost] any problem.
6. To me the poem was like a [rich, richly] colored painting.
7. This auditorium is constructed so [perfect, perfectly] that a person can hear a pin drop fifty yards away.
8. The thought of the drought makes them feel [bad, badly].
9. I was glad to escape so [easily, easy].
10. If we get into a habit of eating [regular, regularly], we have much better health.
11. Walk [careful, carefully] across the street.
12. That is a [really, real] becoming dress.

5 ca

5. Give to each noun or pronoun the case required by its function in the sentence.

Note: An appositive takes the same case as the noun or pronoun with which it is in apposition.

RIGHT We — *John* and *I* — are responsible for the damage. [The appositives *John* and *I* are in the nominative case, in agreement with *we*.]

RIGHT The damage was caused by us — *John* and *me*. [The appositives *John* and *me* are in the objective case, in agreement with *us*.]

Nouns and pronouns have case to indicate their functions in the sentence as subjects (nominative case), possessors (possessive case), or objects (objective case).

EXAMPLE   Nominative   Possessive   Objective   Nominative
        I   furnish   my   labor   and   you   pay

Objective   Possessive   Objective
me   for the   day's   work.

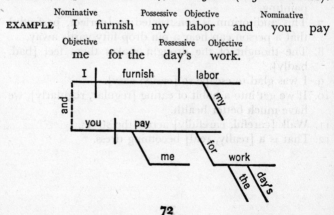

72

NOUN

	Nominative	Possessive	Objective
SINGULAR	day	day's	day
PLURAL	days	days'	days

PRONOUNS

	Nominative	Possessive	Objective
	Singular		
FIRST PERSON	I	my, mine	me
SECOND PERSON	you	your, yours	you
THIRD PERSON	he, she, it	his, her, hers, its	him, her, it
	Plural		
FIRST PERSON	we	our, ours	us
SECOND PERSON	you	your, yours	you
THIRD PERSON	they	their, theirs	them

Nominative	Possessive	Objective
Singular and Plural		
who	whose	whom

As this table shows, nouns are inflected only in the possessive case, and consequently require little attention. The personal pronoun (*I, you, he, she, it*) and the relative-interrogative pronoun (*who*) must be used with more care because they are inflected in all three cases.

NOMINATIVE CASE

5a. Subjects of verbs (but not of infinitives) are put in the nominative case.

RIGHT   *He* is old.   *She* is kind.   *They* work diligently.

In certain types of sentences care must be taken to prevent mistaking the subject for the object:

(1) Do not allow the pronoun *who* to be incorrectly changed to *whom* by a following parenthetical expression such as *I think* or *He says.*

WRONG   She is a very dependable person *whom* I think will prove worthy of every trust.

RIGHT   She is a very dependable person *who* I think will prove worthy of every trust.

who | will prove

WRONG   The man *whom* he says is coming to help us build the cabin is Mr. Smith.

RIGHT   The man *who* he says is coming to help us build the cabin is Mr. Smith.

who | is coming

(2) Use the nominative case when the pronoun is the subject of a clause the whole of which is the object of a verb or preposition.

WRONG   Employ *whomever* is willing to work.

RIGHT   Employ *whoever* is willing to work. [*Whoever* is the subject of *is willing.* The object of *employ* is the whole clause *whoever is willing to work.*]

WRONG   He had respect for *whomsoever* was in power.

RIGHT   He had respect for *whosoever* was in power. [The complete clause, not merely the pronoun *whosoever*, is the object of the preposition *for.*]

(3) Use the nominative case after the conjunctions *than* or *as* if the pronoun is the subject of an elliptical clause.

RIGHT   He is older than *I.*

RIGHT   He is as wise as *they.*

5b. Pronouns used as predicate complements of verbs should be put in the nominative case.

RIGHT   It is *I, (she, he, they).* [Informal usage accepts *It is me.*]

POSSESSIVE CASE

5c. Use 's (plural s') to form the possessive of nouns and indefinite pronouns, but do not use the apostrophe to form the possessive of personal pronouns (*my, mine, your, yours, his, hers, its, our, ours, their, theirs*) nor of the relative-interrogative pronoun *whose*.[1]

RIGHT *boy's* (singular); *boys'* (plural)

RIGHT *his, hers, its, yours, whose* (singular); *ours, yours, theirs, whose* (plural). [Remember that *hi's* (an error no one would make) is no more incorrect than *her's* or *it's* (possessive). Of course *it's* is correct colloquially as a contraction of *it is:* "It's cold today."]

5d. A noun or pronoun preceding the gerund is usually in the possessive case.

RIGHT *His* coming was not expected.

RIGHT He objected to *Mary's* accepting the position.

RIGHT The *army's* camping along the river caused much anxiety.

In these sentences the verbals ending in *ing* (*coming, accepting*) are used as nouns and are called *gerunds*. But the verbal ending in *ing* is also used as an adjective, called a *participle*. Compare the following:

RIGHT Just imagine *Mary's flying* [possessive + gerund] an airplane. [Emphasis is on the act of flying.]

RIGHT Just imagine *Mary flying* [objective + participle] an airplane. [Emphasis is on *Mary*.]

[1] See further details for forming the possessive case under section 15.

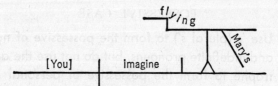

[*Flying* is a gerund, the object of the verb *imagine*.]

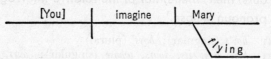

[*Flying* is a participle modifying *Mary*, the object of the verb *imagine*.]

> *Exceptions:* In informal writing the nominative + gerund construction is occasionally used. Even in formal writing it is used when the substantive lacks a possessive form or when the substantive is separated from the gerund.
>
> RIGHT The chance of *anyone* in the party *falling* out was not good.

EXERCISE. Point out each verbal ending in *ing* and determine whether it is a gerund or a participle. Make any needed corrections of case.

1. A woman seldom passes by an attractive window display without it getting her attention.
2. I should not mind anyone inspecting our apartment.
3. As a result of the people disagreeing, Langley's money supply was discontinued.
4. Hardy shows his power of description when he tells of Eustacia appearing on Egdon Heath.
5. I could not picture a statesman coming easily into his rôle.

5e. An of-phrase instead of the possessive is regularly used (1) with inanimate objects and (2) with a noun which is the object of an action.

(1) WRONG The house's roof; the wall's surface; the property's value.

    RIGHT The roof of the house; the surface of the wall; the value of the property.

  Exceptions: Usage justifies the possessive with a number of inanimate objects.

        RIGHT Month's pay, day's work, rope's end, boat's length, etc.

(2) WRONG The Indian's capture was impossible.

    RIGHT The capture of the Indian was impossible.

OBJECTIVE CASE

5f. The object of a verb or preposition should be put in the objective case.

RIGHT All of *us* (not *we*) students bought *tickets*. [*Us* is the object of the preposition *of; tickets* is the object of the verb *bought*.]

Especially troublesome are the relative and interrogative pronouns:

WRONG The artist and the model who he loved had a quarrel.

RIGHT The artist and the model whom he loved had a quarrel. [*Whom* is the object of loved.]

he	loved	whom

WRONG Who should the United States befriend?

RIGHT Whom should the United States befriend? [*Whom* is the object of *should befriend*.]

United States	should befriend	Whom

Note: Before the verb the interrogative *who* is acceptable colloquial English, but formal English requires the objective *whom*.

Pronouns following the conjunction *and* are frequently put in the wrong case.

WRONG Last summer my father took Tom and I on a camping trip.

RIGHT Last summer my father took Tom and me on a camping trip. [*Me* is the object of the verb *took*.]

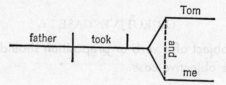

WRONG This is a secret between you and I.

RIGHT This is a secret between you and me. [*Me* is the object of the preposition *between*.]

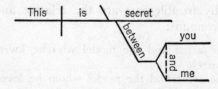

EXERCISE. Correct all errors in case. Show by diagramming that you have used the proper case for each pronoun.

1. Will you go with Tom and I?
2. Is it not a great satisfaction to have a person who you can trust and depend upon at all times?
3. He pretended that his younger brother, who he named Ernest for convenience, was forever getting into trouble.
4. All of we children grew up devoid of any form of religion.
5. Many people are robbed by the innocent looking people who they pick up.

5g. The subject, the object, or the predicate comple-ment of an infinitive should be put in the objective case.

RIGHT   Whom do you think him to be?   [*Whom* is the objective complement and *him* the subject of the infinitive *to be*. *Whom to be him* is the object of the verb *do think*.]

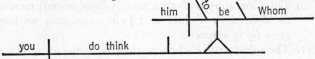

RIGHT   He asked me to help him.   [*Me* is the subject and *him* the object of the infinitive *to help*.]

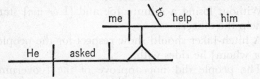

EXERCISE ON CASE

Supply the proper case, giving the reason for your choice.

1. All of [we *or* us] students would appreciate a perfect record.

79

2. Jack pretends to have a very wild brother [who *or* whom] he is constantly coming to the city to look after.

3. Knowing that he had a girl at home [who *or* whom] he should marry, Mrs. Hauksbee stepped in to save him.

4. Poetry is the [poet *or* poet's] expressing his thoughts in verse.

5. Although Brown knew the militia was coming and would destroy [he, his, *or* him] and his followers, he would not retreat.

6. They believe that the angels talk and behave in the same manner as [them *or* they].

7. Robert Browning is a poet [who *or* whom] we can use as an example.

8. I have just heard about [you *or* your] planning to run for mayor.

9. One soon learns the true meaning of the [witches *or* witches'] love.

10. This biography is about a man [who *or* whom] most of us idolized as a child and [who *or* whom] we later grew up to respect.

11. The salesman feels better when he sends away a customer [who *or* whom] he knows will be pleased with the articles purchased.

12. He thought of his poor brother [who *or* whom] this woman had sent to his death.

13. Without losing a minute Joe and [I *or* me] started to help the officer.

14. A hitch-hiker should show respect for the people [who *or* whom] he rides with.

15. The people did not approve of the [government *or* government's] donating money to Langley to carry on his experiments.

16. Many objected to [him *or* his] being in the house.

17. No one knows [who *or* whom] our next mayor will be.

18. [He, his, *or* him] and his father had been reared on a farm.

AGREEMENT

6. Make every verb agree in number[1] with its subject; make every pronoun agree in number[2] with its antecedent.[3]

Note: If you have repeated difficulty with matters of agreement, you should first master the fundamentals of the sentence treated in section **2e, Sentence Sense,** and then study **Agreement.**

[1] A verb also agrees with its subject in person: *I go, he goes.* But agreement in person demands little attention since hardly anyone is illiterate enough to say *I goes.*

[2] A pronoun also agrees with its antecedent in person and in gender. The relative pronoun *who* usually refers to persons, *which* to things, and *that* to either persons or things. Lack of agreement in person causes a shift in point of view.

WRONG   *One* must help his neighbors during *your* spare time. [Shift from third person to second person.]
RIGHT   *One* must help his neighbors during *his* spare time.
See further discussion under **27, Point of View.**

Agreement in gender is usually easy and natural: "The *boy* lost *his* kite." "The *girl* tore *her* dress." The masculine pronoun may be used to refer to common gender: "Every *person* in the audience raised *his* head." Paired antecedents of different genders may call for two pronouns; but such sentences are often better recast.

PERMISSIBLE   Each man or woman should make his or her contribution to the fund.
BETTER   Each man or woman should make a contribution to the fund.

[3] Complete mastery of section **6** will eliminate the fourth most common error in the average student theme.

RIGHT   The *engine runs* smoothly.   [Singular subject —
        singular verb.]

RIGHT   The *engines run* smoothly.   [Plural subject — plural
        verb.]

RIGHT   The *woman* washes *her* clothes.   [Singular ante-
        cedent — singular pronoun.]

RIGHT   The *women* wash *their* clothes.   [Plural antecedent
        — plural pronoun.]

Make a diagram, or at least form a mental picture,
of each subject and its verb (engine | runs ,

engines | run) and of each antecedent and its

pronoun (*woman ← her, women ← their*).   This practice
will make it easy to avoid errors in agreement.

SUBJECT AND VERB

6a. Make every verb agree in number with its subject.

(1) Do not be misled by nouns or pronouns intervening between the subject and the verb.

WRONG   The *recurrence* of identical sounds *help* to awaken the
        emotions.

RIGHT   The *recurrence* of identical sounds *helps* to awaken
        the emotions.

WRONG   The *wings* of the average bird *enables* it to fly.

RIGHT   The *wings* of the average bird *enable* it to fly.

recurrence | helps   wings | enable

Note that the number of the subject is not changed
by the addition of parenthetical expressions introduced

by such words as *with, together with, as well as, no less than, including, accompanied by.*

RIGHT *He,* as well as his two brothers, *was* (not *were*) a skillful mason.

RIGHT *John,* together with James and William, *was* (not *were*) *drafted* into the army.

EXERCISE. Find the verb, then its subject, and make the two agree in number.

1. The discomforts in a pit is clearly described.
2. The crooked streaks of lightning seems to split the sky open.
3. The manifestations of college spirit as seen at a football game is an inspiring sight.
4. The cool days of autumn seems to fill one with vitality.
5. The schedule of the street cars are uncertain.

(2) Two or more subjects joined by *and* take a plural verb.

RIGHT Hoes, rakes, and plows *are* garden tools.

RIGHT Mary, Jane, and I *were* tired after our morning's work.

But note that a compound subject referring to a single person or thing takes a singular verb.

RIGHT My best friend and adviser *is gone.*

RIGHT The tumult and shouting *dies.*

(3) Two or more singular subjects joined by *or* or *nor* take a singular verb. If one subject is singular and one plural, the verb agrees with the nearer.

RIGHT Neither the boy nor the girl *is* to blame for the accident.

RIGHT Either the man or his wife *knows* the exact truth of the matter.

RIGHT Neither the teacher nor the pupils *are* in the building. [The plural *pupils* is nearer the verb.]

RIGHT Neither the pupils nor the teacher *is* in the building. [The singular *teacher* is nearer the verb.]

EXERCISE. Make the verb agree with its subject or subjects.

1. The improved library system and the comfort of reading rooms induces one to read more.
2. Neither the girls nor Jim were willing to give up anything for one another.
3. Both the body and the mind needs a certain amount of exercise.
4. Ceremony and ritual is essential to the spiritual side of man.
5. He found that some inner voice or urging were present in his mind.

(4) When the subject follows the verb (as in sentences beginning with *there is, there are*) special care is needed to determine the subject and to make sure that it agrees with the verb.

RIGHT The crowd began coming to town Friday night, and by game time Saturday there *were* approximately twenty-five thousand *fans* to witness the match.

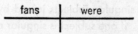

| fans | were |

RIGHT Along the water's edge there *are found* many wild *flowers*.

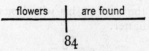

| flowers | are found |

RIGHT   In families where there *are several* who like to hear the radio, it is difficult to select a program pleasing to all.

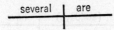

RIGHT   Because of the small number attending school, there *are* only three *teachers needed*.

teachers	are needed

RIGHT   Incessantly *fall* the *snow* and the *sleet*.

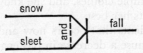

EXERCISE.   Make subject and verb agree.   Then diagram the subject and predicate of each sentence to show agreement.

1. There has been very few changes in my life.
2. Then there is two other types of drama.
3. There has been written many sonnet cycles.
4. In some families there is several who would like to hear the radio.
5. From these small dishonesties develops thieves and criminals.

(5) A relative pronoun used as a subject is plural or singular in accord with its antecedent.

RIGHT   This is one of the warmest days that have come (*not* has come) this summer.   [The antecedent of the relative pronoun *that* is *days*, not *one*.]

that (days)	have come

RIGHT Christmas is one of the holidays that have (*not* has) a significant meaning. [The antecedent of *that* is *holidays*, not *one*.]

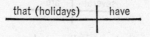

that (holidays)	have

EXERCISE. Point out the antecedent of each relative pronoun. Then make the pronoun agree with its verb.

1. It is this quality which most of us have that make other nations think twice before antagonizing us.
2. She chooses simple clothes, and she knows the types and colors that suits her best.
3. The few accidents that occurs now and then scare the patrons and cause a decrease in passenger trade.
4. The detector which accomplish these changes of frequency may be a crystal or a vacuum tube.
5. The jury tends to feel kindly toward a witness who answer the lawyers politely.

(6) *Each, every, either, neither, anyone, anybody, someone, somebody, everyone, one, no one, nobody,* etc., regularly take singular verbs.

RIGHT Someone is unable to hear the signal.
RIGHT Nobody cares to listen to worries.
RIGHT Neither likes the friends of the other.
RIGHT Each takes his turn at rowing.
RIGHT Every person finds people that he likes.

None is plural or singular according to the meaning of the sentence.

RIGHT None are so blind as those who will not see.
RIGHT None is so blind as he who will not see.

(7) Collective nouns take singular verbs when, as is usually the case, the group is regarded as a unit; but plural verbs when the individuals of the group are regarded separately.

RIGHT   The council has ordered his arrest. [Council regarded as a unit.]

RIGHT   The council have adjourned and have gone to their several homes. [Individuals of the council regarded separately.]

(8) A verb agrees with its subject, not with its predicate noun.

RIGHT   His chief support is (*not* are) his brother and sister.

RIGHT   His brother and sister are (*not* is) his chief support.

But such sentences are often better recast so as to avoid the disagreement in number between subject and predicate noun.

BETTER   His support came chiefly from his brother and sister.

(9) Nouns plural in form but singular in meaning usually take singular verbs. In all doubtful cases a good dictionary should be consulted.

RIGHT   The *news* from China is encouraging.

RIGHT   The *whereabouts* of the fugitive is unknown.

EXERCISE.   Consult your dictionary to determine the number of the verb required for each of the following nouns.   Use each noun correctly as the subject of a sentence.

athletics	news
mathematics	acoustics
measles	tactics
politics	riches
scissors	mumps

(10) A title of a book or a word used in a special sense, even when plural in form, takes a singular verb.

RIGHT   *Twice Told Tales* was written by Hawthorne.
RIGHT   *They* is a pronoun.

PRONOUN AND ANTECEDENT

6b. Make every pronoun agree in number with its antecedent.

(1) Use a singular pronoun to refer to such antecedents as *man, woman, person, one, anyone, anybody, someone, somebody, every, everyone, everybody, each, kind, sort, either, neither, no one, nobody.*

WRONG *Each* of the sons followed *their* father's occupation.
RIGHT   *Each* of the sons followed *his* father's occupation.
WRONG An outstanding trait of primitive *man* was *their* belief in superstitions.
RIGHT   An outstanding trait of primitive *man* was *his* belief in superstitions.

(2) Two or more antecedents joined by *and* are referred to by a plural pronoun; two or more singular antecedents joined by *or* or *nor* are referred to by a singular pronoun. If one of two antecedents joined by *or* is singular and one plural, the pronoun usually agrees with the nearer.

RIGHT   Henry and James have completed *their* work.
RIGHT   Neither Henry nor James has completed *his* work.
WRONG When a *boy or girl* enters college, *they* find it different from high school.
RIGHT BUT CLUMSY   When a *boy or girl* enters college, *he or she* finds it different from high school.
BETTER When *boys and girls* enter college, *they* find it different from high school.

RIGHT   Neither the *master* nor the *servants* were aware of *their* danger. [The plural *servants* is the nearer antecedent.]

(3) Collective nouns are referred to by singular or plural pronouns, according as the collective noun is considered singular or plural.

WRONG   The *family* does *their* best to make a living. [The singular verb shows that *family* is considered as a unit.]

RIGHT   The *family* does *its* best to make a living.

WRONG   The *family* separate each morning to do *its* work in various parts of the city.

RIGHT   The *family* separate each morning to do *their* work in various parts of the city.

EXERCISE. Make every pronoun agree with its antecedent.

1. Everyone should read the life of Daniel Boone, if they have not already done so.
2. Most students consider the first week of each quarter the most difficult, because he has different teachers and rooms in which to meet his classes.
3. A person can worship in church, and, at the same time, have a code of ethics entirely foreign to the teachings of the church which they attend.
4. A country may believe in neutrality, but they must be heavily armed to enforce it.
5. If England or the United States were in France's situation, they might do the same thing.
6. I do not mind helping someone by telling them what I know.
7. In college one has a chance to apply themselves and increase their knowledge.

8. When one is living in a dormitory, they must depend upon themselves for every comfort.
9. A vain woman thinks they are beautiful.
10. All of the women want to make an impression on those around them, and of course she wants it to be a good one.

EXERCISE ON AGREEMENT

Point out and correct the errors in agreement between subject and verb and between pronoun and antecedent.

1. I became interested in some very peculiar drawings which was on the ceiling.
2. Each of these powers claims that they are building armaments only for defense against invasion.
3. Many a student have been misled into believing that they can conquer the world.
4. Almost every school in this country have some kind of student dances.
5. One may achieve success in spite of any handicap they possess.
6. Limited boundaries for all officers is desirable.
7. Many people goes to church just to make an impression on other people.
8. Each of us are somewhat temperamental.
9. Since perfume have been known, all nations of the world have used it lavishly.
10. If a student can get benefit from attending every class, I think they should attend.
11. When a man is drinking, they are not safe drivers.
12. Success is one of those things which is exceedingly difficult to define.
13. If a board of directors controls the company, they may vote themselves bonuses.
14. Guns and airplanes, newer and better than any other nation possesses, is the order of the day.

15. The crew was soon aboard and fighting their enemies.
16. The parts that I thought was the best of all was the balcony scene and the duel.
17. In the group there was a doctor, a lawyer, and a merchant.
18. Neither William nor Jane could finish their assigned work.
19. The best quality are gentility and kindness.
20. What is a few demerits to a freshman?
21. Each part must fit in their groove.
22. The size of the houses vary in the different sections of the village.
23. The cause of many diseases are poverty and ignorance.
24. Any student may withdraw from college if they wish.
25. The boy needs some food, don't he?
26. Not one of the players dare break the training rules.
27. There seem to be a great deal of employment in the city.
28. A hammer, nails, and a long board is needed.
29. Everybody did their best to cheer the team.
30. The many noises made by the saw confuses the workmen.

7 t

TENSE

Mood; *Shall* and *Will*

7. Use the correct form of the verb.

TENSE

7a. Select the correct part of the verb to express the desired tense. Avoid confusing the principal parts of similar verbs. In case of doubt, consult a good dictionary.

The six tenses are built on three forms (principal parts): the present stem (infinitive), the past, and the past participle.

Irregular Verb	*Regular Verb*
do, did, done	use, used, used

Built on the Present

1. PRESENT	I do	I use
2. FUTURE	I shall do	I shall use

Built on the Past

3. PAST	I did	I used

Built on the Past Participle

4. PRESENT PERFECT	I have done	I have used
5. PAST PERFECT	I had done	I had used
6. FUTURE PERFECT	I shall have done	I shall have used

For all irregular verbs (such as *do*) the dictionary gives the past tense (*did*), the past participle (*done*), and also the present participle (*doing*). For regular verbs (such as *use*) the past tense and the past participle, when not given, are understood to be formed by adding *d* (or *ed*). Writers usually know the tense desired. They should use the dictionary more freely to make sure of the form.

WRONG Tom Sawyer *done* very much as he pleased. [Past tense desired; dictionary gives *did* as the correct form.]

RIGHT Tom Sawyer *did* very much as he pleased.

WRONG I *use* to live in the country. [Past tense desired; consult dictionary for correct form.]

RIGHT I *used* to live in the country.

WRONG She *knowed* something was wrong. [Past tense desired; dictionary shows the principal parts to be *know, knew, known*.]

RIGHT She *knew* something was wrong.

Some verbs are frequently confused because of similarity in spelling or meaning.

Present	*Past*	*Past participle*
[I] lie (recline), *intransitive*	[I] lay	[I have] lain
lay (deposit), *transitive*	laid	laid
lie (falsify), *intransitive*	lied	lied
rise, *intransitive*	rose	risen
raise, *transitive*	raised	raised
sit, *intransitive*	sat	sat
set, *transitive*	set	set

WRONG He *layed* (or *laid*) down on the bed. [Past tense of the intransitive verb *lie* needed.]

RIGHT He *lay* down on the bed.

WRONG He *lay* the book on the table. [Past tense of the transitive verb *lay* needed.]

RIGHT He *laid* the book on the table.

RIGHT He *rose* (*has risen*) from the table. [Intransitive.]

RIGHT He *raised* (*has raised*) the bucket from the well. [Transitive.]

RIGHT He *sat* (*has sat*) in the chair. [Intransitive.]

RIGHT He *set* (*has set*) the bucket on the table. [Transitive.]

EXERCISE A. The verbs listed below are among those which cause most difficulty. Write out the principal parts of each verb.

awake	drink	show
begin	drive	sit
bite	eat	spring
blow	go	steal
break	lay	swear
burst	lie	swim
catch	rise	take
dive	run	throw
do	see	wake
drag	set	write

EXERCISE B. Keep a list of all verbs which you use incorrectly in your themes. Master the verbs by writing out the principal parts and by using them correctly in sentences.

7b. Make a subordinate verb, an infinitive, or a participle agree logically with the main verb.

Common sense and reasonable care will solve most problems involving the agreement of tenses.

VERBS

WRONG The people *begin* to realize how much she *had contributed*.

RIGHT The people *begin* to realize how much she *has contributed*. [*Has contributed* until the present time of the verb *begin*.]

WRONG The people *began* to realize how much she *has contributed*.

RIGHT The people *began* to realize how much she *had contributed*. [*Had contributed* before the past time of the verb *began*.]

WRONG He *was fishing* where the river *was dredged*.

RIGHT He *was fishing* where the river *had been dredged*. [Change necessary to show the time relationship to the main verb.]

WRONG Since I *heard* no more rumors, I *have ceased* worrying.

RIGHT Since I *heard* no more rumors, I *ceased* worrying.

RIGHT Since I *have heard* no more rumors, I *have ceased* worrying.

RIGHT Since I *hear* no more rumors, I *cease* worrying.

WRONG I *hoped* that I *could have gone*.

RIGHT I *hoped* that I could go. [In the past time indicated by *hoped* I was still anticipating going.]

INFINITIVES

WRONG I hoped *to have gone*.

RIGHT I hoped *to go*. [At the time indicated by the verb I was still expecting *to go*, not *to have gone*.]

WRONG I intended *to have helped*.

RIGHT I intended *to help*.

PARTICIPLES

WRONG *Arriving* at the camp before noon, he *was ready* to fish early in the afternoon.

95

RIGHT *Having arrived* at the camp before noon, he *was* ready to fish early in the afternoon.

WRONG *After having accepted* the position, he *began* work promptly. [*After* is redundant.]

RIGHT *Having accepted* the position, he *began* work promptly.

7c. Statements permanently true are regularly put in the present tense, even when illogically used with the tense of the main verb.

RIGHT Corn *grows* well in fertile soil.

RIGHT The early settlers knew that crops *grow* well in fertile soil.

The present tense is commonly used in discussions of literary works.

RIGHT Dickens *introduces* one eccentric character after another.

RIGHT In *David Copperfield* Dickens draws heavily on his early experiences. David *represents* Dickens himself, who *had* many hardships as a boy. [Note that the past tense *had* is used to refer to events in the author's life.]

7d. Avoid needless shifts in tense.[1]

WRONG He *came* to the river and *pays* a man to ferry him across.

RIGHT He *came* to the river and *paid* a man to ferry him across.

EXERCISE ON TENSE

Correct all errors in tense.

1. I wish I had been able to have played in the band.
2. Did hours of hard, grilling work lay there for me?

[1] See also section **27, Point of View.**

3. I had secured an old corncob pipe which had been laying around the house for years.

4. When Romeo appears below Juliet's window, she was probably expecting him.

5. A wicked smile comes over her face, and she tells him she would strangle him sometime when he was sleeping.

6. He was swimming near the place where the bridge collapsed.

7. Imagine the thrill you would have when you see the ocean for the first time.

8. He was so tired that he laid down on the bed.

9. Wordsworth's poem is written in such simple form that it would be easy for people to understand it.

10. The man and his wife had a little girl who is five years old.

11. Uncle sent a telegram to our parents, telling them we missed the train.

12. The radio has not yet grew old to the public.

13. We have often heard that history repeated itself.

14. Coming into the harbor before night, the boat was ready to sail early next morning.

15. We knew that food was necessary for life.

16. After having lost my job I decided to go home.

17. I lay the pipe down, stumbled to the bed, and lay down.

18. He intended to have accepted the invitation.

19. His descriptions are vivid and his style was pleasing.

20. He will gladly die so that she might marry her captain.

SUBJUNCTIVE MOOD

7e. Use the subjunctive mood to express (1) a condition contrary to fact, (2) a doubt or uncertainty, especially in clauses introduced by *as if* or *as though*, (3) a wish or regret, a concession, a necessity, or a parliamentary motion.

The subjunctive mood has largely been displaced by the indicative mood, especially in colloquial and in informal English. Only in the verb *to be* is there now much difference between indicative and subjunctive forms. In the paradigms below, boldface indicates the special form used for the subjunctive.

Present Indicative		*Present Subjunctive*	
I am	We are	I **be**	We **be**
You are	You are	You **be**	You **be**
He is	They are	He **be**	They **be**

Past Indicative		*Past Subjunctive*	
I was	We were	I **were**	We were
You were	You were	You were	You were
He was	They were	He **were**	They were

In ordinary verbs only the third person singular of the present subjunctive has a distinctive form.

Present Indicative		*Present Subjunctive*	
I come	We come	I come	We come
You come	You come	You come	You come
He comes	They come	He **come**	They come

Past Indicative	*Past Subjunctive*
I, you, he, we, they came	I, you, he, we, they came

(1) Use the subjunctive mood to express a condition contrary to fact.

RIGHT If he *were* (not *was*) here, he would assist us.
RIGHT If he *were* (not *was*) eligible, he would be elected.

(2) Use the subjunctive mood to express a doubt or uncertainty, especially in clauses introduced by *as if* or *as though*.

RIGHT   If this disease *be* contagious, we may expect an epidemic. [*Informal:* If this disease *is* contagious, etc.]

RIGHT   The man looks as if he *were* sick.

(3) Use the subjunctive mood to express a wish or regret, a concession, a necessity, or a parliamentary motion.

RIGHT   Would that he *were* here.

RIGHT   Even though he *desert* me, I will still support him.

RIGHT   It is urgent that he *leave* in haste.

RIGHT   I move that he *go* alone.

EXERCISE ON THE SUBJUNCTIVE MOOD

Select the correct form and give the reason for your choice.

1. The manager acted as if he [was *or* were] very worried.
2. Even though he [comes *or* come], we shall need other help.
3. He would not run from an unpleasant accusation even if he [was *or* were] guilty.
4. My wish is that she [go *or* goes] to Europe.
5. If I [was *or* were] there, I could assist him.
6. The tailor asked that he [pay *or* pays] his bill before leaving town.
7. I wish I [was *or* were] wealthy enough to provide for all my friends.
8. It is not necessary that one [is *or* be] a pianist in order to teach public school music.
9. I often write many themes before one sounds as though it [was *or* were] fairly good.
10. War demands that men [are *or* be] trained for action.
11. When Roderick came in, he looked as if he [was *or* were] angry.

12. John suggested that Frances [bring *or* brings] the food in a container.
13. If everyone [was *or* were] careful to avoid throwing away burning cigarettes, there would be fewer fires.
14. If all [is *or* be] lost, there is no use trying.
15. If the invitation [comes *or* come], I will forward it to you.

SHALL AND *WILL*

7f. Use the correct form for *shall (should)* and *will (would).*

Informal English is rapidly dropping the distinctions between *shall* and *will*, *should* and *would*. Except for the use of *should* to express an obligation (see below) the tendency is to use everywhere *will* and *would*. But careful usage still observes the following rules:

(1) To express the simple future tense use *shall (should)* in the first person and *will (would)* in the second and third.

RIGHT   I *shall* stay. He *will* go. You *will* find me at home. We *shall* expect you.

(2) To express determination (or in making a promise) use *will (would)* in the first person and *shall (should)* in the second and third.

RIGHT   I *will* help. You *shall* have your reward. He *shall* not obstruct our passage.

(3) In questions, use the form expected in the answer.

RIGHT   *Shall* you remain longer in the country? [Answer expected: *I shall, or I shall not.*]

RIGHT   *Will* you go in spite of all the dangers? [Answer expected: *I will; I am determined to go.*]

(4) Use *should* in all persons to express an obligation.

RIGHT   I (you, he, we, they) *should* help the needy.

(5) Use *would* in all persons to express customary or habitual action.

RIGHT   I (you, he, we, they) *would* take a vacation at the end of summer.

EXERCISE ON *SHALL* AND *WILL* (*SHOULD* AND *WOULD*)

Which of the words in parentheses would be used by careful writers? If more than one word may be used, explain the meaning of the sentence with each word.

1. I [should, would] like him to have a sense of humor.
2. Where [shall, will] we be ten years from now?
3. Last summer I went on a camping trip that I [shall, will] never forget.
4. I [should, would] be afraid to say how many times this jug has been upset.
5. In it we learn the things that we [shall, will, should, would] do in later life.
6. He [should, would] rather live here than in any other place.
7. Don't think I [shall, will] forget you!
8. I [shall, will, should, would] continue.
9. I [shall, will] never forget entering New York City by way of the Holland Tunnel.
10. He [should, would] take a walk every afternoon.
11. I [shall, will] take care of the equipment for you.
12. I hope that I [shall, will] be asked to go along.
13. He [should, would, shall, will] apply for a loan.
14. The book was rather interesting, but I [should, would] have enjoyed another book more.
15. When [shall, will] he leave?

8 ms

MECHANICS

MANUSCRIPT
FORM AND REVISION

8. Put your manuscript in acceptable form. Make revisions with care.

MATERIALS

8a. Use the proper materials.

(1) **Paper.** Unless you are given other instructions, use standard theme paper, size 8½ by 11 inches, with lines about half an inch apart. (The usual notebook paper, even if it is the standard size, should be carefully avoided because the narrow spaces between lines make hard reading and allow insufficient space for corrections.) For typewritten themes use the unruled side of the theme paper; or, if you prefer, use regular typewriter paper, size 8½ by 11 inches.

(2) **Ink.** Use black or blue-black ink and write on the ruled side of the paper only.

(3) **Typewriter.** Submit typewritten themes only if you do your own typewriting. Use a black ribbon and make sure that the type is clean.

ARRANGEMENT ON THE PAGE

8b. Arrange the writing in clear and orderly fashion on the page.

(1) **Spacing.** Leave sufficient margins — about an inch and a half at left and top, an inch at right and bottom — to prevent a crowded appearance. The ruled lines on theme paper indicate the proper margins at left and top. In typewritten themes use double spacing between lines. Leave one space after a comma or semicolon, one or two after a colon, and two or three after a period, question mark, or exclamation point.

(2) **Indention.** Indent the first lines of paragraphs uniformly, about an inch in longhand and five spaces in typewritten copy. Leave no long gap at the end of any line except the last one in the paragraph.

(3) **Paging.** Use Arabic numerals in the upper right-hand corner to mark all pages after the first.

(4) **The Title.** Center the title on the page about an inch and a half from the top or on the first ruled line. Leave the next line blank and begin the first paragraph on the third line. In this way the title will be made to stand off from the text. Ordinarily the text should not begin with a reference to the title. For proper capitalization of titles see section **9c.**

(5) **Poetry.** Quoted lines of poetry should be arranged and indented as in the original.

(6) **Punctuation.** Never begin a line with a comma, a colon, a semicolon, or a terminal mark of punctuation.

(7) **Endorsement.** Manuscript for publication carries the author's name and address in the upper left-hand corner. Themes are endorsed in the way prescribed by the instructor to facilitate handling. Usually themes carry the name of the student, the date, and the number of the theme.

SYLLABICATION

8c. Whenever possible avoid the division of a word at the end of a line. When a division is necessary, make the break only between syllables (parts naturally pronounced as separate units of the word) and mark the break by a hyphen at the end of the line — not at the beginning of the next line.

WRONG the-ir, ignit-ion, class-ify.

RIGHT their, igni-tion (*or* ig-nition), clas-sify (*or* classi-fy).

A good dictionary should be consulted freely to determine the proper syllabication of individual words.

(1) Never divide a word to set off a single letter. The saving of space is not sufficient to justify the break.

WRONG e-nough, a-gainst, e-vade.

WRONG man-y, show-y, dyspepsi-a. [The final letter can be written as readily as the hyphen.]

(2) Never confuse the reader by setting off an -ed pronounced as a part of the preceding syllable.

CONFUSING enjoy-ed, gleam-ed, watch-ed, remember-ed.

(3) Divide hyphenated words only at the break already marked by the hyphen. A second hyphen is awkward.

WRONG fire-eat-er, mass-pro-duced, Pre-Rapha-elite.

RIGHT fire-eater, mass-produced, Pre-Raphaelite.

(4) Never divide a word of a single syllable.

WRONG Thr-ough, lea-ve, wro-ught.

RIGHT Through, leave, wrought.

LEGIBILITY

8d. Write legibly.

The only purpose of writing is that it may be read.

(1) **Spacing for Legibility.** Proper spacing on the page adds to the legibility as well as to the general attractiveness of the manuscript. Adequate space between lines and between the words in the line is essential to easy reading. In typed copy use double space between lines. Single-spaced copy is difficult for the instructor to read and even more difficult for the student to revise. In longhand make each word a distinct unit: join all the letters of a word and leave adequate space in the line before beginning the next word.

(2) **Shaping for Legibility.** Shape each letter distinctly. Avoid flourishes. Many pages of manuscript generally artistic and attractive to the eye are almost illegible. Dot the *i*'s, not some other letter near by. Cross the *t*'s, not the adjoining *h* or some other letter. Make dots and periods real dots, not small circles. Let all capitals stand out distinctly as capitals and keep all small letters down to the average of other small letters. Remember that you will not be present to tell the reader which letters you intend for capitals, which for lower case.

BAD: *anne gave this book to Walter and me.*

IMPROVED: *Anne gave this book to Walter and me.*

REVISION OF THEMES

8e. Revise the manuscript with care.

(1) **First Step: Revision before Submission to the Instructor.**
The first problem is to write down the facts in as clear
and orderly a way as possible. If time permits, the
writer should put the theme aside for a day or more.
Then he will be able to read the theme more objec-
tively, to see what parts need to be expanded, what to
be excised. If extensive revisions are necessary, he
should make a full, clean copy to submit to the instructor. If only a few changes are needed, the paper
may be handed in — after corrections have been made
— without rewriting. The changes should be made
as follows:

    i. Draw one line horizontally through any word to be
       deleted. Do not put it in parentheses or brackets.

    ii. In case of a short addition of one line or less, place
       a caret (∧) in the line where the addition comes and
       write just above the caret the part to be added.

(2) **Second Step: Revising the Theme after the Instructor's
Criticism.** A student learns how to write chiefly by correcting his own errors. Corrections made for him are
of comparatively little value. Therefore the instructor
points out the errors but allows the student to make
the actual revision for himself.

The instructor usually indicates a necessary correction by a number (or symbol) from the handbook
marked in the margin of the theme opposite the error.
If a word is misspelled, the number **18** (or the symbol
sp) will be used; if there is a fragmentary sentence,
number **2** (or the symbol **frag**); if there is a faulty
reference of a pronoun, number **28** (or the symbol
ref). The student will then consult the handbook,

master the principle underlying each correction, and make the necessary revisions with red ink. He will draw one red line through words to be eliminated, but he will allow such words to remain legible in order that the instructor may compare the original with the revised form.

The comma. Whenever the instructor indicates the need for a comma by the number **12** (or the symbol **,/**), the student should insert the comma and also indicate the specific use of the comma by writing after the number (or symbol) in the margin the appropriate letter from the handbook — **a, b, c, d,** or **e.** By inserting the appropriate letter, the student shows his understanding of the principle involved.

The following pages reproduce part of a typewritten theme, the first showing the instructor's suggestions by means of numbers, the second by means of symbols. The third page shows (in longhand) the revisions made by the student.

		In the rapidly changing world with
12		which we are now familiar chivalry is
18	*2*	becomeing a thing of the past. Something
	25	which we only know as it exists in our
		books and moving pictures. Why does
		chivalry mean so little to the average
17	*22*	person. First, one should try determine
		what chivalry really is. According to
	18	most authoritys on the subject it is the
		practice of observing the rules of
18	*28*	knight errantry. This readily produces

[From a typewritten theme, showing the instructor's suggestions by means of numbers.]

In the rapidly changing world with

which we are now familiar chivalry is

sp / *frag*   becomeing a thing of the past. Something

coh   which we only know as it exists in our

books and moving pictures. Why does

chivalry mean so little to the average

?/ ∧   person. First, one should try determine

what chivalry really is. According to

sp   most authoritys on the subject it is the

practice of observing the rules of

sp *ref*   knight errantry. This readily produces

[From a typewritten theme, showing the instructor's
suggestions by means of symbols.]

In the rapidly changing world with

12 b   which we are now familiar, chivalry is

18   2   *becoming* ~~becomeing~~ a thing of the past/, Something

25   which we ~~only~~ know, *only* as it exists in our

books and moving pictures. Why does

chivalry mean so little to the average

17   22   person/? First, one should try *to* determine

what chivalry really is. According to

18   most ~~authoritys~~ *authorities* on the subject it is the

practice of observing the rules of

18   28   knight—errantry. This *definition* readily produces

[From a typewritten theme, showing the instructor's suggestions
by means of numbers and the student's revisions in longhand.
Revisions are usually made in red ink.]

ms 8

8f. Use the following marks in correcting proof for the printer.

ẟ̃	Delete and close up	en|	En dash
ꝺ	Reverse	;|	Insert semicolon
⌒	Close up	⊙	Insert colon and en quad
#	Insert space	⊙	Insert period and en quad
¶	Paragraph	?|	Insert interrogation point
▢	Indent one em	⑦	Query to author
⌐	Move to left	⌒	Use ligature
⌐	Move to right	ⓢⓟ	Spell out
⊔	Lower	tr	Transpose
⊓	Elevate	wf	Wrong font
∧	Insert marginal addition	bf	Set in **bold face** type
∨∧	Even space	rom	Set in ⓡoman type
✕	Broken letter	ital	Set in *italic* type
↓	Push down space	caps	Set in **CAPITALS**
—	Straighten line	sc	Set in SMALL CAPITALS
‖	Align type	lc	Set in lower case
⋏	Insert comma	ⱡ	Lower-case letter
⌄	Insert apostrophe	stet	Let it stand
⌵	Insert quotes	no ¶	Run in same paragraph
=|	Hyphen	ld⟩	Insert lead between lines
em	Em dash	hr#	Hair space between letters

— From *A Manual of Style*, The University of Chicago Press.

9 cap

9. Capitalize (a) proper names, (b) titles preceding the name and other words used as an essential part of a proper name, (c) the chief words of titles of publications, (d) the pronoun *I*, the interjection *O*, and (e) the first letter of sentences or lines of poetry. Avoid unnecessary capitals.

9a. Capitalize proper names, including derivatives of proper names and abbreviations of them.

1. SPECIFIC PERSONS OR PLACES: Mary, John, Mr. Smithson, Smithsonian, Charles Dickens, Chicago, Maine, the South (referring to a specific section of the country), the Orient, an Oriental custom, the Pacific, Japan.

2. ORGANIZATIONS OF ALL KINDS: Woodmen of the World, Masons, Presbyterians, Protestants, Quakers, Methodists, General Motors, the Standard Oil Company, the Republican Party, the House of Representatives, the Kiwanis Club.

3. RACES AND LANGUAGES: Caucasian, Indian, Negro, Spanish, Dutch, Norwegian.

4. DAYS OF THE WEEK, MONTHS, SPECIAL DAYS: Monday, Wednesday, March, June, Christmas, Easter, Thanksgiving.

5. HISTORICAL PERIODS, EVENTS, OR DOCUMENTS: The Dark Ages, the Stone Age, the Battle of Waterloo, the Spanish War, the Revolution, the Magna Carta, the Declaration of Independence.

6. WORDS PERTAINING TO DEITY: God the Father, the Son, the Lord, the Savior, the Virgin, the Almighty, the Creator.

7. PERSONIFICATIONS:

> Can Honor's voice provoke the silent dust,
> Or Flattery soothe the dull cold ear of Death?

Note: In general, abbreviations are capitalized or not according to the capitalization of the word abbreviated. One important exception is *number*, *No.* *A.M.* and *P.M.* may be capitalized or written with small letters. A good dictionary, such as the fifth edition of *Webster's Collegiate Dictionary*, "Abbreviations," pp. 1175–1181, will show the usage in given instances.

EXERCISE. Use capitals wherever needed.

1. The music was furnished by the knights, a popular dance orchestra.
2. He escaped in the disguise of a negro woman.
3. I intend to give my life and my service to god.
4. I will go to school on monday if i can get the books.
5. The bible is a library within itself.
6. Journalism developed more slowly in the south than in the north.
7. They wanted to give each other an appropriate christmas present.
8. This type of lathe is still used in many of the spanish settlements.
9. Arrowhead, an indian, used his knowledge of the forest to guide the frenchman to the spot.
10. Above the surface a large diesel engine is used.

9b. Capitalize titles preceding the name, or other words used as an essential part of a proper name.

(1) Titles preceding the name are regularly capitalized as an essential part of the name. Titles immediately following, or used alone as a substitute for the name, are capitalized only to indicate pre-eminence or high distinction.

RIGHT   Mr. Smith, Judge Jones, King George, Aunt Mary, Mother Hubbard.   President Roosevelt; the President of the United States; the President; William Smith, president of the First National Bank; the president of the bank.

Note: Words denoting family relationship (*father*, *mother*, *brother*, *aunt*, *cousin*) follow the general rules for titles except that, when used alone as a substitution for the name, they may be capitalized or not according to the writer's preference.

RIGHT   Brother James; Sister Mary; Mary, my sister; my brother; my sister; my father.

A trip with Father (*or* father); a letter for Mother (*or* mother); a letter for my mother.

(2) Such words as *college, high school, club, river, street, park, lake, county, company, railroad,* and *society* are usually capitalized when used as an essential part of a proper name. They are not capitalized when used alone as a substitute for the name.

RIGHT   Knox College, the college, Central High School, the high school, Madison Street, the street, the Pennsylvania Railroad, a railroad in Pennsylvania.

Note: Many newspapers omit capitals in such cases. *Examples:* Madison street, the Pennsylvania railroad.

EXERCISE. Insert all necessary capitals. State the reason for the use of each capital.

1. Horton's bay was once the scene of a prosperous lumber camp.
2. John's father was a democrat and supported the new deal.
3. I joined the 105th observation squadron.
4. The town is called the "gateway to the great smoky mountains national park."
5. I entered the seventh grade at carter school.
6. I became a member of the beaver club during my last year in high school.
7. The prince banished romeo from the city.
8. The chinese and japanese follow oriental customs.
9. He is a member of the house of representatives.
10. The standard oil company has branches all over the world.

9c. Capitalize the first word and all important words (all except the articles *a, an, the,* conjunctions, and prepositions) in the titles of books, articles, or themes.

RIGHT   *Treasure Island, The Yearling, A Tale of Two Cities,* the Boston *Herald.*

9d. Capitalize the pronoun *I* and the interjection *O.*

RIGHT   If *I* forget thee, *O* Jerusalem, let my right hand forget her cunning. — *Psalms.*

9e. Capitalize the first word of every line of poetry and the first word of every sentence, including quoted sentences, questions, and complete statements inserted in sentences.

RIGHT   But I was one-and-twenty,
No use to talk to me.   — HOUSMAN

RIGHT   He answered, "We have no choice."

RIGHT   He answered that he had "no choice." [A fragmentary quotation is not capitalized.]

RIGHT   The question is, Shall we go?

RIGHT   He took a necessary precaution: He sent a present to the chief. [The colon may be followed by either a capital or a small letter.]

9f. Avoid unnecessary capitals.

Many students write unnecessary capitals more frequently than they fail to use necessary ones. If you have a tendency to overuse capitals, you should study the five principles treated above (9a, b, c, d, e) and use a capital letter only when you can justify it.

WRONG   Winter, Spring, Summer, and Autumn are the four seasons. [The seasons are not capitalized.]

RIGHT   Winter, spring, summer, and autumn are the four seasons.

WRONG   He went South during winter. [Mere direction is not capitalized.]

RIGHT   He went south during winter, *or* He lived in the South during winter.

WRONG   I studied History, Geography, and Spanish. [Names of studies are capitalized only when specific — *History 2* — or when derived from a proper name — *Spanish*.]

RIGHT   I studied History 2, geography, and Spanish.

WRONG   I went to High School.

RIGHT   I went to high school (*or* Dover High School).

WRONG   My Father and my Cousin were with us.

RIGHT   My father and my cousin were with us.

EXERCISE. Indicate which of the capitals should be changed to small letters.

1. My home is located in the Southern part of the State.
2. During the Civil War The Confederate Army was stationed at Market Street.
3. The boy's Family consisted of his Mother, his Father, and his two younger Brothers.
4. The first Thanksgiving was in the Fall of 1621.
5. Ulysses, Ruler of Ithaca, muses over the fact that he is now an idle King.
6. My oldest Brother lives on a ranch in Eastern Oregon.
7. Any soil contains some Iron ore.
8. Every day we meet in the Gymnasium.
9. During the Summer I read all day.
10. I am taking five Major Subjects, which include English, History, Psychology, Physics, and Greek.

EXERCISE ON CAPITALS

Insert necessary capitals and change unnecessary capitals to small letters. State the reason for each change.

1. The prettiest Season of the year is the Spring.
2. Will you please go to the Bakery for me?
3. We took the Trophy right out of the hands of the canadian mounted police.
4. I enjoy living in the south in the Winter and in the north in the Summer.
5. Blanche knelt at the Altar, weeping.
6. The Story is about the eve of st. agnes.
7. Romeo went to friar laurence and arranged for the marriage.
8. All zoologists classify Whales as Mammals.
9. General houston had ability in controlling the indians.
10. My Father bought a farm west of the City.

11. Booker T. Washington is responsible for the advancement of the negro race.
12. His Father, his Mother, and his Aunt came to his Graduation.
13. The bible has been translated into every important language.
14. Madame Curie discovered a great many uses for Radium.
15. Baffin bay is icebound during the Fall and Winter.
16. Mr. Smith is a member of the senate and lives in washington.
17. We shall leave tuesday if Mother can get ready.
18. I worked on my Theme all Summer long.
19. Chivalry as an Institution flourished in the middle ages.
20. Of all my Studies I like History best.
21. Mr. brown goes to England in the Spring and stays until Winter.
22. My son william is a freshman at yale.
23. Corn is grown in the south, in the middle west, and in other sections of the country.
24. The Ambassador called to see the president.
25. Use either arabic or roman numerals.
26. My Father went to new york before returning to his home in southern florida.
27. Please come here, mother, and see aunt linda.
28. He belongs to the lutheran church.
29. Voltaire was a noted french writer.
30. John smith, esq., is a native of cornwall, england.

ITALICS

In longhand or typewritten papers, italics are indicated by underlining. The printer sets all underlined words in italic type.

LONGHAND *In David Copperfield Dickens writes of his own boyhood.*

PRINT In *David Copperfield* Dickens writes of his own boyhood.

10. Italicize (underline) titles of publications, foreign words, names of ships, or works of art, and words spoken of as words. Use italics sparingly for emphasis.

10a. Titles of separate publications — such as books, bulletins, magazines, newspapers, musical productions — are put in italics (underlined) when mentioned in writing.

Note: Quotation marks are sometimes interchanged with italics, but are preferably reserved for articles from periodicals and for subdivisions of books. A title is not italicized when it stands at the head of a book, bulletin, etc. Accordingly, a student should not italicize (underline) the title standing at the head of his own theme.

RIGHT   Many people have read Margaret Mitchell's *Gone with the Wind.* [The author's name is not italicized.]

RIGHT   He put aside Scott's *The Talisman* and took up Churchill's *A Roving Commission.* [The articles *a, an, the* are capitalized and italicized whenever they belong to the title; otherwise not, as in "He read the *Sonnets* of John Keats."]

RIGHT   He pored over *Time*, the *Atlantic Monthly*, the *Saturday Evening Post*, and the New York *Times*. [As a rule italics are not used for articles standing first in the titles of magazines and newspapers nor for the name of the city in the titles of newspapers.]

10b. Foreign words are put in italics (underlined).

RIGHT   One of the common mushrooms is known to botanists as *Agaricus campestris.*

RIGHT   She had a *joie de vivre* distinctly her own.

RIGHT   We enjoyed a good meal *à la française.*

RIGHT   The explorers moved into the mysterious *terra incognita* of the Arctic.

10c. Names of ships and titles of works of art are put in italics (underlined).

RIGHT   The *Queen Mary* and the *Princess Elizabeth* sailed from New York.

RIGHT   Rodin's *The Thinker* stands in one of the Parisian gardens.

10d. Words, letters, or figures spoken of as such are put in italics (underlined).

RIGHT   The article *the* has lost much of its demonstrative force.

RIGHT   The final *e* in *stone* is not pronounced.

RIGHT   The first *3* and the final *o* of the serial number are barely legible.

10e. Very seldom should italics (underlining) be used to give special emphasis to a word or a group of words.

Frequent use of italics for emphasis defeats its own purpose and becomes merely an annoyance to the reader. This use of italics has been almost abandoned by good contemporary writers. Emphasis on a given word or phrase can best be secured by careful arrangement of the sentence. See section **29**.

RIGHT   The differences of primal importance which I observed between the nature of this garden, and that of Eden, as I had imagined it, were, that, in this one, *all* the fruit was forbidden; and there were no companionable beasts. — Ruskin.

EXERCISE ON ITALICS

Underscore all words that should be italicized.

1. Seventeen is a novel with a very simple plot.
2. I really enjoyed The Return of the Native.
3. We christened the two boats Tony and Lisbeth.
4. He found a volume entitled How Shall I Word It?
5. Chorus comes from the Greek word choros.

6. The word gavelkind is a legal term.
7. I subscribe to the American Boy and to the Springfield Republican.
8. Jane Austen's Pride and Prejudice has been successfully dramatized.
9. The Odyssey is said to have furnished ideas for Tennyson's Ulysses.
10. In our group he was facile princeps.
11. The Majestic sailed from New York to Liverpool.
12. The letter i in the word believe is silent.
13. The Atlantic Monthly is recognized as an excellent magazine.
14. The Good Earth was written by Pearl Buck.
15. Ipso jure is a term used in law.
16. Be sure to dot your i's.
17. Robert always reads the Sunday edition of the New York Times.
18. Rebecca is one of the outstanding books of the year.
19. He meant to write affect, not effect.
20. Should one italicize the word résumé?

ABBREVIATIONS
AND NUMBERS

11. In ordinary writing avoid abbreviations (with a few well-known exceptions), and write out numbers whenever they can be expressed in not more than two or three words.

11a. In ordinary writing spell out all titles except *Mr.*, *Messrs.*, *Mrs.*, *Mmes.*, *Dr.*, and *St.* *(saint,* not *street).* Spell out even these titles when not followed by proper names.

WRONG The Dr. made his report to the Maj.

RIGHT The doctor (*or* Dr. Smith) made his report to the major (*or* to Major Brown).

11b. In ordinary writing spell out names of states, countries, months, and days of the week.

WRONG He went to Neb. on the last Sat. in Dec.

RIGHT He went to Nebraska on the last Saturday in December.

11c. In ordinary writing spell out *Street, Road, Park, Company,* **and similar words used as part of a proper name.**

WRONG The procession moved down Lee St. between Central Pk. and the neon signs of the Ford Motor Co.

RIGHT The procession moved down Lee Street between Central Park and the neon signs of the Ford Motor Company.

11d. In ordinary writing spell out references in the text to volume, pages, chapters, subjects.

WRONG The notes on chem. are taken from ch. X, p. 346. [Many abbreviations not acceptable in the text are preferable in footnotes. See section 33.]

RIGHT The notes on chemistry are taken from chapter X, page 346.

11e. In ordinary writing spell out Christian names.

WRONG Jas. Smith, Geo. White.

RIGHT James Smith, George White.

General Exceptions: The following abbreviations are permissible and usually desirable.

1. *Before proper names:* Mr., Messrs., Mrs., Mmes., Dr., St. (*saint,* not *street*).

    RIGHT Mr. Smith, Messrs. Smith and Jones, St. Mark.

    In informal writing *Hon.* and *Rev.* may be used before the surname when it is preceded by the Christian name or initials, never before the surname alone.

    WRONG Hon. Smith, Rev. Jones.

    RIGHT Hon. George Smith, Hon. G. E. Smith, Rev. Thomas Jones, Rev. T. E. Jones, Rev. Dr. Jones.

RIGHT (more formal): The Honorable George Edward Smith, the Reverend Thomas Everett Jones, the Reverend Dr. Jones.

2. *After proper names:* Jr., Sr., Esq., D.D., LL.D., M.A., M.D., etc.

RIGHT Mr. Sam Jones, Sr., Sam Jones, Jr., Thomas Jones, M.D.

3. *With dates or numerals:* B.C., A.D., a.m., p.m., No., $.

RIGHT In 450 B.C.; at 9:30 a.m.; in room No. 6; for $365.

WRONG Early this a.m. he asked the No. of your room. [The abbreviations are correct only with the numerals.]

RIGHT Early this morning he asked the number of your room.

4. *In general use, but spelled out in formal writing:* i.e. (*that is*), e.g. (*for example*), viz. (*namely*), cf. (*compare*), etc. (*and so forth*), vs. (*versus*).

Note: Use *etc.* sparingly. Never write *and etc.* The *et* means *and*.

Special Exceptions: Many abbreviations are desirable in footnotes, in tabulations, and in certain types of technical writing. In such special writing the student should follow the practice of the better publications in the field. If he has any doubt regarding the spelling or capitalization of any abbreviation, he should consult a good dictionary such as *Webster's Collegiate Dictionary*, Fifth Edition, "Abbreviations Used in Writing and Printing," pages 1175–1181.

EXERCISE. Correct all errors in abbreviations.

1. Mt. Mitchell is higher than other mts. east of the Miss.
2. Vacation begins at Xmas. and lasts until Jan. 1.

3. U.S. and Gt. Britain are democratic countries.
4. He lives at 1165 Main St., Chicago, Ill.
5. Swimming classes come on Mon. and Fri.
6. Frank. D. Roosevelt was nominated for Pres. in 1940.
7. He was prof. of history at Northwestern U.
8. The collection was made on the fifth Sun. in Dec.
9. Wm. and Jas. Baker enlisted in the army.
10. Chas. Smith has gone to S. America.

11f. In general write out all numbers that can be expressed in not more than two or three words; otherwise use figures.

RIGHT The boy had four dollars.
RIGHT The boy has $2.27.
RIGHT The car has been driven fifty thousand miles.
RIGHT The car has been driven 53,568 miles.
RIGHT He lost seventy-five cents.
RIGHT He lost $1.75.
RIGHT The man is sixty-seven years old.
RIGHT The moon is over two thousand miles in diameter.
RIGHT The moon is 2,160 miles in diameter. [In numbers of four or more digits commas are used to separate hundreds, thousands, millions, etc.]
RIGHT 3,456,560.

11g. In ordinary writing do not repeat in parentheses a number that is spelled out.

This practice, usually reserved for legal or commercial writing, should be used logically if at all.

ILLOGICAL I enclose twenty ($20) dollars.
LOGICAL I enclose twenty (20) dollars.
LOGICAL I enclose twenty dollars ($20).

Exceptions: The general rule for the treatment of numbers does not hold in the following instances:

1. *Use figures for dates.*

RIGHT   May 1, 1940; July 2, 1648; April 3, 1850. The letters *st, nd, rd, th* should not be added to the day of the month when the year follows; they need not be added even when the year is omitted. CORRECT: May 1, July 2. When the year is omitted, the day of the month may be written out. CORRECT: May first, July second. Ordinal numbers to designate the day of the month may be written out or expressed in figures. CORRECT: He came on the fifth (*or* 5th) of May. But the year is never written out except in very formal social announcements or invitations.

2. *Use figures for street numbers, for pages and divisions of a book, for decimals and percentages, and for the hour of the day when used with* a.m. *or* p.m.

RIGHT   26 Main Avenue, 460 Fourth Street.

RIGHT   The bar is .63 inches thick.

RIGHT   She gets 10 per cent of the profits.

RIGHT   He arrived at 4:30 p.m.

3. *Be consistent in spelling out or using figures.*

RIGHT   He earned $15 weekly, spent $3.50 for a room, $7 for board, and saved $4.50.

4. *Spell out any numeral at the beginning of a sentence. If necessary, recast the sentence.*

WRONG   993 freshmen entered the college last year.

RIGHT   Last year 993 freshmen entered the college.

WRONG   25 boys made the trip.

RIGHT   Twenty-five boys made the trip.

EXERCISE. Write out the numbers which should be written out.

1. 800 new students swarmed on the campus.
2. My father came to America 60 years ago.
3. He was born on May 12, 1920, exactly 2 years after his sister.
4. He caught a 20 pound catfish in the lake.
5. Classes start on the campus at 8 o'clock.
6. The fare to the center of the city is $.05.
7. He graduated from the 8th grade when he was 12.
8. The Atlantic Ocean is about 3000 miles wide.
9. He paid $2 for a hat and $15 for a suit.
10. Harry is 6 inches taller than his brother.

EXERCISES ON ABBREVIATIONS
AND NUMBERS

Correct all errors in the use of abbreviations and numbers.

1. Mr. Jno. Baker lives at twelve Central Blvd.
2. 15 years ago the Smiths moved to N. Mexico.
3. He paid $10 for a football ticket.
4. The lights in the dormitory are turned off at 10 o'clock.
5. Jim has worked for the Power and Light Co. for 10 years.
6. Fairs were held in Cal. and N.Y. during the same year.
7. About 6000 people attended the county fair.
8. Geo. Tate is prof. of chem. at the college.
9. He had a master's degree from the U. of Wis. and a doctor's degree from Yale U.
10. Jas. is 4 lb. heavier and 2 inches taller than his brother.
11. Mr. Wm. Davis was made Sec. and Mr. Chas. Fuller was made Treas.
12. The mts. in E. Tenn. are covered with forests.
13. 30 people were crowded into two boats.

14. The price of milk is $.12.
15. My father sent me $10 as a birthday present.
16. I live at fourteen Elm St.
17. The lodge was 7 miles from town and 3 miles from the gravel road.
18. All Americans celebrate the 4th of July.
19. I am sending you ten ($10) dollars in this envelope.
20. The 1st., 2nd, 3rd, and 4th. grades are to be transferred.
21. The Eng. Lab. is on the first floor of the main bldg.
22. Doctor Smith lost four thousand nine hundred fifty dollars last Sat. eve.
23. 4 officers appeared on Key St. after the accident.
24. When Wm. was four years old, he went to N. O., La., to live.
25. Milk sells for $.04 a pt. in the small towns of New Mexico.
26. Geo. Williams was made Sec. of the Co. at the convention in N.Y.
27. One can buy 6 car tokens for $.30.
28. He held a 200-lb. wt. in each hand.
29. You will find the reference in Chap. six, p. 40, l. 9.
30. The catfish weighed 10 lb. and 2 oz.
31. Geo. Moore, Prof. of Sociology, will deliver a lecture on the operations of the A. F. of L.
32. Pasadena, in So. Cal., is the seat of a great U.
33. The rod is 2 in. long and .05 of an in. in diameter.
34. The mts. in Col. are much more rugged than those in the eastern part of the U.S.
35. The class in math. will be excused on Tues.
36. Deliver this U.S. bond to the bank at eight Elm St.
37. Tom worked for the Lee Mfg. Co. for 3 yrs.
38. I shall get fifty per cent of all the income for my labor.
39. I shall be at the P.O. early in the a.m.
40. 55 men were waiting in the St.

12 '/

PUNCTUATION

THE COMMA

12. Use the comma where it is demanded by the structure of the sentence.

A very few principles control the uses of the comma, the one mark of punctuation that causes serious trouble.[1] The rules given below make no effort to cover all uses of skilled writers to express delicate shades of meaning. But the fundamentals are there, quite enough for the average student. As he becomes more proficient in expressing himself, he will learn possible variations in the use of the comma. These variations are easily and safely made by the writer who has first learned to apply the fundamentals here explained.

The uses of the comma may be grouped under four major rules:

a. For separating main clauses joined by *and, but, or, nor,* or *for.*
b. For setting off introductory clauses (or phrases).
c. For separating items in a series (and co-ordinate adjectives).
d. For setting off nonrestrictive (parenthetical, interrupting) elements.

[1] Complete mastery of section **12** will eliminate the most common error in the average student theme.

128

[A fifth rule, much less important than the others, provides for inserting commas, even though not called for by any other rule, to separate parts of the sentence that might erroneously be read together.]

The application of these rules is easy for anyone who understands the structure of the sentence — almost impossible for anyone who does not. If a student cannot readily distinguish main clauses, subordinate clauses, and the various kinds of phrases, he does not have the proper foundation on which to build. He should first develop his "Sentence Sense" (see section 2e), and then he can readily master the principles underlying the uses of the comma.

COMPOUND SENTENCES

12a. Main clauses joined by one of the co-ordinating conjunctions (*and, but, or, nor, for*) [2] should be separated by a comma.

[If the conjunction is omitted, the main clauses must be made into separate sentences, or at least separated by a semicolon. See section 3.]

RIGHT   The boy came for the book, but I did not permit him to have it. [Note that the comma comes before the conjunction *but*, not after it.]

RIGHT   There are good roads all over the country, and the farmer can haul his goods to market.

[2] Until the student is sure of his punctuation, he should probably limit himself to these five conjunctions as the ones which, preceded by a comma, may join main clauses. Later he may take more liberty with such words as *so, yet,* and *also,* which are less generally recognized as co-ordinating conjunctions. Students have a tendency to overwork *so.* See section 19, Glossary.

RIGHT He left the heavy pack, for the guide had warned him of the steep climb. [The conjunction *for* may be mistaken momentarily for the preposition *for* if the comma is omitted.]

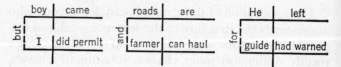

Caution: Main clauses should be distinguished from parts of a compound predicate, which are not ordinarily separated by a comma.

RIGHT The boy came for the book but was not permitted to have it.

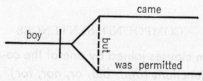

Even more objectionable would be the use of a comma before a conjunction which joins merely two words (*men* and *women*, *white* and *black*) or two phrases (*out of the pan* and *into the fire*, *to see* and *to believe*).

Exception 1: The comma before the co-ordinating conjunction *and* or *or* (seldom before *but*) may be omitted if the main clauses are very short. In colloquial style, especially in narrative writing, the comma is frequently omitted even when the clauses are longer.

RIGHT The women rode and the men walked.

Exception 2: A semicolon is often preferable when the main clauses are very long or when one of them contains a comma. The semicolon enables the reader to see at a glance the main divisions of the sentence.

RIGHT   The apples are green, we must admit; but they make good cider.

EXERCISE.   Determine whether a comma or a semicolon (or possibly no comma at all) is needed to separate the main clauses.

1. It was a hot day but he wore a heavy overcoat.
2. He ate all that was left on the plate for he was very hungry.
3. The lake is at its normal level and the water is clear but the fish are not plentiful enough to encourage fishing.
4. The boys looked up to me for some reason or other and I naturally became the leader.
5. We worked and we played.
6. One night I remember very well for I thought I would never live to tell the story.
7. Mary cooked and Laura served.
8. Very simple diction is used and the descriptions are most impressive.
9. I had often seen this girl before but I never liked her.
10. Of course there were tests of various kinds, some of which were not altogether pleasant but everyone seemed to survive them quite easily.

INTRODUCTORY CLAUSES (OR PHRASES)

12b. An adverbial clause (or long phrase) preceding the main clause is usually set off by a comma.

RIGHT   *When he found that his companions had deserted him,* he refused to go farther. [Adverbial clause preceding the main clause.]

RIGHT *If I were elected president of this group,* I should enforce the rules. [Adverbial clause preceding the
main clause.]

RIGHT *Far across the lake and directly on top of a flat hill,* one
solitary oak marks the site of an old home. [Long
phrase preceding the main clause.]

When the preceding phrase contains an infinitive, a
participle, or a gerund, it is generally set off by a
comma. In such sentences the comma is frequently
necessary to prevent misreading.

RIGHT Because of his effort *to escape,* the punishment was
increased. [Phrase containing infinitive.]

RIGHT At the time of his *leaving,* the students assembled at
the station. [Phrase containing gerund.]

Exception: Short introductory clauses and phrases are
frequently better left without punctuation when there
is no danger of misreading.

> RIGHT *When the order comes* he will go.
> RIGHT *After the first attack* only the men remained.

EXERCISE. Insert a comma where it is necessary,
leave it out where it is better omitted, and insert a question
mark where the use of the comma is optional.

1. Whenever a stranger walked into a place of business
   he was treated with due courtesy.
2. When I was about four we moved to a little town in
   the West.
3. If I see a boy who is hurt I want to do something for
   him.
4. If you do this you will not have bad luck.
5. When he was coming in from his position in left field
   he would run until he came to the foul line.
6. To climax my summer vacation I visited my grand-
   mother for two weeks.

7. Although she is not yet the best actress in the land she has the qualifications to become the best some day.
8. During his early days he was granted a license to preach.
9. Since there is no longer a definite type of work for the different sexes men and women often specialize in the same type of work.
10. After a person has gone one day without having to get up early he will surely want to do the same thing the next morning.

ITEMS IN SERIES

12c. Words, phrases, or clauses in series (and co-ordinate adjectives modifying the same noun) are separated by commas.

(1) Words, phrases, or clauses in series are separated by commas.

RIGHT *Men, women, children* crowded into the square. [Form *a, b, c.*]

RIGHT *Men, women,* and *children* crowded into the square. [Form *a, b,* and *c.*]

Note 1: The use of the comma before the conjunction (as in the sentence above) is preferable, but the comma may be omitted unless required for clarity.

CONFUSING The natives ate beans, onions, rice and honey. [Was the rice and honey a mixture?]

RIGHT The natives ate beans, onions, rice, and honey; *or,* The natives ate beans, onions, and rice and honey.

RIGHT He walked up the steps, across the porch, and into the hallway. [Phrases in series.]

133

RIGHT   We protested that the engine used too much oil, that the brakes were worn out, and that the tires were dangerous. [Subordinate clauses in series.]

RIGHT   He burst open the door, he rushed into the house, but he could not find the gun. [Main clauses in series.]

Note 2: Main clauses without the co-ordinating conjunction are usually separated by semicolons. But short main clauses closely related in idea or parallel in structure may be separated by commas.

RIGHT   I came, I saw, I conquered.

(2) Co-ordinate adjectives modifying the same noun are set off by commas.

RIGHT   An old, dilapidated, unpainted house. . . . [The three adjectives modify the noun *house.*]

RIGHT   An old, dilapidated house. . . . [The two adjectives modify the noun *house.*]

RIGHT   A thin, aging, emaciated man. . . . [The three adjectives modify the noun *man.*]

RIGHT   A thin, aging man. . . . [The two adjectives modify the noun *man.*]

But note that the comma is omitted before the last adjective when it is thought of as a part of the noun. In such cases the last adjective is not co-ordinated with the preceding one.

RIGHT   A thin old man. . . . [*Old man* has the force of a single noun, like *postman.* *Thin* and *old* are not co-ordinate; instead, *thin* modifies *old man.*]

RIGHT   The wide, rusty folding doors. . . . [*Folding doors* has the force of a single noun. *Wide* and *rusty* are co-ordinate and are separated by a comma.]

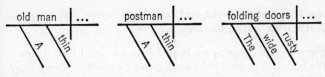

EXERCISE. Use commas where they are needed. Explain the reason for each comma.

1. Mrs. Wharton had a career as well as a home a husband and social prestige.
2. She was carrying a pail of milk a loaf of bread and a dressed chicken.
3. There were four needy families to clothe feed and take care of.
4. He was a good looking intelligent neat individual.
5. The heavy rolling pin fell to the floor.
6. She has seen lamps hills and country farmhouses all of her life.
7. Poetry deals with the higher more beautiful things in life.
8. One bright sunny morning in early June, my father my mother my cousin and I left my home and drove toward Lake Michigan.
9. Did hours of hard grilling work lie there for me?
10. Ethan is a tall stooped man, with a large scar under his eye.

NONRESTRICTIVE (PARENTHETICAL, INTERRUPTING) ELEMENTS

12d. Nonrestrictive clauses (or phrases) and other parenthetical elements (" interrupters ") are set off by commas. Restrictive clauses (or phrases) are not set off.

[To *set off* means to put the comma after a parenthetical element that stands at the beginning of the sentence, before

135

one that stands at the end, and both before and after one that stands within the sentence.

Everything being ready, we hoped that we could start at once.
We hoped that we could start at once, *everything being ready.*
We hoped, *everything being ready,* that we could start at once.]

---

(1) Nonrestrictive clauses and phrases are set off by commas. Restrictive clauses (or phrases) are not set off.

A nonrestrictive clause (or phrase) adds information about a word already defined. It is parenthetical; that is, it can be omitted without changing the meaning of the main clause. A restrictive clause (or phrase) limits or defines the main clause and cannot be omitted.

NONRESTRICTIVE CLAUSE Our newest boat, *which is painted red and white,* has sprung a leak. [The *which* clause, adding information about a boat already identified, is parenthetical. It is not essential to the main clause, *Our newest boat has sprung a leak.*]

NONRESTRICTIVE PHRASE Our newest boat, *painted red and white,* has sprung a leak.

RESTRICTIVE CLAUSE (NO COMMAS) A boat *that leaks* is of little use. [The clause *that leaks* is essential to the meaning of the main clause.]

RESTRICTIVE PHRASE (NO COMMAS) A boat *with a leak* is of little use.

NONRESTRICTIVE CLAUSE William Jones, *who is lazy,* will lose his job.

RESTRICTIVE CLAUSE (NO COMMAS) A boy *who is lazy* deserves to lose his job.

Sometimes a clause (or phrase) may be either restrictive or nonrestrictive, according to the meaning of the writer.

NONRESTRICTIVE He spent hours caring for the Indian
           guides, who were sick with malaria. [He cared
           for all the Indian guides.   Incidentally they were
           sick with malaria.]

RESTRICTIVE (NO COMMA) He spent hours caring for the
           Indian guides who were sick with malaria. [Some
           of the Indian guides were sick with malaria.   He
           cared for the sick ones.]

EXERCISE. Determine whether each clause (or phrase)
is restrictive or nonrestrictive.   Set off only the nonrestrictive clauses or phrases.

1. This ode which was written by Shelley expresses many
   of his thoughts.
2. The law permitted banks to borrow money from the
   Federal Reserve Banks which were twelve in number.
3. Stephen Leacock wrote "My Fishpond" which is a
   humorous essay.
4. The smoke that had filled the house was now gone.
5. He lived at the capital which is a seaport.
6. He betrayed the man who had helped him build his
   fortune.
7. At the piano which her mother gave to her she spent
   many happy hours.
8. The fumes from the motor added to the roll of the boat
   made him seasick.
9. Opening the door of the cabin he looked into the
   darkness.
10. Along the streets which ran north and south moved
    most of the traffic.

**(2) Appositives, geographical names, and items in dates and
    addresses are set off by commas.**

Note that these may be readily expanded into nonrestrictive clauses.   In other words, the principle under-

lying the use of commas to set off nonrestrictive clauses
also applies here.

APPOSITIVES

RIGHT Jesse, *the caretaker*, is a good fellow. [The appositive *caretaker* is equivalent to the nonrestrictive
clause *who is the caretaker*.]

RIGHT Vinie, *the cook*, wears red dresses. [The appositive *cook* is equivalent to the nonrestrictive clause
who is the cook.]

RIGHT Sandburg, *the biographer of Lincoln*, was awarded
the Pulitzer Prize. [The appositive is equivalent
to the nonrestrictive clause *who is the biographer of
Lincoln*.]

Appositives are usually nonrestrictive (parenthetical),
merely adding information about a person or thing already defined.   Such appositives are set off by commas.
But when an appositive is restrictive, commas are
usually omitted.

RIGHT The poet Sandburg has written a biography.
[*Sandburg* restricts the meaning, telling what poet
has written a biography.]

RIGHT His son James is sick. [*James*, not his son *William*.]

RIGHT William the Conqueror invaded England in 1066.
[An appositive that is part of the title is restrictive.]

RIGHT The word *malapropism* is derived from Sheridan's
The Rivals.

EXERCISE.   Determine whether the appositives are
restrictive or nonrestrictive.   Set off all nonrestrictive appositives.

1. Martha his second wife was the daughter of a judge.
2. His second wife Martha was the daughter of a judge.
3. His wife Martha was the daughter of a judge.

4. Henry the Eighth was married five times.
5. Tommy the young pup is as playful as a kitten.
6. Jackson the capital of Mississippi is near the center of the state.
7. My son William is now in college.
8. The word *mob* was once slang.
9. Dickens the author of *David Copperfield* was born in southern England.
10. My youngest son John will soon return home.

GEOGRAPHICAL NAMES, ITEMS IN DATES AND ADDRESSES

RIGHT   Shreveport, Louisiana, is a center of the oil industry. [*Louisiana* is equivalent to the nonrestrictive clause *which is in Louisiana*.]

RIGHT   He works at 20 Tremont Street, Boston, Massachusetts. [Tremont Street, *which is in Boston, which is in Massachusetts*.]

RIGHT   On Sunday, June 30, 1940, he returned. [Sunday, *which was June 30, which was in the year 1940*.]

EXERCISE. Use commas where they are needed.

1. Detroit Michigan is the center of the automobile industry.
2. He was born at Los Angeles California on May 25 1905.
3. He will return home on Saturday January 4 1941.
4. Please send the package to 224 North State Street Chicago Illinois.
5. The accident occurred in De Soto Parish Louisiana on Monday September 9 1940.
6. My best friends live in Denver Colorado and in Kansas City Missouri.
7. He was born in Brattle Street Cambridge Massachusetts at the beginning of the last century.
8. He died on May 1 1874.

(3) Parenthetical words or phrases (inserted expressions), words in direct address (vocatives), absolute phrases, and mild interjections are set off by commas.

PARENTHETICAL EXPRESSIONS

As a matter of fact, the term "parenthetical" is correctly applied to everything discussed under **12d**; but the term is more commonly applied to such expressions as *on the other hand, in the first place, in fact, to tell the truth, however, that is, for example, I hope, I report, he says.* The term would apply equally well to expressions inserted in dialogue: *he said, he observed, he protested,* etc.

RIGHT   *To tell the truth,* we anticipated bad luck.

RIGHT   The work is, *on the whole,* very satisfactory.

RIGHT   "We believe," *he replied,* "that the contract should be forfeited."

Note 1: Some parenthetical expressions causing little if any pause in reading are frequently not set off by commas: *also, too, indeed, perhaps, at least, likewise, nevertheless,* etc. The writer must use his judgment.

RIGHT   I am *also* of that opinion.

RIGHT   He is *perhaps* the best swimmer on the team.

RIGHT   I am *indeed* glad that you returned.

Note 2: At the other extreme, some parenthetical expressions loosely connected with the rest of the sentence call for punctuation stronger than the comma — for dashes or parentheses. See section **17**.

DIRECT ADDRESS

RIGHT   Come here, *Mary,* and help us.

RIGHT   I refuse, *sir,* to believe the report.

RIGHT   This, *my friends,* is the whole truth.

ABSOLUTE PHRASES [1]

RIGHT *Everything being in readiness,* we departed promptly.

RIGHT He ran swiftly, *the dog in front of him,* and plunged into the forest.

RIGHT I fear the encounter, *his temper being what it is.*

MILD INTERJECTIONS

RIGHT *Well,* let him try if he insists.

RIGHT *Ah,* that is my idea of a good meal.

Note: Strong interjections call for the exclamation point. See section **17**.

EXERCISE. Use commas to set off all parenthetical expressions, words in direct address, absolute expressions, and mild interjections.

1. He has no doubt reached his destination.
2. To tell the truth I never intended to go.
3. Please come here James and help me.
4. "I am confident" he replied "that I can please you."
5. I shall be glad sir to help you.
6. Thomas was also in the group.
7. The ship having arrived the soldiers embarked.
8. Oh I am indeed glad that you have come.
9. She was in fact entirely too frank.
10. There are however many exceptions to this rule.
11. She is going I know.
12. I hope my dear sir that you are convinced.
13. Well he may come whenever he pleases.
14. I enjoyed the trip the day being clear and mild.
15. "After I return" he promised "you may expect a reply from me."

[1] See section **1, Grammatical Terms.**

EXERCISE. Use commas to set off all nonrestrictive or parenthetical elements. Do not set off restrictive elements.

1. The safety man attempting to get away let the ball slip from his hands.
2. In August 1930 my family moved to Atlanta Georgia.
3. You are surprised I know to learn of his arrival.
4. The switch that controlled the lights was out of order.
5. Above all a teacher should have a sense of humor.
6. Children of all ages eager to get home watched for the school bus.
7. Many students graduating from college fail to find work.
8. Christianity soon won control of the Empire forcing the Jews into a subordinate position.
9. Dormitory life as I said before should be a chapter in every girl's life.
10. To the latter circumstance perhaps he owed the meekness of spirit for which he became so famous.
11. Only a few such as Charlie Chaplin and Douglas Fairbanks could appeal to the public under these circumstances.
12. The characters are vividly portrayed each one representing a type.
13. Late in March 1933 a cyclone hit the town.
14. It is evident of course that a person can find little employment here.
15. *Macbeth* written by William Shakespeare was another drama in the Great Plays Series.
16. Come do not object to such trifles.
17. William his youngest son enlisted in the army.
18. The trees along the shores of the lake were covered with moss.
19. The clowns who frolicked in the circus ring made the children shriek with joy.
20. Hurry James and close the door.

21. Madison Wisconsin is the seat of a great university.
22. A lighthouse built on a rocky ledge protects the passing ships.

12e. Even though a comma is not called for by any other rule, insert a comma between sentence elements that might otherwise be incorrectly read together.

CONFUSING Inside the room was gaily decorated. [*Inside* may be at first mistaken for the preposition.]

CLEAR Inside, the room was gaily decorated. [*Inside* clearly the adverb.]

CONFUSING After all the conquest of malaria is a fascinating story.

CLEAR After all, the conquest of malaria is a fascinating story.

EXERCISES ON THE COMMA

A. In the following sentences explain each comma by writing above it the appropriate symbol from section **12**: **a, b, c1, c2, d1, d2, d3,** or **e.** (Use **e** only when no other symbol will apply.)

1. My aunt, who had not heard the car drive up, continued reading.
2. The dam adds to the wealth, power, and efficiency of the country.
3. Well, what does it matter anyway?
4. Mary, where did you go last night?
5. The university is made up of law, commercial, liberal arts, and agricultural colleges.
6. The visitors, by the way, were some old-time friends.
7. This is where you live, isn't it?

8. A group of hungry, wet, bedraggled hikers reached the inn.

9. The box was sent to Jim Smith, 19 Elm Street, Chicago, Illinois.

10. Instead of ten, forty volunteers appeared.

11. The study of law, which touches every phase of life, is always changing.

12. Although John is honest and progressive, he is not an executive.

13. The game having ended, the crowd left the stadium.

14. Mr. Smith, the electrician, will repair the doorbell.

15. The band played a stirring march, and the students joined the parade.

16. As soon as he received the telegram, he left for home, for his mother was sick.

17. The bomb hit the cathedral, filling the air with debris.

18. Well, when you reach the place, write me.

19. The oak tree, which was a mass of golden-brown foliage, stood on the top of the hill.

20. Since missiles were coming from every direction, the cellar was the only safe place.

21. My good friend, Alice, will take charge.

22. The specifications called for steel, not aluminum.

23. The airplane rose, gained speed, and quickly disappeared.

24. Robert Lee, the commander of the Confederate army, was respected by the North and by the South.

25. Before starting to cook, the maid peeled the potatoes.

26. The next afternoon, after driving for six hours, we reached Yellowstone Park.

27. The bell rang, but no one came.

28. "Father," she answered, "is not at home."

29. In his manner were pride, confidence, and conceit.

30. The rain ceased, and the sun came out.

B. Insert all necessary commas. Explain each comma by writing above it the appropriate symbol from section **12**: **a, b, c1, c2, d1, d2, d3,** or **e.** (Do not use **e** when any other symbol is appropriate.)

1. The letter was addressed to Jack Smith 6 Oak Street Boston Massachusetts.
2. The lodge which is reached by a gravel road belongs to my brother.
3. Well what do you think of the plan now?
4. Mrs. Jones the dietitian will take charge of the food.
5. Before starting to drive William completely overhauled the car.
6. The rain fell heavily all day long and the trees swayed to and fro.
7. I asked for steak sausage and liver.
8. As soon as he reached his destination he wrote to his mother for she was anxiously awaiting word.
9. Although Tom is clever and quick he is not accurate.
10. A group of cold hungry Boy Scouts reached camp after dark.
11. The successful author brought fame prestige and honor to his native town.
12. The Confederate soldiers although outclassed and outnumbered fought bravely to the end.
13. After months of planning we finally started on our journey.
14. Mary by the way will preside at the meeting.
15. Mr. Jones our neighbor is a well-known artist.
16. This is where you saw her is it not?
17. Sociology a study which interests everyone deals with facts of everyday life.
18. In spite of the evidence I do not believe it.
19. The little town is made up of retired farmers missionaries and tradespeople.
20. The boy gave a shrill whistle and the dog came running.

21. John who had no key tried to open the door by force.
22. The play being over the cabs filled the streets.
23. The boat hitting the water with a splash almost capsized.
24. "Are you sure" she asked "that you can go?"
25. Men who were going to work filled the car.
26. Bob where are you going?
27. I hope son that you are pleased with your job.
28. Since he was neither at home nor at the park we had to go without him.
29. A knowledge of birds and plants and animals adds to the enjoyment of a camping trip.
30. When you arrive Jim ring the bell.
31. The soldiers filled the streets and the houses were filled with anxious people.
32. Magnesium a silver-white metallic element burns with a dazzling light.
33. Since the bridge was washed away we had to make a detour.
34. Several ragged unkempt boys asked for money to buy food.
35. To tell the truth I want to stay at home.
36. When you knock the maid will open the door.
37. As a matter of fact Mary will be glad to sing for you.
38. For supper he had oatmeal honey and toast.
39. The game having ended the crowd left.
40. Cultivate the flowers and weeds will not grow.

C. Select several paragraphs from a book or from an article in a magazine, and explain each comma by writing above it the appropriate symbol from section 12: **a, b, c1, c2, d1, d2, d3,** or **e.** (Do not use **e** when any other symbol is appropriate.)

SUPERFLUOUS COMMAS

13. Do not use superfluous commas.[1]

If you have a tendency to use unnecessary commas, consider each of your commas and omit it unless you can justify it by one of the principles treated under section 12.

Another way — perhaps less satisfactory — to avoid unnecessary commas is to observe the following rules:

13a. Do not use a comma to separate the subject and its verb, the verb and its complement, or an adjective and its noun.

Omit the commas in parentheses:

Rain at short intervals(,) is productive of mosquitoes. [Needlessly separating subject and verb.]

Many people who are loyal members(,) will refuse to believe the report.

He learned at an early age(,) the necessity of economizing.   [Needlessly separating verb and object.]

The book says(,) that members of the crew deserted. [Indirect discourse: needless separation of verb and object.]

He was a bad, deceitful, unruly(,) boy.   [Needless separation of adjective and its noun.]

[1] Complete mastery of section 13 will eliminate the fifth most common error in the average student theme.

13b. Do not use a comma to separate two words or two phrases joined by a co-ordinating conjunction.

Omit the commas in parentheses:

The poem has nobility of sentiment(,) and dignity of style.
The players work together(,) and gain a victory. [Compound predicate: *and* joins two verb phrases.]

He had decided to work(,) and to save his money. [*And* joins two infinitive phrases.]

13c. Do not use commas to set off words or short phrases (especially introductory ones) that are not parenthetical or that are very slightly so.

Omit the commas in parentheses:

On last Monday(,) I went to a baseball game.
Maybe(,) he had a better reason for leaving.
The center passes the ball(,) through his legs(,) to a man in the backfield.
In our age(,) it is easy to talk(,) by wire(,) to any continent.
I am(,) also(,) convinced of his sincerity.

13d. Do not use commas to set off restrictive clauses, restrictive phrases, or restrictive appositives.

Omit the commas in parentheses:

A man(,) *who hopes to succeed*(,) must work hard. [Restrictive clause.]

A man(,) *hopeful of success*(,) will work hard. [Restrictive phrase.]

That man(,) *Jones*(,) will overcome his opponents. [Restrictive appositive.]

13e. Do not put a comma before the first item of a series, after the last item of a series, or after a co-ordinating conjunction.

Omit the commas in parentheses:

I enjoy the study of(,) history, geography, and geology.

History, geography, and geology(,) are interesting subjects.

I enjoy these subjects, but(,) for others I have less appreciation.

EXERCISE ON SUPERFLUOUS COMMAS

In the following sentences some of the commas are needed and some are superfluous. Strike out all unnecessary commas. Explain each comma that you allow to stand.

1. The girl spent too much time playing tennis, and other games, instead of working on her studies.
2. Love songs, nature poems, and satires, were written by Burns.
3. In our day there are a number of ways to communicate, by wire, that our forefathers did not know.
4. After all, the conquest of malaria, is a fascinating story.
5. He had been pushed lower, and lower, into the blackest depth of ignominy.
6. The word, *ode*, comes from a Greek word, meaning *song*.
7. Then, Lady Bracknell and Algernon went into another room.
8. The only encouragement, I have had, was looking forward to the day when I would receive your daughter's hand in marriage.
9. This is an annual event, and arouses much interest.
10. If this were not true, I should not feel proud, when I walk with her.

11. I enjoyed, the second, fifth, and tenth chapters of the book.
12. Both are women who are capable of handling people.
13. He has learned during this time, the necessity of work.
14. Last Friday afternoon, I went to a football game.
15. The Indians called it, "The Crow's Nest," because it was surrounded by mountains.
16. He worked hard when he was doing something, that he wanted to do.
17. I like to sit on the bank of a brook, and hear the rippling water.
18. I was very much impressed by the quietness of the study hall, and the ease with which the students selected their reference books.
19. A boy secretly worships the ball player as an idol, and considers him an ideal.
20. The many, who had been criticized by Hazlitt, were later able to secure their revenge.
21. One must remember, that Kean was one of the best actors of his era.
22. Most of the men spent their leisure time gambling, and loafing at the only store in the camp.
23. Benjamin Franklin was a man, who enjoyed serving his country.
24. Some course, that deals with citizenship, should be required of every student.
25. The contraption then called radio, would not be recognized as such today.
26. I recall the time, when my father took me to the circus.
27. Egdon Heath, at twilight, already had the appearance of night.
28. First, is the problem of budgeting.
29. Another example, is that of a person who promises to make good in college.
30. Although he was stingy, and denied himself many things, he always lavished gifts on others.

THE SEMICOLON

14. Use the semicolon to separate (a) main clauses not joined by a co-ordinating conjunction and (b) phrases or clauses containing commas, even when joined by co-ordinating conjunctions.

Note: If you make repeated errors in the use of the semicolon, you should first master the fundamentals of the sentence treated in section **2e, Sentence Sense,** and then study section **14** again.

The semicolon may be used only between parts of equal rank: between two main clauses, two subordinate clauses, or two phrases. *Be careful not to use a semicolon between a clause and a phrase or between a main clause and a subordinate clause.*

WRONG A bitter wind swept the dead leaves along the street; casting them high in the air and against the buildings. [Between the main clause and the phrase a semicolon is impossible.]

RIGHT A bitter wind swept the dead leaves along the street, casting them high in the air and against the buildings.

WRONG The doctors admitted that the disease was a new one**;** unknown to them.

RIGHT The doctors admitted that the disease was a new one unknown to them. [Since the phrase is restrictive, not even a comma is needed.]

WRONG Tennessee was the second Southern state to establish schools for Negroes**;** although it was not much in favor of Negro education. [Between the main clause and the subordinate clause a semicolon is impossible.]

RIGHT Tennessee was the second Southern state to establish schools for Negroes**,** although it was not much in favor of Negro education.

14a. Use the semicolon to separate main clauses not joined by one of the co-ordinating conjunctions: *and, but, or, nor, for.*

WRONG Many people have the ability to write themes**,** others have not.

RIGHT Many people have the ability to write themes**;** others have not.

WRONG She was easily impressed she liked whatever she looked at.

RIGHT She was easily impressed**;** she liked whatever she looked at.

Note particularly that the **conjunctive adverbs** (such as *therefore, then, so, also, thus, still, instead, hence, however, accordingly, moreover, nevertheless, furthermore, consequently, otherwise, besides,* and *notwithstanding*) are not co-ordinating conjunctions. Thus, in accordance with the rule, main clauses joined by these *adverbs* must be separated by a semicolon. Only the *co-ordinating conjunctions* may join clauses separated by a comma. Many writers now use *so* with the comma, but the more conservative ones still employ the semicolon. Students tend to overwork *so*. See section **19, Glossary.**

WRONG The B-rays are not to be recommended for use, however, they are used in many hospitals today.

RIGHT The B-rays are not to be recommended for use; however, they are used in many hospitals today.

ALSO RIGHT The B-rays are not to be recommended for use, but they are used in many hospitals today. [A comma is correctly used with the co-ordinating conjunction *but*.]

Note: The co-ordinating conjunctions are called "pure" conjunctions because they make a close connection and have no other function in a sentence. The conjunction *but*, for example, could occupy no position except the one it holds — directly between the two clauses. The adverb *however*, on the other hand, may readily be shifted to a position nearer the verb.

RIGHT The B-rays are not to be recommended for use; they are used, *however*, in many hospitals today.

Explanatory expressions (such as *namely, that is, in fact, on the contrary,* and *on the other hand*) are used just as the conjunctive adverbs; that is, main clauses joined by them must be separated by a semicolon.

WRONG He is coming today, in fact, he is due here now.

RIGHT He is coming today; in fact, he is due here now.

14b. As a rule the semicolon should be used to separate phrases or clauses which themselves contain commas, even when such phrases or clauses are joined by co-ordinating conjunctions.

This use of the semicolon makes for clarity, showing the reader at a glance the main divisions.

RIGHT The lake is useful as a source of electrical energy, pouring its waters through the mighty turbines; as a reservoir, holding back the floods from the swollen rivers; and as a place of recreation, providing bathing, boating, and fishing. [Semicolons separating phrases.]

RIGHT The life and ambition of a young girl are probably not very interesting to anyone except to the young girl herself; and sometimes, even to that young girl, her past life is not interesting. [Semicolon separating two main clauses.]

Note: Very long main clauses, even when neither clause contains commas, are sometimes separated by a semicolon in addition to the co-ordinating conjunction. Occasionally a semicolon instead of a comma is used between shorter main clauses to emphasize balance or contrast.

RIGHT Goldsmith died a pauper and in debt; but after his death he won recognition from the whole world.

EXERCISES ON THE SEMICOLON

A. Insert semicolons where they are needed. Do not allow a semicolon to stand between parts of unequal rank.

1. He would not let us pay him for it, so we thanked him and started on our way.
2. The "mill" of that time consisted of two stones, one of these was a flat stone with a convex top, the other a pestle-shaped rock which was held in hand.
3. I have lived at Miami only one month, hence I am not well acquainted with the city.

4. He had been married only a short time, therefore he did not like to leave his wife alone at home.

5. I prefer literature to composition, for I should much rather read than write, but since both are required, I will not neglect composition.

6. In the early days of shipping, long before David wrote of Tyre and Sidon, the Mediterranean was the center of the world's commerce, and that commerce consisted chiefly of linen.

7. America absorbs a great deal of her own products, therefore, a prolonged strike would result in depression.

8. There were tears in her eyes when Kathryn walked into the room where she was to have her lessons, and tears remained in her eyes, for she continued to cry almost all day.

9. Someone jerked off his beard, soon there was no Santa Claus.

10. I have not attended any of the formal dances, therefore I cannot pass judgment on them.

11. He worked as an apprentice to a printer, then he became a pilot on the Mississippi.

12. Robert created in himself a wanderlust, that is, he wanted to see more of the world.

13. Juliet awoke and saw Romeo dead, then she killed herself.

14. We arrived there about dinnertime, so we ate our lunches to avoid carrying them any farther.

15. It is well known that some soils erode more easily than others, some subsoils have greater ability to absorb water.

16. The visitors finally accomplished their task, they made the final touchdown and won the game.

17. If she had married Andrew, the picture might have been entirely different; because he was a thrifty young man.

18. Changes in civilization did not disturb Egdon Heath, in fact, civilization was regarded as an enemy.

19. These companies do not consider the exorbitant prices they charge, instead, they think only of getting more customers.

20. Colesville was rather a collection of farms than of houses; with the nearest village seven miles away.

21. Sift about two cups of sugar over the mixture, then begin the folding process.

22. Some squaws prepared meals, others looked after the wigwams, hides, and children.

23. After graduating from high school, I faced one of the most difficult tasks I had ever known; the task of choosing a course in college.

24. They went back to the lake and began fishing, they had very little success.

25. As he climbs toward that ideal, he may stumble or fall, he may have to stop to rest or to get a clearer vision of the right path.

26. They can never be together, still they will never be far apart.

27. Tolerance is not enough, we must go farther and do away with all differences and misunderstandings.

28. Reading broadens the mind, therefore, it gives one a feeling of security when talking with other people.

29. Three men and a boy sailed away four men came back.

30. It looked as if it might rain so I took an umbrella with me.

B. From some book or magazine, copy five sentences in which the semicolon is properly used. Explain the reason for each semicolon.

C. Compose five sentences to illustrate the proper use of the semicolon.

THE APOSTROPHE

15. Use the apostrophe (a) to indicate the possessive case of nouns and indefinite pronouns — but not of personal pronouns; (b) to mark omissions in contracted words or numerals; and (c) to form the plurals of letters, figures, or symbols.[1]

15a. Avoid careless omission of the apostrophe in the possessive case of nouns and indefinite pronouns.

Caution: As a rule the possessive is not used with inanimate objects. See section 5e.

(1) Unless the ending is in *s,* add the apostrophe and *s* for either singular or plural.

RIGHT   The boy's top; the girl's doll; John's ball. [Singular.]
The men's hats; the women's dresses; the children's toys. [Plural.]

(2) If the plural ending is in *s,* add only the apostrophe.

RIGHT   The boys' wagon; the girls' party.

[1] Complete mastery of section 15 will eliminate the seventh most common error in the average student theme.

(3) If the singular ending is in *s,* add either the apostrophe and *s* or, if the second *s* would make for difficult pronunciation, add only the apostrophe.

A student who wishes a more specific rule may follow *Webster's Collegiate Dictionary*, Fifth Edition, under **possessive**:

> Singular nouns ending in an *s–* or *z–* sound, when of one syllable, add *'s* (*James's*); when of two or more syllables taking accent on the last, add *'s* (*Hortense's*); when of two or more syllables taking no accent on the last, add *'s* if the last syllable is not preceded by an *s–* or *z–* sound (*Thomas's*); but when the last syllable is preceded by an *s–* or *z–* sound, they add simply the apostrophe (*Moses'; for conscience' sake; Xerxes'*); proper nouns ending in *–es* [*pron. –ēz*], add only the apostrophe if the accent is on the penult (*Achil'les'*); but add *'s* otherwise (*Hercules's*).

(4) In the case of compounds or of nouns in joint possession the possessive form is taken by the last word only. In case of individual possession each noun takes the possessive form.

RIGHT   My father-in-law's house.
RIGHT   Helen and Mary's piano. [Joint ownership.]
RIGHT   Helen's and Mary's clothes. [Individual ownership.]

15b. Do not use the apostrophe with the personal pronouns (*his, hers, its, ours, yours, theirs*) or with the relative-interrogative pronoun *whose.*

WRONG He buttoned *hi's* coat. [No one would make this error.]
RIGHT   He buttoned *his* coat.

WRONG Virtue is *it's* own reward. [Fully as incorrect as *hi's*.]

RIGHT Virtue is *its* own reward.

WRONG hi's, his', her's, hers', it's (possessive), its', our's, ours', your's, yours', their's, theirs', who's, whose'.

RIGHT his, hers, its (possessive), it's (meaning *it is*, as in *It's cold today*), ours, yours, theirs, whose.

15c. Use an apostrophe to mark omissions from contracted words or numerals.

RIGHT Didn't, can't, won't, o'clock.

Caution: Place the apostrophe exactly where the omission occurs.

WRONG Is'nt, does'nt, have'nt.
RIGHT Isn't, doesn't, haven't.

15d. Use an apostrophe and *s* to form the plurals of letters, figures, and words referred to as words.

(Such expressions are always italicized.)

RIGHT Watch your *p's* and *q's*.
RIGHT He ate the grapes by *2's* and *3's*.
RIGHT There were no *if's* or *and's* about his proposal.

EXERCISES ON THE APOSTROPHE

A. Insert necessary apostrophes and mark out unnecessary ones.

1. Nothing was said to him about the familys unhappiness.
2. A nurses life cannot satisfy me.
3. Do'nt use so many *sos* and *buts*.

4. Its easy to drive.
5. Edwards first job was washing windows for a baker.
6. I didnt get to sleep until after twelve oclock.
7. I cant go on Thursday.
8. They wont affect her as they do me.
9. Reading increases ones knowledge.
10. The readers mind must be alert.
11. He eliminated all the 5s and 7s.
12. Keat's poetry stirs the readers imagination.
13. Its not our's.
14. Johns hat still remained on his mothers bed.
15. Alls well at the mens club.
16. Miss Prism said that she thought it was her's.
17. I have enjoyed many a summers visit there.
18. It may be the poets own experience.
19. The moon cast it's gleam upon the waves.
20. I like to watch the expressions on students faces while they are studying.
21. The boys dog scratched up all the neighbors lawns.
22. Her months pay was sufficient to buy the childrens clothes.
23. A birds chief occupation is getting its food.
24. The book was her's, not his.

B. Write the possessive singular and the possessive plural of each of the following words:

1. mother-in-law	2. jockey	3. Andrews
4. father	5. lady	6. Myers
7. lackey	8. mouse	9. ox
10. man	11. sailor	12. deer
13. child	14. family	15. sheep
16. goose	17. will-o'-the-wisp	18. woman
19. jury	20. fox	21. committee
22. spoonful	23. genius	24. aviatress
25. princess	26. army	27. passer-by
28. class	29. bellman	30. chief

QUOTATION MARKS

16 Use quotation marks to set off all direct quotations, some titles, and words used in a special sense. Place other marks of punctuation in proper relation to quotation marks.

Caution: Be careful not to omit the second set of quotation marks: the first set, marking the beginning of the part quoted, must be followed by another set to mark the end.

WRONG **"I have no intention of staying, he replied.

RIGHT **"I have no intention of staying," he replied.

WRONG **"I do not object, he said, to the tenor of the report."

RIGHT **"I do not object," he said, "to the tenor of the report." [Two parts are quoted. Each must be enclosed, leaving *he said* outside of the quotation marks.]

16a. Direct (but not indirect) quotations are enclosed by double quotation marks.

WRONG He said **“**that he had no intention of staying.**”** [Indirect quotation.]

RIGHT He said that he had no intention of staying.

RIGHT He said, **“**I have no intention of staying.**”** [Direct quotation.]

16b. A quotation within a quotation is enclosed by single quotation marks; one within that, by double marks.

RIGHT Mr. Jones replied to Mr. Smith: **“**I resent your statement **‘**You bought the stock illegally.**’** I know that the purchase was regular in every detail.**”**

RIGHT After a short pause the witness continued his story. **“**Mr. Jones replied to Mr. Smith: **‘**I resent your statement **“**You bought the stock illegally.**”** I know that the purchase was regular in every detail.**’** But Mr. Smith would not alter his statement.**”**

16c. If the direct quotation consists of two or more paragraphs, the quotation marks come before each paragraph and at the end of the last; they do not come at the end of intermediate paragraphs.

RIGHT **“**And so the talk ended. There was no doubt that the expedition had been an utter failure. Adrian was a ruined man; and Amyas had lost his venture.

“Adrian rose, and begged leave to retire; he must collect himself.

“ ‘Poor gentleman!**’** said Mrs. Hawkins; **‘**it is little else he has left to collect.**’ ”**

— KINGSLEY, *Westward Ho!*

162

Many writers prefer to avoid quotation marks with passages of more than two or three lines, indicating the quotation by means of indention and single-spacing. In print such passages are usually set in type smaller than that of the regular text. Quoted lines of poetry are sufficiently marked by the verse form without the aid of quotation marks.

RIGHT

> And so the talk ended. There was no doubt that the expedition had been an utter failure. Adrian was a ruined man; and Amyas had lost his venture.
>
> Adrian rose, and begged leave to retire; he must collect himself.
>
> "Poor gentleman!" said Mrs. Hawkins; "it is little else he has left to collect."
>
> — KINGSLEY, *Westward Ho!*

RIGHT

> A thing of beauty is a joy forever:
> Its loveliness increases; it will never
> Pass into nothingness; but still will keep
> A bower quiet for us, and a sleep
> Full of sweet dreams, and health, and quiet breathing.
>
> — KEATS, *Endymion.*

16d. **Phrases borrowed from others, words used in a special way, and slang introduced into formal writing are enclosed in quotation marks.**

RIGHT   He called himself "emperor," but he was only a thief.

16e. **Titles of literary, artistic, and musical works are sometimes put in quotation marks, but are more commonly italicized.**

RIGHT   "Treasure Island," Chopin's "Prelude."

RIGHT (*more common*)   *Treasure Island*, Chopin's *Prelude*.

RIGHT   The third chapter of *Treasure Island* is entitled **"The Black Spot."** [The title of a chapter or an article from a magazine is regularly put in quotation marks.]

16f. Do not overuse quotation marks. In general do not enclose in quotation marks common nicknames, well-known phrases and technical terms, or slang used in informal writing.

NEEDLESS PUNCTUATION   **"Old Hickory"** was wrought up over the dismissal of his friend.

BETTER   Old Hickory was wrought up over the dismissal of his friend.

16g. In using marks of punctuation with quoted words, phrases, or sentences, place

(1) The period and the comma always within the quotation marks.

(2) The colon and the semicolon always outside the quotation marks.

(3) The dash, the question mark, and the exclamation point within the quotation marks when they apply to the quoted matter only; outside when they refer to the whole sentence.

RIGHT   **"I** will go**,"** he insisted.   **"I** am needed**."** [Comma and period always inside quotation marks.]

RIGHT   He spoke of his **"old log house"**; he might have called it a mansion. [Semicolon (and colon) always outside quotation marks.]

RIGHT   He asked, **"When** did you arrive**?"** [The question mark applies only to the quoted part of the sentence.]

164

RIGHT   What is the meaning of **"the open door"?** [The question mark applies to the whole sentence.]

RIGHT   The captain shouted, **"Halt!"** [The exclamation point applies only to the quotation.]

RIGHT   Save us from his **"mercy"!** [The exclamation point applies to the whole sentence.]

EXERCISE ON QUOTATION MARKS

Insert quotation marks where they are needed.

1. The woman, Alice explained, cried Fire! and ran from the house.
2. You need not go to town today, Sara, said Mrs. Jones. I have enough food on hand.
3. The captain shouted, Man the boats!
4. Keeping up with the Joneses is a costly business.
5. The phrase Let George do it has been used for many years.
6. I cannot explain, she said, why I distrust the agent.
7. Buck up and do your best, urged the old man.
8. She added, Mr. Smith said, I just can't buy the property.
9. What are you trying to do? he asked.
10. War seems inevitable, the sergeant said, and we must accept the fact.
11. Come, let us go, said Jane. Perhaps we can find the house.
12. Then the conductor shouted, All aboard!
13. At any rate, said Jim, I have finished one year's work.
14. It is no use. I can't go. Jack spoke desperately. What shall I do?
15. Can you take it on the chin, son? asked Mr. Jones.

THE PERIOD
AND OTHER MARKS

17. Use the period, the question mark, the exclamation point, the dash, the colon, parentheses, and brackets in accordance with accepted usage.

THE PERIOD (.)

17a. Use the period after declarative and imperative sentences, after indirect questions, and after most abbreviations. Use periods (or dots) to mark omissions from quoted passages.

(1) Use periods to mark the end of declarative sentences.

RIGHT   He obeyed the rules.
RIGHT   He delivered the prisoners to the guard.

(2) Use periods to mark the end of imperative sentences.

RIGHT   Obey the rules.
RIGHT   Deliver the prisoners to the guard.

(3) Use periods to mark the end of indirect questions.

RIGHT   He asked whether the rules had been obeyed.
RIGHT   He inquired whether the prisoners had been delivered to the guard.

(4) Use periods to follow most abbreviations.

RIGHT Mr., Dr., M.D., etc., Maj., *i.e.*, Cal., A.D., B.C., a.m., p.m., *viz.*, Jr.

Use no period after such contractions as *I've, doesn't, isn't* or after letters standing for such recently created governmental agencies as *CCC, TVA, WPA*. If you have any doubt in regard to a given abbreviation, consult a good dictionary. See, for example, the list of "Abbreviations Used in Writing and Printing," *Webster's Collegiate Dictionary*, Fifth Edition, pp. 1175–1181.

(5) Use periods (or dots) to indicate the omission of words from a quoted passage.

At the beginning of a sentence or within it three dots are used; at the end, four dots, the last serving as the period.

RIGHT "Ingratitude is among them a capital crime • • • for they reason thus, that whoever makes ill returns to his benefactor, must needs be a common enemy to the rest of mankind. • • •"

— JONATHAN SWIFT, *Gulliver's Travels*

THE QUESTION MARK (**?**)

17b. Use the question mark (1) to follow direct questions and (2) to indicate the writer's uncertainty.

(1) Use the question mark to follow every direct (but not indirect) question.

RIGHT Who started the riot**?** [Direct question.]
RIGHT He asked who started the riot. [Indirect question, followed by a period.]

RIGHT   Did he ask who started the riot? [The sentence as a whole is a direct question despite the indirect question at the end.]

RIGHT   "Who started the riot?" he asked.

RIGHT   He asked, "Who started the riot?"

RIGHT   You started the riot? [Question in the form of a declarative sentence.]

RIGHT   To ask the question Who started this riot? is unnecessary. [The inserted sentence is a direct question, followed by a question mark.]

RIGHT   To ask who started the riot is unnecessary. [Indirect question, requiring no question mark.]

RIGHT   Did you hear him say, "What right have you to ask about the riot?" [Double direct question followed by a single question mark.]

RIGHT   Did he plan the riot? employ assistants? give the signal to begin? [Question marks cause full stops and give separate emphasis to each interrogative element.]

RIGHT   Did he plan the riot, employ assistants, and give the signal to begin? [A single question mark throws less emphasis on the separate parts.]

Note: "Courtesy" questions common to business letters are usually followed by a period.

     RIGHT   Will you write me again if I can be of further service. [But the question mark is also in good use.]

   (2) Use the question mark (within parentheses) to express the writer's uncertainty as to the correctness of the preceding word or fact.

RIGHT   Alaric was born in 376(?) and died in 410.

Caution: The question mark within parentheses is no longer correctly used to express the author's wit or sarcasm.

> WRONG This kind(?) proposal caused Gulliver to slip away to Blefuscu.
>
> RIGHT This harsh proposal caused Gulliver to slip away to Blefuscu.

THE EXCLAMATION POINT (!)

17c. Use the exclamation point after an emphatic interjection and after a phrase, clause, or sentence to express a high degree of surprise, incredulity, or other strong emotion.

Caution: Avoid overuse of the exclamation point. Use a comma after mild interjections, and end mildly exclamatory sentences with a period.

> RIGHT What! I cannot believe it!
>
> RIGHT What a range, what a grasp, there was in his glowing, various mind!
>
> — CHRISTOPHER MORLEY
>
> RIGHT Forbid it, Almighty God! I know not what course others may take, but as for me, give me liberty, or give me death!
>
> — PATRICK HENRY

EXERCISE. Supply periods, question marks, and exclamation points where needed.

1. "Where are you going" he asked
2. Oh, how can you say such a thing
3. He asked whether the trees had been sprayed

4. Alas we see that the small have always suffered for the follies of the great
5. One goes to the right   One goes to the left   Both are wrong
6. It is true, is it not, that we need men for defense
7. Did he ask who wanted to go
8. Send the scouts on an errand
9. "Do you know," he asked, "where the gymnasium is"
10. Dr Young has been out of town
11. "What do you want" he asked
12. You will find the references on pp 775 and 826
13. What You are not going
14. He replied that he lived on Concord Avenue
15. You know you can do it if you try

THE COLON (:)

17d. The colon is used after a formal introductory statement to direct attention to what follows.

Caution: Colon and semicolon, notwithstanding the similarity of the names, differ widely in use. The semicolon is a strong "separator" almost equal to a period and is used only between equal parts. The colon is an "introducer," pointing to something that is to follow.

(1) The colon may direct attention to an appositive or a series of appositives.

RIGHT   He had only one pleasure: eating. [Very formal. A dash or a comma would be more frequently used.]

RIGHT   We may divide poetry into three classes: narrative, lyric, and dramatic. [A dash may be used; a comma would be confusing.]

RIGHT   We have one chance for escape: we may retreat by the lower road. [The second clause explains the first.]

(2) The colon may direct attention to a formal explanation or to a long quotation.

RIGHT   Her plans were as follows: to travel in France, to increase her knowledge of the language, and to return to her teaching.

RIGHT   He replied: "I enjoy hunting and fishing. During next summer I am planning to hunt in the southern part of Texas and to fish off the coast of Louisiana." [A comma is used to follow *he said* when it introduces a short quotation.]

(3) The colon may separate two main clauses when the second clause explains or amplifies the first.

RIGHT   With what was universal in all these efforts, Whitman could sympathize: Homer and Shakespeare and the Bible had been his daily food.
— LEWIS MUMFORD

RIGHT   These, however, were not for sale: these were decoys; the saleable birds lay, packed far too close, in little wooden boxes in a man's bag. — E. V. LUCAS. [The colon may be followed by either a small letter or a capital.]

(4) The colon, in its more conventional uses, may direct attention to a business letter following the salutation, to the title following the name of the author, to the verse following the Biblical chapter, or to the minute following the hour.

EXAMPLES   Dear Sir**:**
             Carl Sandburg**:** *The People, Yes.*
             John 4**:** 10.
             8**:**30 p.m.

Caution: Omit the colon when there is no formal introduction.

       WRONG   In the boat were**:** a man, two boys, and a girl.

       RIGHT   In the boat were a man, two boys, and a girl.

       WRONG   He had**:** two horses, a cow, and a hog.

       RIGHT   He had two horses, a cow, and a hog.

       WRONG   They caught such fish as**:** mackerel, tarpon, and bass.

       RIGHT   They caught such fish as mackerel, tarpon, and bass.

EXERCISE.   Supply colons where needed.

1. There are various departments in the college of engineering mechanical, electrical, and chemical.
2. His plan was as follows first he would find a job, then he would save his money, and later he would go to college.
3. Joseph Conrad Lord Jim
4. I shall be there at 9 20 p.m.
5. There is only one thing left for us to do go back the way we came.

THE DASH (—)

17e. The dash is used to mark a sudden break in thought, to set off a summary, or to set off a parenthetical element that is very abrupt or that has commas within it.

172

[For a comparison of the dash, the comma, and parentheses, see section 17f.]

RIGHT   But you think that I ——

RIGHT   He opened the book and said —— what did he say?

RIGHT   We shall need —— let's see, what shall we need?

RIGHT   They climbed the hill, played tennis, and went boating —— all before breakfast.

RIGHT   The tools that we need —— a hammer, a saw, and a chisel —— are all here.   [Commas might be used except for the commas within the interrupter.]

RIGHT   We need three tools —— a hammer, a saw, and a chisel.   [A colon may be used instead of the dash.]

RIGHT   A hammer, a saw, and a chisel —— all these we shall need.

RIGHT   Some exercise —— tennis, for example —— would be good for him.

Caution: The dash is used more extensively in an informal style, but even there it becomes ineffective when overused.

PARENTHESES ( )

17f. Parentheses are used to set off parenthetical, supplementary, or explanatory matter.

Parentheses, dashes, commas —— all are used to set off parenthetical matter.   Parentheses set off parts loosely joined to the sentence and tend to obscure the parts thus set off.   Dashes set off sharply abrupt parts and tend to emphasize them.   Commas are the mildest, most commonly used separators and tend to leave the parts more intimately connected with the sentence.   Parentheses and dashes should be used sparingly, only when commas will not serve equally well.   (For the use of the comma to set off parenthetical matter, see section **12d**; for the use of the dash, see section **17e**.)

RIGHT   It is strange (as one reviews all the memories of that good friend and master) to think that there is now a new generation beginning at Haverford that will never know his spell. — CHRISTOPHER MORLEY

RIGHT   Another [reason] is that it has no buttons (it didn't have any buttons after the first week) and is extremely difficult to manage in a head wind. — JAMES THURBER. [After a complete sentence in parentheses the period may be either used or omitted.]

RIGHT   "No, never," I answered. (Neither him nor any other.)   — STEPHEN LEACOCK

When the sentence demands other marks of punctuation with the parenthetical matter, these marks are placed after the second parenthesis. The comma is never used before the first parenthesis.

RIGHT   He was not yet of legal age (if we may believe the records), but he was already a council member.

BRACKETS [ ]

17g. Brackets are used to set off corrections or interpolations made in a quotation by the person using the quotation.

RIGHT   Every man who loved our vanished friend [Professor Gummere] must know with what realization of shamed incapacity one lays down the tributary pen.   — CHRISTOPHER MORLEY

RIGHT   At the office he found a note from the janitor:
         "Last night i [*sic*] found the door unlocked." [A
         bracketed *sic* (meaning *thus*) tells the reader that
         the error appears in the original — is not merely
         a misprint.]

EXERCISE.   Supply dashes, parentheses, or brackets
where needed.
1. It is strange when one thinks back how events have
   transformed our thinking.
2. The war *la guerre* is to blame for all our troubles.
3. You would never think that I
4. He had three tools an augur, a hammer, and a chisel.
5. How many are there let's see, how many are there who
   can go?
6. There are many myself included who do not like war.
7. Games golf, tennis, and baseball especially were his
   delight.
8. I started to say but what did I want to say?
9. Badminton a less strenuous game than tennis, for example would be good for the boy.
10. "Come on, all of you and" but no one heard him shout.
11. She gave her son good advice to work hard, to save
    money, and to pay his debts promptly.
12. Charles promised that but what is the use of recalling
    his promises?
13. The old man said that he was born in Georgia actually
    in Mississippi before the Civil War.
14. His oldest friends James and Henry, for example still
    have confidence in him.
15. The events of the past year had left him no choice he
    was forced to remain on the little farm.

18 sp

SPELLING

18. Spell every word according to established usage as shown by a good dictionary.[1]

When a misspelled word is pointed out, do not guess at the correct spelling or ask a friend. The dictionary is the authority.

SPELLING BY OBSERVATION

18a. Give special attention to your individual difficulties with spelling, listing for further study each misspelled word as it is pointed out.

(1) Write down in a list the correct form of each word that you misspell and master the correct spelling by means of the ear, the eye, and the hand.

THE EAR   Look up the pronunciation in a good dictionary and pronounce the word several times accurately and distinctly. Have you misspelled the word because of mispronunciation? If so, you can learn both correct pronunciation and correct spelling at the same time. But many English words are not spelled and pronounced in the same way. Careful sounding of the word with the correct spelling in mind will prove helpful.

[1] Complete mastery of section **18** will eliminate the second most common error in the average student theme.

THE EYE Look carefully at the word as it appears in the dictionary and again as you write it *correctly* in your list. Visualize the correct form of the word.

THE HAND After you are sure of the pronunciation of the word and of the correct form as it appears on the printed or written page, write the word correctly several times. This manual exercise is unusually helpful for some persons.

Any person who records the words he misspells and who studies them intelligently and persistently will steadily improve his spelling.

(2) Do not allow careless, inaccurate pronunciation to cause misspelling.

SPELLING LISTS: 69 WORDS

Wrong (*Careless omission*)	*Right*	*Wrong* (*Careless omission*)	*Right*
accidently	accident*a*lly	lible	li*a*ble
artic	ar*c*tic	libary	lib*r*ary
boundry	bound*a*ry	literture	liter*a*ture
canidate	can*d*idate	occasionly	occasion*a*lly
considable	consid*e*rable	probly	prob*a*bly
curosity	cur*i*osity	relly	re*a*lly
everbody	ever*y*body	reconize	recog*n*ize
Febuary	Feb*r*uary	representive	represen*tative*
genrally	gen*e*rally	sophmore	soph*o*more
goin'	goin*g*	stricly	stric*t*ly
goverment	gover*n*ment	suprise	su*r*prise
histry	hist*o*ry	temperment	temper*a*ment
labratory	lab*o*ratory	usally	us*u*ally
lenth	len*g*th		

Wrong (*Careless* *addition*)	*Right*	*Wrong* (*Careless* *addition*)	*Right*
atheletics	athletics	mischievious	mischievous
disasterous	disastrous	momentious	momentous
elem	elm	rememberance	remembrance
enterance	entrance	similiar	similar
grievious	grievous	sufferage	suffrage
hinderance	hindrance	umberella	umbrella
lightening	lightning		

Wrong (*Careless* *transposi-* *tion*)	*Right*	*Wrong* (*Careless* *transposi-* *tion*)	*Right*
Britian	Britain	preform	perform
calvary	cavalry	prespiration	perspiration
childern	children	perfer	prefer
gaurd	guard	perscription	prescription
hunderd	hundred	perserve	preserve
irrevelant	irrelevant	tradegy	tragedy
marraige	marriage		

Wrong (*Careless* *change*)	*Right*	*Wrong* (*Careless* *change*)	*Right*
accerate	accurate	formally	formerly
advisor	adviser	humerous	humorous
begger	beggar	interduce	introduce
docter	doctor	optermistic	optimistic
conquerer	conqueror	particalar	particular
discription	description	predudice	prejudice
dispair	despair	privalege	privilege
devide	divide	seperate	separate

EXERCISE. Pronounce each word in the preceding lists, noting and correcting any tendency you may have to make improper omissions, additions, transpositions, or changes.

(3) Distinguish between words of similar sound or spelling, and use the spelling demanded by the meaning.

SPELLING LISTS: 179 WORDS

accent, ascent, assent
accept, except
advice, advise
affect, effect
all ready, already
all together, altogether
allowed, aloud
allusion, illusion
ask, asked
aught, ought
baring, barring, bearing
berth, birth
born, borne
breath, breathe
buy, by
canvas, canvass
capital, capitol
choose, chose
cite, sight, site
close, clothes, cloths
coarse, course
complement, compliment
conscience, conscious
corps, corpse
council, counsel, consul
dairy, diary

decent, descend, descent
desert, dessert
device, devise
dining, dinning
dual, duel
dyeing, dying
fair, fare
formally, formerly
forth, forty, fourth
hear, here
heard, herd
hole, whole
holy, wholly
instance, instants
irrelevant, irreverent
its, it's
knew, new
know, no
later, latter
lead, led
lessen, lesson
loath, loathe
loose, lose
luxuriant, luxurious
mind, mine
of, off

passed, past
peace, piece
plain, plane
precede, proceed
presence, presents
principal, principle
prophecy, prophesy
quiet, quite
respectfully, respectively
reverend, reverent
right, rite, wright, write
sense, since
shone, shown
staid, stayed
stationary, stationery
statue, stature

steal, steel
straight, strait
than, then
their, there, they're
therefor, therefore
threw, through
till, until
to, too, two
track, tract
troop, troupe
waist, waste
weak, week
weather, whether
which, witch
whose, who's
your, you're

EXERCISE A. Use the following words correctly in sentences.

accept
assent
except
fare
formally

instants
irrelevant
its
quite
too

B. Keep a list of all words you misspell during the first month, master the spelling, and ask your instructor at conference period to test you.

SPELLING BY RULES

18b. Apply the more important rules for spelling.

Some students will find helpful the detailed rules for spelling given by such dictionaries as *Webster's New*

International Dictionary, Second Edition, pp. lxxviii–lxxx, or *Webster's Collegiate Dictionary,* Fifth Edition, pp. xx–xxi. Most students will do well to master at least the more important rules for spelling listed below. There are, unfortunately, many exceptions.

(1) **Drop the final e before a suffix beginning with a vowel but not before a suffix beginning with a consonant.**

SPELLING LISTS: 54 WORDS

Drop the final *e* before a suffix beginning with a vowel.

allure	+ –ing	= alluring
bride	+ –al	= bridal
combine	+ –ation	= combination
fame	+ –ous	= famous
move	+ –able	= movable
plume	+ –age	= plumage
prime	+ –ary	= primary
precede	+ –ence	= precedence

Retain the final *e* before a suffix beginning with a consonant.

care	+ –ful	= careful
care	+ –less	= careless
entire	+ –ly	= entirely
place	+ –ment	= placement
rude	+ –ness	= rudeness
stale	+ –mate	= stalemate
state	+ –craft	= statecraft
sure	+ –ty	= surety

Some Exceptions: due, duly; awe, awful; hoe, hoeing; singe, singeing. After *c* or *g* the final *e* is retained before suffixes beginning with *a* or *o*: notice, noticeable; courage, courageous.

181

EXERCISE. Add the suffixes as indicated.

confine + –ing =
confine + –ment =
arrange + –ing =
arrange + –ment =
love + –ing =
love + –ly =
love + –able =
like + –ness =
like + –ing =
like + –ly =

(2) Double a final single consonant before a suffix beginning with a vowel.

Double a final single consonant before a suffix beginning with a vowel (1) if the consonant ends a word of one syllable or an accented syllable and (2) if the consonant is preceded by a single vowel.

SPELLING LISTS: 45 WORDS

Monosyllables		Dissyllables	
		(Accented on last syllable)	
flag	flagging	abet	abetting
fret	fretting	abhor	abhorring
mop	mopping	admit	admitted
slap	slapping	concur	concurred
spin	spinning	confer	conferred
throb	throbbed	expel	expelled
trot	trotted	regret	regrettable
wet	wettest		

EXERCISE. Write the present participle and the past tense of each of the following verbs: throb (throbbing, throbbed), spin, fix, unravel, drive, stay, occur, place, conceal, let, stop, admit, transpose, confer.

sp 18

(3) Avoid confusion of *ei* and *ie*.

SPELLING LISTS: 41 WORDS

When the sound is *e*, write *ie* (except after *c*).

Right	*Right* (after *c*)
relieve	conceit
priest	ceiling
relief	deceive
chieftain	perceive
grievous	receipt
field	deceit

When the sound is other than *e*, usually write *ei*.

eight	weight	neigh
rein	their	skein
veil	sleigh	neighbor
heir	vein	reign

Exceptions: Either, neither, financier, leisure, seize, species, weird.

EXERCISE.   Complete the spelling of the following words.

cash—r	conc—ve	w—r	bes—ge	shr—k
bel—f	p—rce	fr—ght	w—gh	repr—ve

(4) Except before a suffix beginning with *i*, final *y* is usually changed to *i*.

SPELLING LISTS: 21 WORDS

defy	+ —ance	=	defiance
happy	+ —ness	=	happiness
mercy	+ —ful	=	merciful
modify	+ —er	=	modifier
modify	+ —ing	=	modifying [Not changed before *i*.]

183

EXERCISE.   Add the suffixes as indicated.

$$
\begin{array}{lll}
\text{crafty} & + -ly & = \\
\text{crafty} & + -ness & = \\
\text{hearty} & + -ness & = \\
\text{beauty} & + -ful & = \\
\text{bounty} & + -ful & = \\
\text{fancy} & + -ful & = \\
\text{fancy} & + -ing & = \\
\text{study} & + -ing & = \\
\end{array}
$$

Exception: Verbs ending in *y* preceded by a vowel do not change the *y* to form the third person singular of the present tense or the past participle: *array, arrays, arrayed.*

(5) Form the plural by adding *s, es,* or *'s.*

SPELLING LISTS: 52 WORDS

Form the plural regularly by adding *s.*

boy, boys	gown, gowns
cap, caps	river, rivers
food, foods	tree, trees

Usually add *es* if the plural forms an extra syllable.

bush, bushes	pass, passes
house, houses	torch, torches
match, matches	watch, watches

If the noun ends in *y* preceded by a consonant, change the *y* to *i* and add *es.*

puppy, puppies   sky, skies   supply, supplies
chimney, chimneys [After a vowel the *y* is not changed to *i*.]

Add *'s* to form the plural of letters, signs, or figures.

RIGHT   His *f's* were like *b's*, and his *8's* were like *3's.*

Consult a dictionary for plurals formed irregularly.

184

EXERCISE. Supply plural forms for words listed below. If necessary, consult the dictionary.

cup	key	ox	valley	room
fence	army	sheep	knife	leaf
box	cameo	foot	radius	goose
child	tomato	son-in-law	passer-by	mouse

HYPHENATED WORDS

18c. Hyphenate words chiefly to express a unit idea or to avoid ambiguity.

Some compounds are written as separate words (*house party*), others are hyphenated (*house-raising*), and still others are written solid (*housework*).

The hyphenated words may be either a new coinage made by the writer to fit the occasion or words still in the process of becoming one word. In the latter case a recent dictionary will assist in determining current usage. Many words now written as one were originally separate words and later hyphenated in the transitional stage. For example, *post man* first became *post-man* and then *postman*. More recently *basket ball* has passed through the transitional *basket-ball* to *basketball*. The use of the hyphen in compounding is in such a state of flux that authorities often disagree. Some of the more generally accepted uses are listed below.

(1) Use the hyphen to join two or more words serving as a single adjective before a noun.

[The dictionary ordinarily cannot help with this use of the hyphen. The writer joins recognized words to coin a new unit idea to fit the occasion.]

RIGHT A well-paved road, a know-it-all expression.

But the hyphen is usually omitted when the first word of the compound is an adverb ending in *ly* or when the words follow the noun.

RIGHT A slightly elevated walk, a gently sloping terrace.
RIGHT The road was well paved.
RIGHT His expression suggested that he knew it all.
RIGHT The man made wooden shoes.
RIGHT The dress was a bluish green.

(2) Use the hyphen with compound numbers from twenty-one to ninety-nine.

RIGHT twenty-two, forty-five, ninety-eight, one hundred twenty.

(3) Use the hyphen to avoid ambiguity or an awkward union of letters or syllables.

RIGHT His re-creation of the setting was perfect.
RIGHT Fishing is good recreation.
RIGHT He re-covered the leaky roof.
RIGHT He recovered his health.
RIGHT Micro-organism, re-enter, semi-independent, shell-like, thrill-less, sub-subcommittee.

(4) Use the hyphen with the prefixes *ex-*, *self-*, *all-*, and the adjective *-elect*.

RIGHT ex-governor, self-made, all-American, mayor-elect.

SPELLING LIST

18d. Many students will find it helpful to master the following list of common words often misspelled. (Of greater importance, however, is the student's mastery of his own list of misspelled words. See 18a.)

COMMON WORDS OFTEN MISSPELLED

SPELLING LIST: 442 WORDS

absence
accidentally
accommodate
accomplish
accustomed
achievement
acquired
across
address
advise
affect
affectionately
again
against
all right
almost
already
altar
although
altogether
always
among
ancestry
angel
announcement
annual
answer
apiece
apologize
apology
apparent
approach
appropriate
arctic
arguing
argument

around
arouse
arrangement
arrive
article
artistically
ascent
asked
asks
athletics
attached
available

bear
beautiful
before
beginning
believe
benefit
benefited
biggest
break
brilliant
bruised
busily
business

captain
carrying
casual
cemetery
census
certain
changeable
channel
choice
chosen

coarse
college
column
comedy
coming
committed
committee
compliment
conceive
concerted
concrete
condescend
conducive
conscious
consistent
conspicuous
contends
continuously
controlled
controlling
corner
counsel
course
courteous
cries
criticism
criticize
crowd
cruising
curiosity

dealt
deceived
decide
decision
definite

definitely
definition
delicate
denies
dependent
descendant
desirable
despair
destroy
detached
develop
development
different
dining
disagree
disappear
disappointed
disapprove
disastrous
discussion
dissatisfaction
distinction
disturb
divide
divine
doesn't
dormitory
double
drunkenness
duly
dying

easily
economic
effect
efficient
eligible
elm
embarrass
enemy

entirely
equipped
etc.
every
evidently
excellent
except
excusable
existence
experience
extremely

familiar
fascinate
February
finally
financial
foresee
foretell
forgotten
formally
formerly
forty
forward
fourteen
friend
front
furnace
further

gayety
generally
goddess
government
governor
grammar
grateful
great
group
guard

happily
heard
heartily
heroes
hers
hoping
humiliated
humorous
hurries

image
imagination
imagine
immediately
immensely
importance
incidentally
instead
insurance
interest
interfere
its

judgment

kindergarten
knew
knocked
know
knowledge

laid
led
lenient
level
library
listen
loneliness
lose
loveliness
luckily

luscious
lying

many
marriage
maybe
meanness
meant
medicine
minute
misspell
morale

narrative
naturally
necessary
Negro
new
nickel
nineteen
ninety
ninth
noticeable
nowhere

occasion
occasionally
occurred
occurrence
occurring
off
official
often
omit
omitted
omitting
once
opinion
ordinarily
originally
ours

paid
parallel
particle
particularly
pastime
peaceable
peculiar
penetrate
perhaps
permanent
pertain
petition
phase
piece
pitiful
pleasant
poison
poisonous
populace
porch
portray
possibly
practical
practically
precede
preparation
prepare
pretty
prevail
prevalent
previous
primitive
principal
principle
prisoner
privilege
probably
problem
procedure

proceed
processes
professor
prophecy
prophesy
propitious
prove
purpose
pursue
pursuing
pursuit

quantity
quarter
quiet
quite

realize
really
receipt
receive
recipe
recognize
recollect
recommend
relief
relieve
religious
reminisce
repetition
replies
review
rhythm
road
rolled
rolling
rough

safety
sarcasm

Saturday
scene
schedule
secede
secretary
sense
sentence
separate
separation
shepherd
shining
shoulder
shovel
shows
shrubbery
significant
similar
simile
since
sincerely
smooth
solely
solemn
speak
spectacle
speech
sponsors
stationary
stationery
stayed
stopped
stopping
straight
strenuous
stretch
studies
studying

succeed
sufficient
suicide
supplies
sure
surely
surprise
suspicious
syllable

tales
tear
than
their
theirs
then
there
thorough
though
thought
threw
through
thrown
till
tired
together
too
toward
tragedy
trail
translate
trial
tries
trouble
truly
tunnel
turns

tying
typical

uncertainty
unconscious
undoubtedly
unmanageable
until
used
using
usual
usually

valuable
vegetable
vengeance
villain
violent

warring
weak
wear
weather
Wednesday
week
weird
welfare
whether
which
wholly
whose
without
woman
women
writing
written

you're
yours

DICTION

GOOD USE — GLOSSARY

Vocabulary and success go hand in hand. Investigation has shown that the man with a large number of words at his command is the one who comes to lead and direct his fellows. Through his knowledge of words, through his ability to make them express the exact shade of his meaning, he gives to his ideas real power.

A knowledge of words is the writer's greatest need. He may increase his knowledge by reading, by careful attention to the speech of others who know more words than he, and by the intelligent use — in connection with his reading and writing — of a good dictionary.

19. Select words that are in general and approved use and that are in keeping with the occasion. [1]

In case of doubt, determine the standing of a word by reference to a good dictionary of recent date.

19a. Use only a good dictionary and consult it intelligently for the meaning and standing of words.

Unless a dictionary is edited with great care, it is not to be trusted. It is reliable only to the extent that it is

[1] Complete mastery of section 19 will eliminate the tenth most common error in the average student theme.

based on a scientific examination of usage. Among the better unabridged dictionaries are:

Webster's New International Dictionary of the English Language, G. & C. Merriam Company, Springfield, Massachusetts, 1934. [This is a new edition, the first thorough revision since the edition of 1909. All issues dated between 1909 and 1934 are practically reissues of the 1909 edition.]

New Standard Dictionary of the English Language, Funk & Wagnalls, New York and London, 1913.

New Century Dictionary of the English Language, 3 vols., P. G. Collier and Sons, New York, 1927.

The Oxford English Dictionary (also called *A New English Dictionary* or *Murray's Dictionary*), 10 vols. and Supplement, Clarendon Press, Oxford, 1888–1933. [This monumental work, on which thousands of scholars have collaborated, furnishes the most detailed study of individual words.]

Dictionary of American English on Historical Principles. [In progress.]

Most students must consult these large dictionaries in the library. But even if the student is fortunate enough to possess one of these, he will still find indispensable, for more convenient use, one of the smaller dictionaries on the college or adult level. He should own one of the following:

Webster's Collegiate Dictionary, Fifth Edition, G. & C. Merriam Company, Springfield, Massachusetts, 1936. [This is the first edition based on the 1934 unabridged edition.]

Winston Simplified Dictionary, Advanced Edition, John C. Winston Company, Chicago, 1926.

College Standard Dictionary, Funk & Wagnalls, New York and London, 1922.

To use the dictionary intelligently the student must refer to the introductory matter whenever necessary for

an interpretation of abbreviations and must note the
various aids for establishing the meaning of a word:
(1) the origin, (2) the meaning (or meanings, if there
are several), (3) the special branding (if any) of the
word, or of one of its meanings, as *colloquial*, *dialectal*,
technical, etc., (4) synonyms, (5) antonyms, and (6)
special paragraphs treating synonyms in more detail.
Let us take, for example:

> **ex·pel'** (ĕks·pĕl'; ĭks-), *v. t.*; EX·PELLED' (-pĕld'); EX·PEL'-
> LING. [L. *expellere, expulsum*, fr. *ex* out + *pellere* to
> drive.] **1.** To drive or force out; to eject. **2.** To cut off
> from membership in or the privileges of an institution or so-
> ciety; as, to *expel* a student from college. — **Syn.** Exile,
> oust, dispossess. See BANISH. — **Ant.** Admit, inject; wel-
> come. — **ex·pel'la·ble**, *adj.*

> By permission; from Webster's Collegiate Dictionary
> Fifth Edition
> Copyright, 1936, by G. & C. Merriam Co.

(1) The origin — also called derivation or etymology
— of the word *expel* is shown in square brackets. The
original Latin, meaning *to drive out*, supplies the fundamental definition of the English word. In many instances the origins give special insight into meanings.
Automobile, for example, originally signified *self-moving;*
to sympathize was *to suffer with; to telegraph* was *to write
far off.* Any student who wishes to get at the heart of a
word cannot afford to overlook its origin.

(2) The two separate meanings of *expel* are shown
under **1** and **2**. In the Webster's dictionaries such
meanings are arranged in the historical order of development, thus enabling the student at a glance to see
something of the history of the word. He should note,
however, that the meaning which developed first, and
is consequently placed first, is frequently no longer the
most common.

(3) Since neither of the two definitions of *expel* has

a special branding — such as *colloquial, dialectal, slang,* or *obsolete* — both are in general and approved use.

(4) The synonyms (**Syn.**) *exile, oust, dispossess* furnish words with meanings similar to that of *expel* and thus help in the interpretation of the word. Furthermore, synonyms often supply the writer with a word expressing more nearly the exact shade of meaning he wishes to convey. They are useful also in the avoidance of awkward repetition.

(5) The antonyms (**Ant.**) *admit, inject, welcome* help define *expel* by giving words of opposite meaning.

(6) Particularly helpful in showing the exact meaning of *expel* is the special paragraph in the dictionary to which reference is made under BANISH. On turning to the word *banish* the student will read that the common element in the synonyms *banish, exile,* and *expel* is enforced removal. *Exile* is different from *banishment* in that it means removal from the home country and stresses enforced absence rather than removal under force. *Banishment* suggests a legal sentence, whereas *exile* suggests the compulsion of circumstances as well. *Expel* means banish summarily, usually in an atmosphere of disgrace. Thus, the student will find himself well repaid for following such references to the end.

EXERCISES IN THE USE OF THE DICTIONARY

A. THE FULL MEANING OF THE WORD

EXERCISE 1. Learn the fundamental meaning of each of the following words by studying its origin.

carnival	mob	curfew	incisive
hippopotamus	graphophone	candidate	neighbor
boycott	bedlam	telegraph	incense

g 19

EXERCISE 2. What was the first meaning developed in the English language for the following words? What meanings developed later?

bully	dunce	craft	property
outlaw	convince	inform	ramble
fiction	mortal	prevent	credit

EXERCISE 3. Which of the following words are limited in use by some branding such as *colloquial*, *dialectal*, *slang*, or *obsolete*? (Note that some meanings of a word may be in good general use while others are branded.)

swell	locate	plug	hot
fix	deal	fetch	bust
calculate	tight	craze	fang

EXERCISE 4. List synonyms for each of the following words.

say	fight	reputation	liberty
go	eat	confinement	affection
think	justice	precise	favor

EXERCISE 5. List antonyms for each of the following words.

concentrate	betray	destroy	cheerful
delay	weaken	militant	revengeful
confine	repel	fast	fault

EXERCISE 6. Study the special paragraphs in the dictionary on the following words. Write sentences to illustrate the exact meaning of each word.

apology, excuse error, mistake
haste, speed discover, invent
grant, concede lawful, legitimate
cause, occasion observation, observance
parcel, package ambition, aspiration

B. OTHER USES OF THE DICTIONARY

EXERCISE 7. Determine the preferred spelling of the following words: *colour, gypsy, inclose, traveler, judgment.* Which of the following words should be written separately, which should be written solid, and which should be hyphenated? *Ablebodied, basketball, presentday, maintopmast, today.*

EXERCISE 8. Determine the pronunciation for each of the following words. Which of the words change the accent to indicate a change in meaning?

impious	contest	italics	vehement	object
precedence	absent	exquisite	condolence	senile

EXERCISE 9. Classify each of the following words as a verb (transitive or intransitive), a noun, an adjective, an adverb, a preposition, or a conjunction. Give the principal parts of each verb, the plural (or plurals) of each noun, the comparative and superlative of each adjective or adverb.

sing	into	since	bite	drag
stratum	bad	tomato	sheep	often

EXERCISE 10. From the following list of words capitalize those which are always capitalized and check those which are capitalized only for certain meanings.

epicurean	platonic	stoical	italic
pastor	symbolic	angelic	juvenalian
spanish	jewish	roman	liberian
lynch	romanesque	italian	easter

EXERCISE 11. Divide each of the following words into syllables.

liberty	distinguish	indistinguishable	interfere
libidinous	vindictive	laboriously	supplement
vocabulary	dangerous	industrious	analytic

EXERCISE 12. Get from your dictionary specific information about each of the following. Note the source of information as (a) general vocabulary, (b) list of abbreviations, (c) gazetteer, (d) biographical dictionary, or (e) list of foreign words.

Frederick William *religio laici*
Zion National Park Semele
S. P. C. A. Thomas Campion
Moravia Zeus
persona non grata Hants

19b. Use freely (and on any occasion) words not branded by the dictionary in some special way, such as *archaic, obsolete, colloquial, dialectal, slang,* or *illiterate.*

As a rule use the simplest word that will express your exact meaning. Words that do not come within the reading vocabulary of the average cultivated person should be avoided as much as possible.

irk (ûrk), *v. t.* [ME. *irken.*] To weary or trouble; to annoy; bore; vex.

By permission; from Webster's Collegiate Dictionary
Fifth Edition
Copyright, 1936, by G. & C. Merriam Co.

pros'pect (prŏs'pĕkt), *n.* [L. *prospectus,* fr. *prospicere, -spectum,* to look forward, fr. *pro-* + *specere* to look, see.] **1.** An extensive view, esp. of landscape. **2.** Relative aspect; outlook; exposure. **3.** An extended region which the eye overlooks at one time; scene. **4. a** Act of looking forward; anticipation. **b** That which is hoped for; expectation; probable result. **5.** A prospective customer, contestant, candidate, applicant, etc. **6.** *Mining.* **a** An unproved mineral occurrence; also, the property on which the mineral is found. **b** A partly developed mine. **c** The gold or other mineral secured in testing a sample of ore or gravel.

By permission; from Webster's Collegiate Dictionary
Fifth Edition
Copyright, 1936, by G. & C. Merriam Co.

The verb *irk*, not branded in any way, may be used freely on any occasion. The noun *prospect* may be used freely with any of the first meanings. But the sixth meaning (or group of meanings), branded as belonging to the special field of *mining*, would be misunderstood by the general reader and should accordingly be avoided in ordinary writing.

19c. Use carefully (and only when occasion permits) words branded by the dictionary as *colloquial, dialectal, slang,* or *technical.*

(1) **Colloquial words or expressions** are correctly used in conversation and in familiar letters. For these purposes colloquialisms often give a desirable tone of informality. But colloquial expressions generally bring to more formal writing a discordant note and are consequently to be avoided in such writing.

> **fix** (fĭks), *v. t.;* FIXED (fĭkst) or FIXT; FIX′ING. [From *fix*, adj., fr. OF. *fixe*, or fr. ML. *fixare*, both fr. L. *fixus*, past part. of *figere* to fix.] **1.** To make firm, stable, or fast. **2.** To hold or direct steadily. **3.** To set or place definitely; establish; settle. **4.** To place or settle (authorship, blame, etc.) *on* or *upon.* **5.** To set or place in order; adjust. **6.** To render permanent; to give an unvarying form to. **7.** *Colloq.* **a** To put to rights; arrange. **b** To repair. **c** To get into a desired position, condition, or the like, by bribing or injuring, etc. (a person), by tampering with (a race horse), or the like. **8.** *Chem.* To render nonvolatile or solid; to cause to form a nonvolatile or solid compound; as, to *fix* ammonia. **9.** *Micros.* To kill, harden, and preserve, as organisms or fresh tissues, as for microscopic study. **10.** *Photog.* To render permanent by removing the unaffected light-sensitive material from a negative or positive. — *v. i.* To become fixed or stable.
> **Syn.** Stabilize, set, confirm. — **Fix, establish.** To **fix** is to give permanence to something, esp. as it already exists; **establish** often implies as well the origination, institution, or demonstration of that which is **fixed** (esp. firmly). — **Ant.** Dislodge; change, alter, unsettle.

By permission; from Webster's Collegiate Dictionary
Fifth Edition
Copyright, 1936, by G. & C. Merriam Co.

COLLOQUIAL   He *fixed* the broken chair.
FORMAL   He *repaired* the broken chair.

COLLOQUIAL	He *fixed* the jury.
FORMAL	He *bribed* the jury.
FORMAL	He *fixed* the picture to the wall. [One of the uses not branded *colloquial*.]

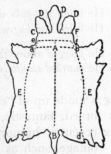

hide, *n.* [AS. *hȳd*.] **1.** The skin of an animal, either raw or dressed. **2.** *Chiefly Humorous.* The human skin. — **Syn.** See SKIN. — *v. t.* **1.** To take the hide from. **2.** *Colloq.* To flog severely.

hide (hīd), *v. t.;* HID (hĭd); HID'DEN (hĭd'n) or HID; HID'ING (hīd'ĭng). [AS. *hȳdan*.] **1.** To conceal; withdraw from sight; put out of view; secrete. **2.** To withhold from knowledge; keep secret. **3.** To obstruct or bar the view of. **4.** To shelter. **5.** To turn away, as the eyes or face, in displeasure, shame, etc. — *v. i.* To lie concealed; keep oneself out of view. — **hid'er** (hīd'ẽr), *n.*

Syn. Cover, mask, veil, cloak, shroud, bury, screen, disguise; dissemble, suppress. — **Hide, conceal, secrete.** Hide (the general term) and **conceal** are often interchangeable. But **conceal** often emphasizes more strongly the element of intention or the effectiveness of the result, and is oftener used of a refusal to divulge; as, the bonnet *hid* her face; the papers were *concealed* in a secret drawer. To **secrete** is to deposit in close hiding. — **Ant.** Expose, show, display, reveal.

Hide, 1. *a b d c* Butt; *A B c a,* *A B d b* Bends; *a b F C* Shoulder; *a b f e* Range; *E, E* Belly Offal; *D, D, D* Cheeks and Faces.

By permission; from Webster's Collegiate Dictionary
Fifth Edition
Copyright, 1936, by G. & C. Merriam Co.

COLLOQUIAL	The teacher gave the boy a good *hiding*.
FORMAL	The teacher gave the boy a severe *flogging*.

(2) **Dialectic words** (also called **provincialisms** or **localisms**) are to be avoided because they are common to only a section of the country. Speakers may safely use dialectic words known to the audience they are addressing; but such words should be carefully eliminated from all writing intended for the general reader.

poke (pōk), *n.* [ME., fr. OF. *poke, poque.*] **1.** *Scot.* A bag; a sack. **2. a** *Scot.* A beggar's wallet. **b** *Archaic & Dial.* A pocket.

By permission; from Webster's Collegiate Dictionary
Fifth Edition
Copyright, 1936, by G. & C. Merriam Co.

prog (prŏg), *v. i.*; PROGGED (prŏgd); PROG′GING. *Dial.* To poke, or search about, esp. in order to steal. — *n. Dial.* Food, esp. that got by begging or filching.

DIALECT   He filled the *poke* with potatoes.
BETTER   He filled the *bag* with potatoes.

DIALECT   He *progged* about the camp.
BETTER   He *searched stealthily* about the camp.

(3) **Slang** is made up of "certain widely current terms having a forced, fantastic, or grotesque meaning, or exhibiting eccentric humor or fancy." Slang may be a special coinage, such as *goofy, hooey, savay, scram,* or *shebang.* But it is more commonly some accepted word given a special meaning, such as *swell* (tiptop), *lousy* (contemptible), *hot* (highly exciting), *to stick* (force to pay), or *to pinch* (arrest). At times slang can hardly be distinguished from a colloquialism, and occasionally it actually passes over into the accepted vocabulary. *Mob, cab, van, sham,* and *banter* are examples. Slang may be apt, vigorous, and refreshing. But it tends to become, from overuse, as trite and distasteful as last year's most popular comic song. Many slangy expressions, moreover, are intelligible only to limited groups.

Slang should be used with great care, always with due regard to its appropriateness and its intelligibility. It is regularly excluded from formal writing unless indicated by quotation marks.

she-bang′ (shĕ-băng′), *n. Slang.* Establishment; contrivance; outfit; concern.

lous'y (louz'ĭ), *adj.*; -i·er (-ĭ·ĕr); -i·est. Infested with or as if with lice. Hence, *Slang*, disgusting or contemptible. — **lous'i·ly**, *adv.* — **lous'i·ness**, *n.*

SLANG   We sold the whole *shebang.*

BETTER   We sold the whole *outfit.*

SLANG   The proposal was *lousy.*

BETTER   The proposal was *contemptible* (or *foolish,* or *unsatisfactory,* or *unpromising,* or *inadequate*).

Slang becomes especially objectionable when it prevents the exact expression of ideas. To some persons everything pleasing is *swell* and everything displeasing is *lousy.*

(4) **Technical words** — expressions peculiar to one profession or group — should usually be avoided in writing intended for the general reader. The ideal is to make the writing readily intelligible to the layman.

ac'ro·car'pous (ăk'rō·kär'pŭs), *adj.* [Gr. *akrokarpos* bearing fruit at the top, fr. *akros* highest + *karpos* fruit.] *Bot.* Bearing fruit at the apex of the main stem.

[This term should be avoided except in writing intended for botanists.]

al'pha (ăl'fà), *n.* [L., fr. Gr.] **1.** The first letter (A, α) of the Greek alphabet. See A. **2.** The first or beginning; formerly, the chief. **3.** *Astron.* The chief or brightest star of a constellation.

[*Alpha* should not be used with its third meaning except in writing intended for astronomers.]

[Even though the dictionary brands *acoustics* as belonging peculiarly to the fields of physics and architecture, the word is well enough known to justify its general use.]

19d. Avoid words omitted by the dictionary or branded by it as *illiterate, vulgar, low, archaic, obsolete, obsolescent,* etc.

(1) **Avoid new (unlisted) words, improprieties, and other illiteracies.** Words not included in the dictionary are in grave danger of being misinterpreted. By the same token, even listed words should not be used in a capacity for which they are not accredited. Such misuse of a word otherwise in good use is known as an impropriety. Vulgarisms, barbarisms, improprieties, and other illiterate expressions should always be avoided.

(2) **Avoid obsolete words.** The dictionary lists words (or meanings of words) no longer used in order that the writers of past centuries may be understood. The modern writer will have no trouble in avoiding words marked *archaic* or *obsolete* (entirely out of use). He should also avoid words marked *obsolescent* (going out of use) unless he wishes on some very special occasion to give an antique flavor to his writing.

pre·vent′ (prē·vĕnt′), *v. t.* ⁀ [L. *praevenire, -ventum,* fr. *prae- + venire* to come.] **1.** *Archaic.* **a** To anticipate, as an occasion by being ready, or a wish by satisfying it. **b** To precede; outrun. **2.** To forestall; frustrate; circumvent. **3.** To keep from happening, existing, etc.; to render impossible esp. by advance provisions; as, rain *prevented* his coming; to *prevent* war. **4.** To hinder (a person); — usually with *from.* — **pre·vent′a·ble, -i·ble,** *adj.* **pre·vent′er,** *n.* — **pre·ven′tion** (-vĕn′shŭn), *n.*

Syn. Prevent, preclude, avert. Prevent is the general term for hindering, checking, or stopping; to *preclude* is to hinder by excluding, or (esp.) to prevent by anticipative action. To *avert* is to prevent or turn aside (esp.) some threatened evil; as, to *avert* war.

[*Whilom* should be avoided entirely; *prevent* should not be used with the first meaning.]

19e. Avoid "fine writing" and the use of words suited only to poetry.

In prose the simpler, plainer words are usually more effective than the unduly ornate ones. Poetic expressions such as *oft, ofttimes, 'twas,* or *'neath* seem unnatural and forced.

UNNATURAL He sat 'neath a tree.
BETTER He sat beneath a tree.

19f. In general avoid abbreviations and contractions.

A few abbreviations are acceptable even in formal writing. See section 11. Others are better omitted in general writing. Contractions such as *can't, don't,* and *isn't* are proper for conversation and for very informal writing. They should be avoided in all formal writing.

19g. Avoid faulty diction such as that treated in the following list.

203

GLOSSARY OF USAGE

(For detailed treatment of any word consult an unabridged dictionary.)

Ability, capacity. *Ability* (used with the preposition *to*) means *power to perform.* "His ability to complete the task was unquestioned." *Capacity* means *power of receiving.* "His capacity for suffering was unlimited."

About. See **At about.**

Above. Used chiefly as a preposition or an adverb. The use of *above* as an adjective (the *above* reference) or as a noun (The *above* refers to . . .) should be restricted to legal or business writing.

Accept. See **Except, accept.**

A.D. Abbreviation for *Anno Domini,* "in the year of our Lord." The abbreviation should be used with due regard to its meaning — always before the date and without the preposition *in* — and only when necessary for clearness.

ABSURD   The second century A.D. [Literally, *The second century in the year of our Lord.*]

RIGHT   The second century after Christ.

REDUNDANT He died in A.D. 30. [Literally, *He died in in the year of our Lord 30.*]

RIGHT   He died A.D. 30.

Ad. Colloquial shortening of *advertisement.* Use the full word.

Affect, effect. Do not confuse. *Affect* (a verb) means *to influence.* "The attack affected the morale of the troops." *Effect* is both a verb and a noun. As a verb it means *to bring to pass.* "The medicine effected a complete cure." As a noun *effect* means *result*. "The effect of the medicine was instantaneous."

After. Redundant with the past participle.

REDUNDANT After having eaten his dinner he left the house.

RIGHT After eating his dinner he left the house.

RIGHT Having eaten his dinner he left the house.

Aggravate. Means *to intensify, to increase.* "Lack of water aggravated the suffering." Colloquially it means *to irritate, exasperate, provoke,* or *annoy.*

COLLOQUIAL He was extremely aggravated by the decision.

BETTER He was extremely annoyed by the decision.

Agree to, agree with. One agrees *to* a plan. "Henry agreed to the delay." One agrees *with* a person. "Henry agreed with the driver as regards the route."

Ain't. An illiterate contraction always to be avoided. In conversation and in very informal writing the following contractions may be used: *I'm not, you (we, they) aren't, he (she, it) isn't.* In formal writing the words should be written out: *I am not,* etc.

All of. *Of* is not used with nouns in formal writing.

COLLOQUIAL All of the trees were bare.

IMPROVED All the trees were bare.

Of is used with pronouns. "All of them have sleds."

All the farther, faster, quicker. Misused for *as far as, as fast as, as quick as.*

WRONG Four miles is all the farther I can walk.

RIGHT Four miles is as far as I can walk.

Allow. Means *to permit.* Do not confuse with *assert, say, think,* or *believe.*

Allude, elude. See **Elude, allude.**

Allude, refer. Do not confuse. *Allude* means *to refer to indirectly.* "When he mentioned dictators, we knew that he was alluding to Hitler and Mussolini." *Refer* means *to mention something specifically.* "I refer you to Mr. Smith, the president."

Allusion, illusion. Do not confuse *allusion*, "an indirect reference," with *illusion*, "an unreal image or false impression."

Almost, most. Do not confuse the adverb *almost* with the adjective *most.*

> WRONG The bus passes most every hour.
> RIGHT The bus passes almost every hour.

Almost quite. A contradiction. *Quite* means *completely.* "The snow is now almost gone," or, "The snow is now quite gone."

Alone, only. *Alone* means *unaccompanied, solitary.* *Only* means *alone in its class.*

Already, all ready. *Already* (one word) means *prior to some specified time, either present, past, or future.* "By noon the theatre was already full." *All ready* (two words) means *completely ready.* "I am all ready to go."

Alright. Not recognized as correct. Use *all right.*

Also. A weak connective. *And* is a better connective. "I bought bread and butter (*not* also butter)."

Altogether, all together. *Altogether* (one word) means *wholly, thoroughly.* "The report is altogether true." *All together* (two words) means *in a group, collectively.* "There were six pups all together."

Alumnus, alumna. *Alumnus*, a male graduate; *alumni*, two or more male graduates. *Alumna*, a female graduate; *alumnae*, two or more female graduates.

Among, between. *Among* implies more than two. "Joseph's brethren divided the spoils among them." *Between* implies only two. "I divided the cake between John and Mary."

And etc. Never place *and* before *etc*. The *and* is redundant since *etc*. is an abbreviation of *et* (and) + *cetera* (other things).

And which. Needless, careless use of *and* to join a subordinate clause to the main statement. See **24d.**

Any place, every place, no place, some place. Vulgar forms used for *anywhere, everywhere, nowhere, somewhere.*

Anyways. Vulgarism for *anyway.*

Anywheres, everywheres. Vulgarisms for *anywhere, everywhere.*

As. (1) Do not use *as* in place of *that* or *whether.*

WRONG I don't feel as I should go.
RIGHT I don't feel that I should go.

(2) As a rule do not use *as* to mean *because.* *For* or *since* is preferable.

VAGUE He worked steadily as the day was cool.
CLEARER He worked steadily, for the day was cool.

(3) In negative statements careful usage prefers *so* . . . *as* to *as* . . . *as*. "I am not so strong as I used to be." "He will go only so far as he is forced to go."

At. Redundant in such sentences as the following.

REDUNDANT Where does he live at? Where are you at now?
RIGHT Where does he live? Where are you now?

At about. Redundant.

> WORDY He arrived at about noon.
> RIGHT He arrived about noon.
> RIGHT He arrived at noon.

Aught. Means *anything*. Do not confuse with *naught* (*0*).

Auto. An abbreviation not yet proper in formal writing.

Awful, awfully. *Awful* means *inspiring with awe*. *Awful* used in the sense of *ugly, shocking, very bad,* and *very great* is slang and should be avoided. Do not confuse the adjective *awful* with the adverb *awfully*.

> IMPROPRIETY AND SLANG He was awful sick.
> BETTER (*but slang*) He was awfully sick.
> RIGHT He was desperately sick.

Back of, in back of. *Back of* (behind) is permissible in informal writing. *In back of* should be avoided.

Badly. Colloquial in the sense of *very much* with verbs signifying *want* or *need*.

> COLLOQUIAL She needs a new coat *badly*.
> IMPROVED She needs a new coat *very much*.

Balance. Not to be used for *rest* or *remainder* (except in reference to a balance at the bank).

> WRONG We enjoyed the balance of the trip.
> RIGHT We enjoyed the remainder of the trip.

Bank on, take stock in. Colloquial expressions for *rely on, trust in*.

Because. Do not use *because* to introduce a noun clause.

> WRONG Because he was sick was no excuse.
> RIGHT The fact that he was sick was no excuse, *or* His sickness was no excuse.

Being as, being that. Use *since* or *because*.

Beside, besides. Do not confuse. *Beside* is a preposition meaning *by the side of.* "Sit beside me." *Besides*, used chiefly as an adverb, means *in addition to.* "We ate apples and other fruit besides."

Between, among. See **Among, between.**

Blame on, blame it on. Faulty idioms. The word *blame* is in itself sufficient to express the meaning.

CRUDE   I blame it on you.
RIGHT   I blame you.
CORRECT IDIOMS I put the blame on you, *or* I blame you for it.

Bunch. Not properly used to refer to a group of people.

CORRECT "A bunch of violets, a bunch of carrots, a bunch of grapes."

Bursted, bust, busted. Incorrect forms for the verb *burst*, which uses the same form for all its principal parts: *burst, burst, burst.*

But, only, hardly, scarcely. These words, negative in implication, should not be used with another negative.

WRONG He didn't have but one hat.
RIGHT He had but one hat; *or*, He had only one hat.

WRONG He wasn't sick only three days.
RIGHT He was sick only three days.

WRONG I don't hardly (scarcely) know.
RIGHT I hardly (scarcely) know.

But what, but that. Avoid the colloquialisms *but what*, *but that*.

COLLOQUIAL There was no doubt but what (but that) Mr. Roosevelt would seek a third term.
IMPROVED There was no doubt that Mr. Roosevelt would seek a third term.

Calculate. Colloquialism for *plan, think,* or *expect.*

Can, may. *Can* means *to be able; may* means *to have permission.*

> RIGHT Mary can (is able to) drive the car.
> RIGHT May I drive the car?

Cannot help but. A faulty idiom because it contains a double negative.

> FAULTY I cannot help but laugh at him.
> RIGHT I cannot help laughing at him.
> RIGHT I cannot but laugh at him.

Can't hardly. A double negative. Use *can hardly.* See **But, only, hardly, scarcely.**

Can't seem to. Illogical. Use *seem unable to.*

> WRONG I can't seem to understand.
> RIGHT I seem unable to understand.

Cause of. Do not say that the *cause of* something was *on account of.* Complete the expression with a noun clause or a predicate noun.

> ILLOGICAL The cause of my inability to work was on account of a bad headache.
> LOGICAL The cause of my inability to work was that I had a bad headache. [Completed by a noun clause.]
> LOGICAL The cause of my inability was a bad headache. [Completed by a predicate noun.]

Caused by. See **Due to, caused by.**

Claim. Means *to demand as a right.* Used colloquially as a synonym for *maintain* or *assert.*

Combine. A colloquialism meaning "a combination of persons or organizations as for commercial or political advantages."

Common, mutual. That thing is *common* in which two or more share equally or alike. That thing is *mutual* which is reciprocally given and received.

Company. A colloquial expression for *guests, visitors, escort.*

Compare to, compare with. "One object is *compared with* another when set side by side with it in order to show their relative value or excellence; *to* another when it is formally represented as like it."

RIGHT He compared the book with the manuscript.
RIGHT He compared the earth to a ball.

Complected. Incorrectly used for *complexioned.*

WRONG He was a light-complected man.
RIGHT He was a light-complexioned man.
RIGHT He was a man of light complexion.

Considerable. Incorrectly used as a noun or adverb. Properly an adjective.

WRONG He lost considerable in the depression.
RIGHT He lost a considerable amount of property during the depression.

WRONG He was considerable touched by the girl's plea.
RIGHT He was considerably touched by the girl's plea.

WRONG Considerable slush made the roads slippery.
RIGHT Much (*or* a good deal of) slush made the roads slippery.

Contact. The use of *contact* as a verb should be avoided in formal writing.

Continual, continuous. Continual means *occurring in steady, rapid, but not unbroken succession.* "The rehearsal was hampered by continual interruptions." *Continuous* means *without cessation.* "The continuous roar of the waterfall was disturbing."

Contractions. Such contractions as *I'm, I'd, we'll, you'll, don't, doesn't, can't,* and *couldn't* should be avoided in formal writing. They may be used in conversation and in such informal writing as familiar letters.

Contrary, contrariness. A colloquial expression for *perverse, stubborn, perverseness, stubbornness.*

> COLLOQUIAL The boy is contrary.
> IMPROVED   The boy is stubborn.

Contrast from. Faulty idiom for *contrast to* or *contrast with.*

Could of. Illiterate corruption of *could have.*

Couple. Implies a linking of two persons or two objects. The use of *couple* to mean the mere number *two* or *a few* is colloquial.

Credible, creditable. *Credible* means *worthy of belief, trustworthy.* "His story was credible." *Creditable* means *deserving of praise.* "His recital was creditable."

Criticize, censure. *To criticize* means *to examine and judge as a critic,* not necessarily to censure. *To censure* means *to find fault with* or *to condemn as wrong.*

Crowd. A colloquialism for *set* or *clique.*

> COLLOQUIAL She is ignored by our crowd.
> IMPROVED   She is ignored by our set.

Cunning. Colloquial for *attractive.*

Cute. Colloquial for *clever, shrewd, attractive, petite.*

Data, strata, phenomena. Plurals of *datum, stratum, phenomenon.*

> RIGHT These data, these strata, these phenomena, this phenomenon.

Date. Colloquial for *appointment, engagement.*

Deal. Colloquial or commercial term for *transaction, bargain.*

Die. Say *die of*, not *die with.* "He died of pneumonia."

Differ from, differ with. Do not confuse. *Differ from* means *to stand apart because of unlikeness.* "The Caucasian race differs from the Mongolian race in color, stature, and customs." *Differ with* means *to disagree.* "On that point I differ with you."

Different than. Faulty idiom. Use *different from.*

Disremember. Colloquial and dialectal. Use *forget.*

Do. Colloquial for *solve* in Do your sums; for *wash* in She will do the laundry.

Done. The past participle of the verb *to do.* *I do, I did, I have done.* *Done* is illiterate for *did* or for the adverb *already.*

ILLITERATE He done well.
RIGHT　　　 He did well.

ILLITERATE He has done sold the dog.
RIGHT　　　 He has already sold the dog; *or,* He has sold the dog.

Don't. A contraction for *do not*, but not for *does not.*

WRONG He don't smoke. [He do not smoke.]
RIGHT He does not smoke. [He doesn't smoke.]

The contraction, if properly made, is correct for conversation and very informal writing.

PROPER CONTRACTIONS I don't, we don't, you don't, they don't. [do not]
　　　　　　　　　　 He doesn't, she doesn't, it doesn't. [does not]

213

Doubt whether, doubt that. Use *doubt whether* when marked doubt exists. "I doubt whether he will come or not." Use *doubt that* when there is no real doubt. "I do not doubt that he will accept the nomination."

Dove. Colloquial for *dived*.

Drownded. Illiterate for *drowned*.

Due to, caused by. Formal English frowns on the use of *due to* or *caused by* except when the phrase refers definitely to a substantive. Careful writers prefer *because of* or *on account of* in adverbial constructions.

WRONG He was tardy due to an accident. [*Due to* modifies the verb.]

RIGHT He was tardy because of (on account of) an accident.

RIGHT His tardiness was due to an accident. [*Due to* modifies tardiness.]

WRONG The crops failed, caused by heavy rains.

RIGHT The crops failed because of (on account of) heavy rains.

RIGHT The failure of the crops was caused by heavy rains.

Each, either. *Each* means *each person; either* means *the one or the other*.

Each other, one another. Used interchangeably. Some writers prefer *each other* when referring to only two, and *one another* when referring to more than two.

Effect, affect. See **Affect, effect.**

Either, neither. Always used with a singular verb, and commonly to refer to one of two persons or things. When the reference is to one of more than two, use *any, anyone, none, no one*.

QUESTIONABLE   Mary, Jane, and Lucy were invited, but neither of them came.

BETTER   Mary, Jane, and Lucy were invited, but none of them came.

Elegant. Means *polished, fastidious, refined.* Do not use for *delicious, good,* as in "This food is elegant."

Elude, allude. *To elude* means *to escape notice of. To allude* means *to refer to indirectly.* The corresponding adjectives are *elusive* and *allusive.*

Emigrate, immigrate. *Emigrate* means *to leave a place of abode for residence in another country. Immigrate* means *to come for permanent residence into a country of which one is not a native.*

Enthuse. Colloquial for *to make enthusiastic, to become enthusiastic.*

COLLOQUIAL   She enthuses over anything.

BETTER   She becomes enthusiastic about anything.

COLLOQUIAL   The game did not enthuse us.

BETTER   The game did not arouse our enthusiasm.

Equally as good. The *as* is redundant. Say *equally good.*

Etc. See **And etc.**

Every. Colloquial in the expressions *every now and then, every so often, every once in a while, every which way.*

COLLOQUIAL   Every so often he opened the door and looked out.

FORMAL   At regular intervals (*or* occasionally) he opened the door and looked out.

Every bit. Colloquial for *entirely, in every way.*

Every place, everywheres. Vulgarisms for *everywhere.*

Exam. Colloquial shortening of *examination*. Use the full word.

Except, accept. Do not confuse. The verb *except* means *to exclude*. *Accept* means *to receive*.

> RIGHT They excepted (*not* accepted) Mary from the invitation.

> RIGHT Mary accepted (*not* excepted) an invitation to dinner.

Expect. Colloquial if used to mean *suppose*.

> COLLOQUIAL I expect the report is true.
> IMPROVED I suppose the report is true.

Extra. Some writers avoid the use of *extra* as an adverb.

> QUESTIONABLE These apples are extra good.
> RIGHT These apples are unusually good.

Falls, woods. Plural nouns, requiring plural verbs. "The falls were at the bend of the river." "The woods were filled with birds."

Farther, further. Some writers prefer *farther* for spatial distance and *further* to indicate degree or quality. "Two miles farther; further development." *Further* is regularly preferred to express the meaning *more*, *in addition*. "Further reports."

Faze. Colloquial for *worry, disconcert, daunt*.

Fellow. Colloquial for *person* or *beau*.

Female. No longer used as a synonym for *woman*.

Fewer, less. *Fewer* refers especially to number. "Fewer than twenty persons attended." *Less* refers especially to value, degree, or amount. "The suit costs less than the overcoat."

Fine. Use sparingly as a vague word of approval. Find an expression to fit the meaning exactly. Avoid *fine* in the sense of *well*.

First-rate. Properly an adjective. Colloquial as an adverb.

> COLLOQUIAL   She cooks first-rate.
> IMPROVED   She cooks very well.
> RIGHT   She is a first-rate cook. [*First-rate* used as an adjective.]

Fix. Colloquial as a verb meaning *to repair, to arrange* and as a noun meaning *predicament, situation*.

> COLLOQUIAL   He fixed the clock. I am in a fix.
> IMPROVED   He repaired the clock. I am in a predicament.

Flunk. Colloquial for *fail*.

Folks. Colloquial for *relatives, persons of one's own family*.

For to. Illiterate.

> WRONG   He went for to buy a house.
> RIGHT   He went to buy a house.

Former. Refers to the first named of two. Not properly used when three or more are named.

Funny. Colloquial for *strange, queer, odd*. Properly *laughable, humorous*.

Gent. A vulgarism. Use *gentleman, man*.

Gentleman, lady. In general prefer *man, woman*. (Use *gentleman, lady* to distinguish persons of refinement and culture from the ill-bred. Use the plural forms in addressing an audience. "Ladies and Gentlemen."

> WRONG   Lady preacher, saleslady, lady clerk, business gentleman, ladies' colleges.
> RIGHT   Woman preacher, saleswoman, woman clerk, businessman, women's colleges.

Get. *Get to go, get a hustle on, get him on the head* (*hit*), *get by with, get away with, get it across, get six months in prison, get behind* (*endorse*), *get next to, get on to,* and *get around* (*evade*) are dialectal, slang, or colloquial expressions.

Getup. Colloquial for *make-up*.

Good. Do not use as an adverb.

> WRONG He reads good. He works good.
> RIGHT He reads well. He works well; *or,* He does good work.

Gotten. Past participle of *get,* the principal parts of which are *get* (present), *got* (past), *got,* or *gotten* (past participle). In England *gotten* is now archaic, but in the United States both *got* and *gotten* are in general use.

Grand. Avoid the vague colloquial use of *grand* to mean *excellent.* Select the exact word to fit the meaning.

> LOOSE We had a grand trip.
> BETTER We had a delightful (pleasant, exciting) trip.

Guess. Colloquial for *think, suppose.*

Gym. Colloquial shortening of *gymnasium.* Use the full word.

Had of. Illiterate for *had.*

> ILLITERATE I wish I had of gone.
> RIGHT I wish I had gone.

Had ought. Illiterate combination.

> WRONG He hadn't ought to have gone.
> RIGHT He ought not to have gone.

> WRONG He ought to go, had he not?
> RIGHT He ought to go, ought he not?

Hardly. See **But, only, hardly, scarcely.**

Have got. Colloquial and redundant.

> COLLOQUIAL I have got ten dollars.
> IMPROVED I have ten dollars.

Healthy. *Healthy* means *having health.* "John is a healthy man." *Healthful* means *giving health.* "Milk is a healthful food."

Heaps. Colloquial for *a great deal.* "They have a great deal (*not* heaps) of food." Also colloquial when used as an adverb. "I like him very much (*not* heaps)."

Help but. See **Cannot help but.**

Hisself. A vulgarism for *himself.*

Homey. Colloquial for *homelike, intimate.*

Horrid. A colloquial and overused word for *offensive.*

How come? A vulgarism for *why.*

If, whether. Some writers prefer *whether* to *if* after such verbs as *say, learn, know, understand, doubt.* "I did not know whether he could come or not."

Ilk. Misused for *family, kind.*

Illusion, allusion. See **Allusion, illusion.**

Immigrate, emigrate. See **Emigrate, immigrate.**

In, into. Do not confuse. *In* indicates *location within.* "He was in the room." *Into* indicates *motion or direction to a point within.* "He came into the room."

In back of. Colloquial for *behind.*

Incredible, incredulous. *Incredible* means *too extraordinary to admit of belief.* *Incredulous* means *inclined not to believe on slight evidence.*

Individual, party, person. *Party* refers to a group, never to a single person, except in legal phraseology. *Individual* refers to a single person, animal, or thing. *Person* is the preferred word for general reference to a human being.

WRONG He is the interested party.
RIGHT He is the interested person.

Inferior, superior. Use *inferior* (*superior*) *to*, not *inferior* (*superior*) *than*.

WRONG These utensils are inferior (superior) than the ones sent last year.
RIGHT These utensils are inferior (superior) to the ones sent last year.

Ingenious, ingenuous. *Ingenious* means *clever, resourceful*. *Ingenuous* means *open, frank, candid*.

Inside, inside of. Colloquial for *within* in reference to time. The *of* is redundant.

COLLOQUIAL He will be here inside of an hour.
IMPROVED He will be here within an hour.

REDUNDANT He locked himself inside of the room.
RIGHT He locked himself inside the room.

Instance, instant. Do not confuse. *Instance* means *an example*. *Instant* means *a moment, an infinitesimal portion of time*.

Invite. Used improperly as a noun.

Its, it's. Do not confuse the possessive *its* and the contraction *it's* (= *it is*).

Just. Colloquial for *simply, quite*.

COLLOQUIAL He was just tired out.
IMPROVED He was quite tired out.

Kind, sort. Singular forms, modified by singular adjectives.

> WRONG I like these kind (*or* sort) of shoes.
> RIGHT I like this kind (*or* sort) of shoes.

Kind of, sort of. Colloquial when used as an adverb to mean *somewhat, rather, after a fashion.*

> COLLOQUIAL I was kind of (sort of) tired.
> IMPROVED I was somewhat tired.

> COLLOQUIAL I kind of (sort of) thought you would go.
> IMPROVED I rather thought you would go.

Kind of a, sort of a. Omit the *a.*

> COLLOQUIAL What kind of a (sort of a) car does he drive?
> IMPROVED What kind of (sort of) car does he drive?

Later, latter. Do not confuse. *Later* is the comparative of *late* and means *more late.* *Latter* refers to the last named of two. If more than two are named, use *last* or *last-mentioned* instead of *latter.*

Lay. See **Lie, lay.**

Learn, teach. *Learn* means *to acquire knowledge; teach* means *to impart knowledge.*

> WRONG She learned him his lesson.
> RIGHT She taught him his lesson.

Leave, let. Do not use *leave* for *let. Leave* means *to depart from; let* means *to permit.*

> WRONG I will not leave you go today.
> RIGHT I will not let you go today.
> RIGHT I will not let you leave today.

Let's. Contraction of *let us.*

> WRONG Let's don't bother him. (Let us do not bother him.)
> RIGHT Let's not bother him. (Let us not bother him.)

Lie, lay. Do not confuse. *Lie*, an intransitive verb, means *to recline*. *Lay*, a transitive verb, means *to cause to lie*.

PRINCIPAL PARTS *I lie* (*down*), *I lay* (*down*), *I have lain* (*down*).

I lay (*a book*), *I laid* (*a book*), *I have laid* (*a book*).

RIGHT I lay a book on the floor and it lies there. [Present.]

RIGHT I laid a book on the floor and it lay there. [Past.]

RIGHT I have laid a book on the floor and it has lain there. [Perfect.]

Like, as, as if. Use *like* as a preposition, not as a conjunction. Use *as* or *as if* as a conjunction.

WRONG It looks like it would rain.
RIGHT It looks as if it would rain.

WRONG Do like I do.
RIGHT Do as I do.

RIGHT He worked like a man.

Likely, liable. Do not confuse. *Likely* states mere probability; *liable* suggests, in addition, the idea of harm or responsibility.

WRONG He is liable to arrive tomorrow.
RIGHT He is likely to arrive tomorrow. [Mere probability.]

WRONG The boy is likely to cut his foot with the ax.
RIGHT The boy is liable to cut his foot with the ax. [Probability + the idea of harm.]

Locate. Colloquial for *settle*.

WRONG He located in Texas.
RIGHT He settled in Texas.

Lose, loose. Do not confuse. *Lose* means *to cease having*. *Loose* (verb) means *to set free*. *Loose* (adjective) means *free, not fastened*.

Lot, lots of. Colloquial for *much, many, a great deal*.

Lovely. Avoid the vague colloquial use of *lovely* to mean *very pleasing*. Select the exact word to fit the meaning.

Mad. Properly *insane*. Colloquial for *angry*.

Math. Colloquial shortening of *mathematics*. Use the full word.

May. See **Can, may.**

May be, maybe. Do not confuse the verb form *may be* with the adverb *maybe*.

May of. Illiterate corruption of *may have*.

Mean. Colloquial for *ill-tempered, indisposed, ashamed*.

Might of. Illiterate corruption of *might have*.

Mighty. Colloquial for *very*.

Most. See **Almost, most.**

Muchly. A vulgarism. Use *much*.

Must of. Illiterate corruption of *must have*.

Mutual. See **Common, mutual.**

Myself, himself, yourself. Properly intensive or reflexive pronouns. Do not use as substitutes for *I* or *me*.

    COLLOQUIAL He gave the dog to John and myself.
    IMPROVED   He gave the dog to John and me.

Neither, either. See **Either, neither.**

Nice. Do not overwork *nice* as a vague word of approval. Find a more exact word.

VAGUE   It was a nice day.
SPECIFIC It was a bright (mild, sunny) day.

No account, no good. Colloquial for *worthless, of no value.*

No place. A vulgarism for *nowhere.*

Nohow. Dialectal for *not at all.*

Nor. See **Or, nor.**

Not anything like, nothing like. Colloquial for *not at all, not in any way, not nearly so.*

Notorious. Means *of bad repute.* Incorrectly used for *famous, noted.*

Nowhere near. Colloquial for *not nearly.*

Nowheres. Dialectal for *nowhere.*

O, Oh. Interjections. *O* is used especially in direct address, is always capitalized, and is never followed by any mark of punctuation. *Oh* is used to express grief, surprise, or a wish and is followed by a comma or an exclamation point.

O.K. An abbreviation used colloquially in business, but not in formal speech or writing.

Off of. *Of* is superfluous.

WRONG He fell off of the platform.
RIGHT   He fell off the platform.

On. Superfluous in such expressions as *later on, plan on, continue on.*

One another, each other. See **Each other, one another.**

Only. Be careful to place *only* so that it modifies the right word. Also see **But, only, hardly, scarcely.**

Or, nor. Correlate *either* with *or*, *neither* with *nor*.

Other times. Use *at other times*.

Ought. See **Had ought.**

Ought to of. Illiterate corruption of *ought to have*.

Out. Superfluous in *win out, lose out, miss out*. Say *win, lose, miss*.

> WRONG You will lose out in the end.
>
> RIGHT You will lose in the end.

Out loud. Colloquial for *aloud, loud, loudly*.

> COLLOQUIAL He cried out loud for help.
>
> IMPROVED He cried loudly for help.

Outside of. *Of* is superfluous. Say *outside*. "The dog was kept outside (*not* outside of) the house." Do not use *outside of* for *except, besides*. "Except (*not* outside of) James, nobody went with him."

Over with. *With* is superfluous. "The rain is over (*not* over with)."

Pair, set. Singular forms, requiring singular verbs.

> WRONG She was given six pair of shoes and two set of china.
>
> RIGHT She was given six pairs of shoes and two sets of china.

Pants. Colloquial for *trousers*.

Per. Used especially in commercial writing. In formal English some authors use *per* only with Latin words, such as *diem, annum, cent*.

> COMMERCIAL His salary was four thousand dollars per year.
>
> FORMAL His salary was four thousand dollars a year.

Per cent. Means *by the hundred*. Better used only after a numeral. "Ten per cent, twenty per cent." In other situations prefer *percentage*. "A large percentage, a small percentage." *Per cent* is not followed by a period except at the end of a sentence.

Phenomena. Plural of *phenomenon*. See **Data, strata, phenomena.**

Phone. Colloquial shortening for *telephone*. Use the full word in writing.

Photo. Colloquial shortening for *photograph*. Use the full word in writing.

Piano. Do not use for *piano lessons*. "She is giving piano lessons (*not* piano)."

Piece. Dialectal for *a short distance*.

Place. See **Any place, every place, no place, some place.**

Plenty. Dialectal or colloquial when used as an adjective or adverb to mean *plentiful, plenty of, amply, quite*.

DIALECTAL We have plenty food (*or* food aplenty).
IMPROVED We have plenty of food.
COLLOQUIAL It is plenty good enough.
IMPROVED It is quite good enough.

Poorly. Colloquial for *in poor health*. "He is in poor health (*not* poorly) this year."

Postal. Colloquial for *postal card*.

Practical, practicable. *Practical* means *useful, sensible*, not simply *theoretical*. *Practicable* means *feasible, capable of being put into practice*.

Prefer. Not to be followed by *than*, but by *to, before, above, rather than*.

WRONG I should prefer that than anything else.
RIGHT I should prefer that to anything else.

Pretty. Dialectal for *moderately large, considerable.*

Principal, principle. Distinguish between *principal*, an adjective or noun meaning *chief* or *chief official*, and the noun *principle* meaning *fundamental truth* or *governing law of conduct.*

Propose, purpose. *Propose* means *to offer for consideration or adoption.* *Purpose* means *to plan, to intend, to resolve.* "His purpose was to propose an amendment."

Proposition. Properly *a thing proposed.* Colloquial with the meaning *a project involving action, venture, difficulty.* "The mine was a paying venture (*not* proposition) from the first."

Put in. Colloquial for *spend.* "I spent (*not* put in) two hours at the work."

Quite. An adverb meaning *entirely, positively.* Used colloquially to mean *to a great extent.*

COLLOQUIAL The lake is quite near.
IMPROVED The lake is rather near.

Quite, quiet. Do not confuse. *Quite* is an adverb meaning *entirely.* *Quiet* is an adjective meaning *calm.*

Quite a few, quite a bit, quite a little, quite a good deal. Colloquial for *a good many, a considerable number, a considerable amount.*

Raise, rear. Formal English prefers *rear* to *raise* in the sense of *bringing up children.* "He reared (*not* raised) the boy from infancy."

Rarely ever. A vulgarism for *rarely, hardly ever.*

Real. Colloquial for *very,* or *really.*

COLLOQUIAL She was real brave.
IMPROVED She was very brave.

Rear. See **Raise, rear.**

Reckon. Dialectal for *think, suppose, guess.*

Refer. See **Allude, refer.**

Refer back. *Back* is superfluous.

Remember of. A vulgarism for *remember.*

Repeat again. *Again* is superfluous.

Respectfully, respectively. Do not confuse. *Respectfully* means *in a courteous manner.* "Yours respectfully." *Respectively* means *each in the order given.* "The soldiers took up their respective positions."

Reverend, Honorable. To be followed by the first name, the initials, or some title of the person referred to.

> WRONG Reverend Smith, The Reverend Smith, Honorable Pope.
>
> RIGHT The Reverend Paul Smith, Reverend Paul Smith, Reverend P. L. Smith, The Honorable James Pope, The Reverend Mr. Smith, The Reverend Dr. Smith.

Right. Dialectal for *very.* "You are very (*not* right) smart."

Right along. Colloquial for *continuously.* "The clock struck continuously (*not* right along)."

Right away, right off. Colloquial for *immediately.* "He will go immediately (*not* right away)."

Right smart, right smart of. Colloquial for *considerable.*

Rile. Colloquial for *annoy.*

Rise, raise. Do not confuse. *Rise* is an intransitive verb. "I rise every morning." "I rose at four o'clock." "I have risen at four o'clock for many months." *Raise* is a transitive verb. "I raise vegetables." "I raised vegetables last year." "I have raised vegetables for many years."

Rumpus. Colloquial for *disturbance*. "The cause of the disturbance (*not* rumpus) was never discovered."

Said. The adjective meaning *before-mentioned* should be used only in legal documents.

Same, said, such. Do not use as pronouns except in legal documents. Prefer *it, this, that, the aforesaid*.

> BAD   When said coat was returned, same was found to be badly torn.
>
> BETTER When this coat was returned, it was found to be badly torn.

Same as. Not to be used for *just as*.

Say. Do not use to mean *give orders*. Do not use *says* for *said*.

> COLLOQUIAL The teacher said to go home.
>
> RIGHT   The teacher told us to go home.
>
> VULGAR   He says to her, "I am tired."
>
> RIGHT   He said to her, "I am tired."

Scarcely. See **But, only, hardly, scarcely.**

Seem. See **Can't seem to.**

Seldom ever, seldom or ever. These terms are vulgarisms for *seldom if ever, seldom or never, hardly ever*.

Shan't. Colloquial for *shall not*.

Shape. Colloquial for *condition, manner*. "He is in a bad condition (*not* shape)."

Should of. Illiterate corruption of *should have*.

229

Show. Colloquial for *play, opera*.

Show up. Colloquial in the sense of *appear, be present, expose*. "I hope that he will appear (*not* show up)." "If you refuse, I will expose you (*not* show you up)."

Sight. Colloquial for *a great deal*. "He left a great deal (*not* a sight) of money." Other colloquialisms are "Not by a long sight," "She looks a sight."

Sit, set. Do not confuse. The transitive verb *set* means *to cause to sit*. The intransitive verb *sit* means *to be seated*.

> PRINCIPAL PARTS *I sit (down), I sat (down), I have sat (down).*
> *I set (the jar), I set (the jar), I have set (the jar).*

> RIGHT I set the jar on the floor and it sits there. [Present.]

> RIGHT I set the jar on the floor and it sat there. [Past.]

> RIGHT I have set the jar on the floor and it has sat there. [Perfect.]

Size up. Colloquial for *form an estimate of*. "I could not form an estimate of him (*not* size him up)."

So. An overworked word. Do not overwork *so* to join co-ordinate clauses. Do not use *so* for *so that* in clauses denoting purpose.

> WRONG He came early so he might see a friend.
> RIGHT He came early so that he might see a friend.

> Do not use *so* to mean *very, exceedingly*.

> WRONG I am so tired.
> RIGHT I am very tired.

Some. Colloquial when used as an intensive or with the meaning *somewhat* or *a little*. "He is making an excellent (*not* some) race." "He feels somewhat (*not* some) better." "He works a little (*not* some) every day."

Some place. See **Any place.**

Somewheres. Vulgarism for *somewhere*.

Sort. See **Kind, sort.**

Sort of. See **Kind of, sort of.**

Sort of a. See **Kind of a, sort of a.**

Species, specie. Do not confuse. *Species* means *kind, class*. *Specie* means *money* (gold and silver). *Species* has the same form for singular and plural. "One species of violets; two species of violets."

Stop. Colloquialism for *stay, visit*.

Such. Note carefully the use of *such* in the dictionary. When *such* is followed by a relative clause, the proper relative is *as*. "I shall give such aid as I think best." When *such* is completed by a result clause, it should be followed by *that*. "There was such a rain that we could not drive." Avoid the weak and vague use of *such*.

> VAGUE We had such a good time.
> BETTER We had a good time.

Suspicion. Incorrectly used as a verb. *Suspect* is the verb.

> WRONG I did not suspicion anything.
> RIGHT I did not suspect anything.

Swell. The adjective is colloquial (stylish, fashionable) or slang (first-rate). "She looks stylish (*not* swell)." "The concert was first-rate (*not* swell)."

Take. Used in many colloquial, provincial, slang, and vulgar expressions. "Take sick" (become sick), "take it in the city" (use the city as an example), "take in a show" (attend a show), "take on" (act violently, pretend).

Take and. Often used unnecessarily.

> WRONG He took and knocked the ball over the base line.
>
> RIGHT He knocked the ball over the base line.

Take stock in. See **Bank on, take stock in.**

Tasty. Dialectal for *attractive*.

Teach. See **Learn, teach.**

Terrible, terribly. Dialectal for *very*.

Than, till, until. Do not misuse for *when*. "He had scarcely entered when (*not* than, till, until) the storm began."

That. Used colloquially as an adverb.

> COLLOQUIAL I can approach only that near.
>
> IMPROVED I can approach only so near.

This here, that here, that there, these here, those here, those there. Vulgarisms. Use *this, that, these, those*.

Those kind, those sort. See **Kind, sort.**

Through. Do not use for *finished*.

> WRONG He is through eating.
>
> RIGHT He has finished eating.

Till. See **Than, till, until.**

Transpire. Means *to exhale, to come to light*. Used by some writers to mean *to happen, to occur*, but this usage is disapproved by many authorities.

QUESTIONABLE It transpired that the two friends met in Scotland.

RIGHT It happened that the two friends met in Scotland.

Try and. Colloquial for *try to*. "Try to (*not* try and) calm yourself."

Ugly. Colloquial for *ill-tempered*. "He was never in an ill-tempered (*not* ugly) mood."

Unique. Means *sole, only of its kind*, and therefore cannot be compared. Misused for *rare, odd, unusual*. "He was a rare (*not* unique) companion."

United States. Always *the United States*, with the article.

Until. See **Than, till, until.**

Up. Often superfluous. "He opened (*not* opened up) the box." "They beat him (*not* beat him up)."

Used to could. A vulgarism for *used to be able*.

Very. Careful writers do not allow *very* to modify a past participle that has not yet established itself as an adjective. They insert some appropriate adverb — such as *much, greatly, deeply* — between *very* and the past participle.

QUESTIONABLE His singing was very appreciated.

RIGHT His singing was very greatly appreciated.

Violin, vocal, voice. Do not use *violin (vocal, voice)* to mean *violin (vocal, voice) instruction*.

COLLOQUIAL He is taking violin.

BETTER He is taking violin lessons.

Wait on. Means *to attend, to serve*. Colloquial for *wait for*. "I waited for (*not* waited on) him to begin."

19 g

Want. Cannot take a clause as its object.

> WRONG I want that he should have a chance.
> RIGHT I want him to have a chance.

Want in, out, down, up, off, through. Dialectal for *want to come* or *get in, out, down, up, off, through*.

Want to. Colloquial for *ought, should, had better*.

> COLLOQUIAL You want to be careful when you go swimming.
> IMPROVED You should be careful when you go swimming.

Way. Colloquial for *condition*. "I left him in a bad condition (*not* way)." The use of *way* for *away* is not permissible.

> WRONG He lives way beyond the river.
> RIGHT He lives away beyond the river.

Way, ways. Dialectal for *distance*. "A long distance (*not* ways)."

What. See **But what, but that.**

Where. Improperly used for *that*.

> IMPROPER I saw in the newspaper where the French had surrendered.
> PROPER I saw in the newspaper that the French had surrendered.

Where at, where to. Illiterate.

> WRONG Where is she at?
> RIGHT Where is she?

> WRONG Where is she going to?
> RIGHT Where is she going?

Which. Use *who* or *that* instead of *which* or *what* to refer to persons.

While. Do not overuse this conjunction. In general do not substitute *while* for *and*, *but*, or *whereas*.

Woods. See **Falls, woods.**

Worst kind, sort, way. Dialectal for *very much.*

Would better. Prefer *had better.*

Would of. Illiterate corruption of *would have.*

You all. A Southern colloquialism for *you* (plural).

You was. A vulgarism for *you were.*

EXERCISE ON USAGE

Correct all errors in usage.

1. I am able to say that I had a swell vacation.
2. I figured I had accomplished enough that day.
3. Most everyone had an excellent time during the week-end.
4. Among the crowd of forty thousand were several big-time sportsmen.
5. She was sort of pretty, though she was old.
6. In the last minutes of the first quarter and again in the third quarter, the "Red Elephants" turned on the steam and went to town.
7. He was a stern man and pretty near ruled the city.
8. She looks kind of like someone I know.
9. All the property was taken to pay the debts, and George was broke and had no job.
10. I have several ambitions which mean a lot to me at the present.
11. I believe that if you dish it out, you should be able to take it.
12. The camp directors were trying to contact me.
13. I read your ad in the paper.

14. There are some people who kick about the R.O.T.C.
15. The Chinese believe in making whoopee at funerals as well as at weddings.
16. I was getting homesick for one real good train ride.
17. Sam and Jimmy had been in a jam during the night.
18. John was kept in bed with coryza.
19. A person breezes along without noticing the length of the verses.
20. She continued to stall about what she had seen.
21. We have no phone at the camp.
22. *Skyward* is a book written by a man completely sold on aviation.
23. The field was filled with grazing kine.
24. The country boy was picked on by the other boys.
25. The minister spake in low accents.
26. It is easy to crash the social world by means of the so-called pull.
27. The lake was a vision of beauty and a delight to behold as the rays of the setting sun made it glow with an ethereal brightness.
28. Any person will find pool a swell means of passing his loafing hours.
29. Perhaps Brown did expect aid, but by some misfortunate chances he did not get it.
30. He is not too dumb to discuss both sides of the question.
31. You will find lockers in the gym.
32. Each candidate tries to win the demotic approval of the people.
33. The prof will give an examination tomorrow.
34. The child evinced a desire to go home.
35. I had a lot of bruises.
36. My idea does not sound so good.
37. I am kind of late today.
38. I feel like my efforts are in vain.
39. I had an invite to the party, but I did not go.

40. The maiden waited eagerly, but her swain did not appear.
41. He calculated that he could leave the job.
42. He filled the bottle with H_2O.
43. War is inevitable, and the only proven remedy for these conflicts is armed resistance.
44. He gave a discussion of the problems of the home and of the affects of the home on a person.
45. Since this experience I have become more enthused to enter this contest.
46. When eve came the birds ceased singing.
47. His innocence had been proven.
48. I wish that you would not aggravate us with all that talking.
49. A lot of excitement is involved in a football game.
50. The Chamber of Commerce claims that its retail trading zone includes over 150,000 persons.
51. He is different than anybody else I know.
52. I don't know as I can go.
53. She don't like her new dress.
54. He could of made the trip if he had thought of it.
55. They had done opened the box before I came.
56. Mrs. Smith enthused over her new house.
57. The farmers raise heaps of vegetables.
58. My father has gone to town for to buy a horse.
59. The little girl swims first-rate.
60. The boy flunked the course in history.

20 e

20. Select the exact word or idiom. Do not be satisfied with vague omnibus words, with trite expressions, or with displeasing combinations of sound.[1]

20a. Find the exact word needed to express the idea.

(1) A general or abstract word should not satisfy the writer when, as is usually the case, a specific or concrete word is needed. Consult a good dictionary for exact shades of meaning.

GENERAL The man *went* along the road.

SPECIFIC The man *rode* (*walked, trudged, slouched, hobbled, sprinted*) along the road.

GENERAL Aviation demands *fine* young men.

SPECIFIC Aviation demands *brave* (*daring, dauntless, plucky; vigorous, energetic, spirited*) young men.

GENERAL The poet *asks* God to direct him.

SPECIFIC The poet *implores* (*supplicates, entreats*) God to direct him.

VAGUE The boy's arguments were *funny*.

BETTER The boy's arguments were *laughable* (*ridiculous, surprising, absurd*).

[1] Complete mastery of section **20** will eliminate the third most common error in the average student theme.

EXERCISE.   Substitute specific or concrete words for general or abstract words.

1. The author's criticism of Blake's work is very good.
2. Many natives proclaim to be charm doctors.
3. The journey was made to obtain information on the aspects of the North American Indians.
4. He wanted to be as fine as his father.
5. It is my prime desire to like all my classes.

(2) Conjunctions and prepositions should be selected carefully to express the exact relation between clauses, phrases, or words.

WRONG There were other candidates, and he was elected.
RIGHT   There were other candidates, but he was elected. [Co-ordination.]
RIGHT   Although there were other candidates, he was elected.   [Subordination.]

WRONG He walked up the steps and in the house.
RIGHT   He walked up the steps and into the house.

WRONG We stayed late so we might evade him.
RIGHT   We stayed late so that we might evade him.

AMBIGUOUS Since I have quit work he has assisted me.
CLEAR   He has assisted me because I have quit work; *or* After I quit work he assisted me.

EXERCISE.   Use the conjunction or the preposition that expresses the idea exactly.

1. The student in college often forgets his exercise, while the student in a boarding school is forced to play games.
2. I do not know as he can go today.
3. He darted in one room and out another.

20 e

4. My statements hold true only to that relatively small group which faces its tasks philosophically.
5. They were interpreting present-day events into thoughts of an older generation.

(3) Words similar in spelling or meaning should not be confused.

WRONG She excepted the invitation.
RIGHT She accepted the invitation.

WRONG Insulin effects the nervous system.
RIGHT Insulin affects the nervous system.

WRONG No one eluded to the misfortune.
RIGHT No one alluded to the misfortune.

WRONG The bell rang continually for five minutes.
RIGHT The bell rang continuously for five minutes.

EXERCISE. Substitute the word that gives the exact meaning.

1. He never reverted to himself as being worthy of praise.
2. This treatment brings about the best responds.
3. James seemed like a man grouping in the dark.
4. The few seconds that lapsed before he came up seemed like hours.
5. There is eminent danger of her losing her position.

20b. Use the exact idiom demanded by English usage.

WRONG Jack is angry at me.
RIGHT Jack is angry with me.

WRONG I cannot help but remember the insult.
RIGHT I cannot help remembering the insult.

WRONG I blame it on you.
RIGHT I blame you for it.

WRONG This vase belongs to be in the drawing room.
RIGHT This vase belongs in the drawing room.

Idioms are homely, vigorous expressions that grow up with a language and are peculiar to it. They are the very heart of the language. Used freely and correctly, they give freshness and life to writing.

Faulty Idiom	*Correct Idiom*
accord to	accord with
according with	according to
accuse with	accuse of
acquitted from	acquitted of
adverse against	adverse to
aim at proving	aim to prove
all-around	all-round
all the farther	as far as
all the faster	as fast as
among one another	among themselves
angry at (a person)	angry with
anyplace, anywheres	anywhere
as a fact	in fact, as a matter of fact
as regards to	as regards
authority about	authority on
belongs to be	belongs
blame it on him	blame him for it
cannot help but say	cannot help saying
comply to	comply with
conform in	conform to, with
correspond with (a thing)	correspond to
desirous to	desirous of
die with	die of
different than	different from
doubt if	doubt whether
entertain to dinner	entertain at dinner
equally as bad	equally bad
feel of	feel
free of	free from

241

Faulty Idiom	*Correct Idiom*
frightened from	frightened by
have got to	must
identical to	identical with
in accordance to	in accordance with
in back of	behind
in search for	in search of
in the city Shreveport	in the city of Shreveport
in the year of 1941	in the year 1941
independent from	independent of
inside of a year	within a year
jealous for	jealous of
kind of a	kind of
listen at	listen to
near enough that	near enough to
no doubt but that	no doubt that
nowhere near enough	not nearly enough
oblivious to	oblivious of
off of	off
out loud	aloud
over with	over
plan on going	plan to go
prior than	prior to
providing	provided
remember of	remember
sensitive about	sensitive to
stay to home	stay at home
superior than	superior to
tend to	attend to
there is no doubt but that	there is no doubt that
to home	at home
treat on	treat of
try and	try to
unequal for	unequal to
very interested	very much interested
vie against	vie with
want in (off, out)	want to get in (off, out)
where are you at?	where are you?
win out	win

EXERCISE. *Correct the faulty idioms.*

1. Mary will be very pleased to attend the party.
2. The carpenter has gone in search for a mason.
3. The team will win out finally.
4. She likes to listen at good music.
5. I cannot help but like him.

20c. Use fresh expressions instead of trite (hackneyed, overworked) ones.

Nearly all trite expressions were once striking and effective. From overuse they have lost their vigor. They no longer stimulate the reader; often they annoy him.

Hackneyed Expressions

a bolt from the blue
abreast of the times
aching void
acid test
after all is said and done
agree to disagree
a long-felt want
all in all
all work and no play
along this line
arms of Morpheus
as luck would have it
at a loss for words
at one fell swoop
bathed in tears
beat a hasty retreat
beggars description
better late than never
bitter end
blood is thicker than water
blushing bride
bolt from the blue

brave as a lion
brawny arms
breathless silence
breathless suspense
brilliant performance
briny deep
brown as a berry
budding genius
busy as a bee
by leaps and bounds
captain of industry
carpet of grass
center of attraction
checkered career
cheered to the echo
clear as crystal
clinging vine
close to nature
cold as ice
completes the picture
conspicuous by its absence
course of true love

Hackneyed Expressions (Continued)

Dame Fortune
deadly earnest
depend upon it
depths of despair
devouring element
doomed to disappointment
downy couch
drastic action
dull thud
each and every
easier said than done
enjoyable occasion
epic struggle
equal to the occasion
everything went along nicely
exception proves the rule
eyes like stars
fair sex
familiar landmarks
fast and furious
favor with a selection
few and far between
fiber of his being
filthy lucre
flower of the Old South
fools rush in
footprints on the sands of
    Time
force of circumstances
goes without saying
golden locks
goodly number
green as grass
green with envy
gridiron heroes
Grim Reaper
heart's content
heartfelt thanks

he-man
holy bonds of matrimony
hoping you are the same
in all its glory
in great profusion
in our midst
in the last analysis
iron constitution
irony of fate
it stands to reason
justice to the occasion
last but not least
last straw
light fantastic
limped into port
lonely sentinel
looking for all the world like
mad as a wet hen
made a pretty picture
mantle of snow
meets the eye
method in his madness
monarch of all I survey
more in sorrow than in anger
Mother Earth
motley crowd
myriad lights
needs no introduction
nestles in the hills
nipped in the bud
no sooner said than done
no thinking man
none the worse for wear
order out of chaos
paramount issue
partake of refreshments
poor but honest
powers that be

Hackneyed Expressions (Continued)

promising future
proud possessor
psychological moment
put in an appearance
red as a rose
reigns supreme
rendered a selection
riot of color
royal reception
ruling passion
sad to relate
sadder but wiser
sea of faces
seething mass of humanity
self-made man
sigh of relief
silence reigned supreme
simple life
single blessedness
skeleton in the closet
sleep of the just
slow as molasses
slow but sure
snow-capped mountains
soul of honor
specimen of humanity
staff of life
stands like a sentinel
strong, silent man
strong as a lion
struggle for existence
sturdy as an oak

sumptuous repast
sun-kissed meadows
sweat of his brow
table groaned
take my word for it
the happy pair
the plot thickens
the time of my life
thereby hangs the tale
tired but happy
to the bitter end
too full for utterance
too funny for words
toothsome viands
tumultuous applause
vast multitude
venture a suggestion
walk of life
was the recipient of
watery grave
wee small hours
wended our way
where angels fear to tread
where ignorance is bliss
with bated breath
words fail me
work like a Trojan
worse for wear
wrapped in mystery
wreathed in smiles
wrought havoc
wry countenance

EXERCISE. Substitute fresh words or phrases for hackneyed expressions.

1. We have to earn our living by the sweat of our brows.
2. The meaning of the sentence is as clear as crystal.

3. James favored us with a musical selection.
4. The sun came out in all its glory.
5. The earth was covered next morning with a mantle of snow.

20d. Avoid clumsy repetition or harsh combinations of sound.

Unpleasant combinations of sound should always be avoided. In prose, the poetic devices of rhyme, alliteration, and a regular rhythm are usually displeasing. Test your sentences by reading them aloud.

DIFFICULT Some people shun the seashore.
BETTER Some people avoid the seashore.

OBJECTIONABLE RHYME He should wait at the gate if it is not too late.
BETTER If he arrives soon enough, he should remain at the gate.

EXERCISE. Rewrite the sentences to avoid displeasing combinations of sound.

1. The glow worms glimmered in the gloom.
2. She sat and listened to the stolid statistician.
3. Roland refused to return the ruler.
4. I will take the boys across the lake when you are awake.
5. The busy bees brought back a bountiful store of honey.

20e. Select words that refer to definite things or ideas; select words that communicate meaning.[1]

(1) Use words that suggest experiences, that evoke specific mental pictures.

[1] The science of the meaning of words, known as semantics, has attracted much attention during the past twenty years. For popular treatments of semantics see Stuart Chase, *The Tyranny of Words*, New York: Harcourt, Brace, 1938; S. I. Hayakawa, *Language in Action*, Chicago: Institute of General Semantics, 1940.

VAGUE   For homes primitive men used anything that afforded shelter.

IMPROVED For homes primitive men used caves.

VAGUE   The cave kept primitive man warm and safe.

IMPROVED The cave kept out the winter cold, the summer heat, and the savage lion.

(2) **Select words that communicate ideas. (What is this thing, where is this thing, when is this thing, how is this thing?)**

VAGUE   Mr. Smith wrote a brilliant account of the War. [The reader gets no new ideas.]

IMPROVED Mr. Smith wrote an account of the war in which he stated the causes, the nations involved, the loss of men and supplies, and the final outcome.

VAGUE   The ball player *was put out of the running.* [Vague idea.]

IMPROVED The ball player broke his leg and was forced to leave the game.

VAGUE   Mary is a *grand* roommate. [*Grand* covers a multitude of things.]

IMPROVED Mary helps me with my lessons, mends my stockings, shops for me when I am rushed with work, and waits on me when I am ill.

VAGUE   The trouble with this city government is politics. [What is politics? Who knows?]

IMPROVED The trouble with this city government is the failure of the city officials to do what they know is right.

(3) **Select words that suit the occasion.**

EXAMPLE The hall was filled with frenzied supporters who were whooping it up for their Alma Mater. [The night before a big game.]

247

"Fourscore and seven years ago our fathers brought forth on this continent a new nation . . . ." [A dignified, sober occasion.]

(4) Select words with due regard to their connotation (power of suggestion).

Words are feelings, emotions, sensations, ideas. Some words, beside their literal meaning, have the power to suggest varied associations. They are surrounded, as it were, by an aura of feelings. They stir up unexplainable emotions, pleasant and unpleasant, and connect the present situation with something remote in consciousness. They seem to be an intrinsic part of ourselves, and are tied up with all our experiences. For instance, the word *hearth*, which literally means *the floor of a fireplace*, suggests in addition *the fireside, warmth, safety, good cheer, a family and friends*, and *the home itself*. *Stove*, on the other hand, is much poorer in suggestive power.

BARREN   He sat musing by the *stove*.
RICHER   He sat musing by the *hearth*.

BARREN   Regas sells *hot* steaks.
RICHER   Regas sells *sizzling* steaks.

BARREN   The boat *stayed* close to the shore.
RICHER   The boat *hugged* the shore.

BARREN   The baby *likes to play*.
RICHER   The baby *is as playful as a kitten*.

BARREN   John *entered* the house quietly.
RICHER   John *sneaked* into the house.

BARREN   The man at the door is an *unemployed person*.
RICHER   The man at the door is a *tramp*.

EXERCISE. Tell briefly what feelings, pleasant or unpleasant, come to you when the following words are read.

1.	pig	13.	Rose Bowl
2.	Ford	14.	honey
3.	Nazi	15.	liberty
4.	Sissy	16.	Finland
5.	duck	17.	expectorate
6.	Fifth Avenue	18.	upper crust
7.	TVA	19.	New Orleans
8.	flag	20.	sport
9.	beans	21.	dog
10.	justice	22.	dirty
11.	date	23.	propaganda
12.	key	24.	courage

EXERCISE ON EXACTNESS

Use the exact word needed to express the thought of each sentence. Make any other necessary corrections.

1. The story would have been very good if he had rounded out the last chapter.
2. The first thing we see as we step in the door of the reference room is a large rubber mat.
3. She is very much rested to know that she will not have to worry any more.
4. These facts should help make a better team this year.
5. As he runs screaming to his mother before the flames sear his lungs, he catches the rug and curtains on fire.
6. It was amusing to watch the people go out in the street to keep from walking under the ladder.
7. When he was a young man, he moved further back into the wilderness.
8. A person is entitled to as much peace and happiness that he is able to get.

9. He is very well adapted for his profession.
10. We have a standing agreement that he was to let me in the show whenever I was broke.
11. During the depression schools were closed from lack of money.
12. Last but not least, the students should be courteous at all times.
13. Religion is living all through the week like you would on Sunday.
14. Perhaps Brown did expect aid and by some misfortunate chances did not get it.
15. His innocence had been proven.
16. He gave a discussion of the problems of the home and the affects of the home on a person.
17. These things tend to take the mind of man off of his work.
18. No one noticed that the drapes were astray.
19. John acted awful about the whole affair.
20. Liquor effects the brain and nervous system.
21. The decorations for Halloween are very unique.
22. When I first entered Girl Scouting, I was impressed over how nice and friendly the girls were.
23. I infringed upon this privilege very much.
24. It seems to me that Germany is already a bit mad over American help to the Allies in this conflict.
25. Her main feature is that she is exceedingly beautiful, and it is this beauty that makes her an important person.
26. One of the characteristics of poetry is the emphasis of beauty.
27. In accord to his plan each group would be isolated.
28. It never seems to occur in the mind of a politician to build onto his reputation, rather than tear down that of an opponent.
29. Later I asked the same question to some of my neighbors.

30. Old Mother Nature was doing her best to make us happy.
31. Everybody says that Jane is a swell girl.
32. There was a sizzling noise that sounded like some one had touched an electric wire.
33. We were not very well supplied with blankets, so when it rained we all got rather chilly.
34. It looks like he would learn sometime.
35. I was surprised when he insisted on toting my books.
36. The property was divided between the three sons.
37. You made a very credible speech last night.
38. You must work hard to finish your work in time.
39. He is relying purely on the patriotism of the people.
40. John was fond of the radio, and so he persuaded his father to buy him a set, and now he is one of the best announcers in town.
41. Frank looked awfully funny when I told him that he had failed.
42. I can't feature myself selling books.
43. Robert is a very nice child.
44. He made an illusion to his former position.
45. The fudge you made last night was grand.
46. I am so tired I am simply dead.
47. Ann felt that she should fix up for the party.
48. I remember of saying that I had seen Tom.
49. Did you have a swell time at the beach?
50. He lost all his money when the bank busted.

21 w

21. Avoid wordiness. Repeat a word or phrase only when necessary to gain force or clearness.[1]

21a. Avoid a careless or needless repetition of the thought in different words.

WORDY The United States is more in debt to a greater degree than ever.

RIGHT The United States is more in debt than ever.

WORDY I always fostered the idea in my own small mind that I could become rich.

RIGHT I always fostered the idea that I could become rich.

WORDY Each writer has his own style which he uses in his own works.

RIGHT Each writer has his own style.

This careless overlapping of thought, called *tautology*, is a common type of wordiness. Note the tautology in each of the following expressions:

WRONG	RIGHT
a mental thought	a thought
and etc.	etc.
as a usual rule	as a rule

[1] Complete mastery of section 21 will eliminate the ninth most common error in the average student theme.

252

ascend up	ascend
circulated around	circulated
combined together	combined
connect up	connect
connect up together	connect
malaria disease	malaria
many frequent	many *or* frequent
meet up with	meet
modern colleges of today	modern colleges *or* colleges of today
more easier	easier
my autobiography of my life	my autobiography
repeat again	repeat
small in size	small
this here	this
total effect of all this	total effect
where . . . at	where

EXERCISE.   Eliminate all needless repetition.

1. As a usual rule the state legislature is filled with shrewd politicians.
2. Mr. McConn divides the students of today into three groups, or classes, that go to the modern colleges.
3. Saturday night was a real pleasure, as I had no lessons for which to study about.
4. During the Renaissance a very large number of words, many of them terms of scholarship, were then taken from the Latin.
5. My desire is to make farm life more easier than that of the ordinary farmer.

21b. Avoid clumsy, roundabout expressions (such as *The reason . . . is because* sentence) and omit phrases that add nothing to the meaning.

WORDY The reason why he stayed behind was because he had no money. [12 words.]

RIGHT He stayed behind because he had no money. [8 words.]

WORDY There were six men who volunteered. [6 words.]

RIGHT Six men volunteered. [3 words.]

WORDY It was during that year that he was elected captain. [10 words.]

RIGHT During that year he was elected captain. [7 words.]

WORDY The treasury was near a state of depletion. [8 words.]

RIGHT The treasury was near depletion. [5 words.]

EXERCISE. Express the thought of each sentence as directly as possible.

1. Roosevelt was elected for a third term by the people who hoped he would continue in the process of creating prosperity.
2. The reason for the usual rarity of these examples is probably due to the fact that the path which leads one to high aspirations is a straight, narrow way which few people succeed in following without side steps and stumbling before reaching the appointed goal.
3. He told the story in a very sober way, trying to make the little things seem as if they were very important.
4. Spaniards are the ones who brought over horses first.
5. Sometimes in our lives we hear the topic of conversation turn to an educated man.

21c. Eliminate needless words by combining choppy sentences or by simplifying clauses and phrases.

WORDY When the Indians made tools, they used flint and bones. [10 words.]

BETTER The Indians made tools of flint and bone. [8 words.]

WORDY Another thing is good health. It is one of our great blessings. It may be had through proper diet and exercise. [21 words.]

BETTER The great blessing of good health may be had through proper diet and exercise. [14 words.]

WORDY A new addition has been built at the side of the house and this addition has been developed into a library. [21 words.]

BETTER A new addition, built at the side of the house, has been developed into a library. [16 words.]

21d. Avoid the double negative and other ungrammatical repetitions.

WRONG The driver *couldn't hardly* miss the way.
RIGHT The driver *could hardly* miss the way.

WRONG We *can't* assist *but* one at a time.
RIGHT We *can* assist *but* one at a time.

WRONG *Tom he* did not like it.
RIGHT Tom did not like it.

21e. Except to gain clearness or force, avoid the repetition of a word or phrase.

FAULTY Since the general committee report has already been reported, only the report dealing with *tenure* will be reported on today.

BETTER Since the committee has already made its general report, it will submit today only its findings on *tenure.*

FAULTY It is impossible to ask me to do the impossible.
BETTER You cannot expect me to do the impossible.

EXERCISE. Eliminate needless repetition.

1. The practice of helping one's neighbor for the enjoyment of it is a very common practice.
2. If one of these programs has an extra good program for the week, I pick that program as the best.
3. The military course should be open to any eligible man desiring the course.
4. In debating, a good debater should decide first on a good subject which is of real interest.
5. A successful man must love his work and be qualified for his work.

EXERCISE ON WORDINESS

Eliminate all wordiness. Revise the sentences as necessary to make them effective.

1. She is very pretty, and she presumably has the qualities of a lady.
2. I held an advantage over most of the others because of the fact that I had been in college for six weeks prior to Freshman Week.
3. His hands were toughened by some kind of hard manual labor of some kind.
4. Just exactly when this pottery-making period was has not been determined and is not known to us.
5. The first horseless carriages were considered as a luxury.
6. When they prepare their lunch, they always prepare more than is necessary to supply their need.
7. In Poe's stories of horror, the setting and environment are always the best to produce the results he wishes to convey to you.
8. Upon entering the building, I found the stage to be decorated very beautifully.
9. Diggory Venn was a very remarkable fellow. He always seemed to happen to be around at the right time.

10. Because of several conditions relative to this composition, the interim of my life between birth and the age of nine we must omit.

11. Denis was a young man of twenty-one years of age.

12. It was in the United States that it was first realized that this method of correction was a profound error.

13. The Big Apple not only includes the people who are dancing but anyone who wishes to enter may do so.

14. Abraham's mother died because of exposure to a frequent malaria disease.

15. The game was exciting, and many fumbles frequently occurred in the game.

16. One of the reasons for my liking *The Glorious Adventure* is because of the humor that the author displays in his book.

17. It seems that Bradford has merely assembled these quotations with a few remarks of his own to connect them together.

18. I wanted to attend camp last summer, but I did not have sufficient funds on which to go.

19. Crown rust is also called leaf rust because the leaves are affected. Crown rust resembles stem rust in that both rusts affects the stems and leaves of the oats.

20. It would seat about one hundred and fifty students, and was usually always full.

21. Another thing that is essential is good health. This is one of the most important things.

22. Living in a dormitory has its advantages and drawbacks. The first advantage to be considered is the economy of living in a dormitory.

23. In facial appearance he seemed to be a man with a lively, active, and somewhat acute face, with slightly sunken but nevertheless roving eyes.

24. The facts about interesting people interest me much.

25. The reason for my lack of preparedness was due to the fact that I had taken a science course in high school.

26. The tobacco is then graded into five grades.
27. The garden was a beautiful place with thousands of beautiful roses which made the place a thing of beauty.
28. Three deciding factors contributed to our decision.
29. During the time that I was in Chicago, which was a period of two weeks, I saw many acquaintances.
30. When one is away from home, one comes in contact with a number of people that one has met many times before on similar excursions.
31. Frank he often drives the car.
32. There were seven inches of rain that fell that day.
33. When the people shout and yell, the shouting and yelling is deafening.
34. The sick man had no appetite to eat heavy foods.
35. John lost his way and had to return back to camp the way he had come.
36. The red rose is equally as beautiful as the white one.
37. William was rather small as to size.
38. The pitcher fell off of the shelf.
39. The stockholders discussed the first necessary transactions in the opening of the new bank which was just being organized.
40. The picture frame was round as to shape.

OMISSION OF
NECESSARY WORDS

22. Avoid the omission of a word or phrase necessary to the meaning of the sentence.[1]

22a. Avoid the omission of a preposition, an article, or some other word through sheer carelessness.

Most faulty omissions in student writing result from oversight. Careful proofreading should be sufficient to eliminate such errors.

EXAMPLES We have learned the importance ∧ using perfume. [Careless omission of the preposition *of*.]

John had been there only ∧ moment ago. [Careless omission of the article *a*.]

I wish I ∧ been able to play football at ∧ university. [Careless omission of *had* (a part of the verb) and of the article *the*.]

22b. Do not omit an article, a possessive adjective, a conjunction, or a preposition when it is needed for clearness.

RIGHT A friend and helper stood at his side; *or*, His friend and helper stood at his side. [The friend and helper are the same person.]

---

[1] Complete mastery of section **22** will eliminate the eighth most common error in the average student theme.

RIGHT	A friend and *a* helper stood at his side; *or,* His friend and *his* helper stood at his side. [To show that the friend and the helper are different persons the article or the possessive adjective must be repeated.]
QUESTIONABLE	Crop rotation puts back certain plant foods other crops have taken away.
SMOOTHER	Crop rotation puts back certain plant foods that other crops have taken away.

Note: Informal writing frequently omits *that* as an introduction to clauses whenever the omission is not confusing.

WRONG	The school burned down my last term.
RIGHT	The school burned down during my last term.

WRONG	He is staying some place in Texas.
RIGHT	He is staying at some place in Texas.
RIGHT	He is staying somewhere in Texas.

Note: Some idiomatic phrases indicating time or place regularly omit the preposition.

RIGHT	They arrived last week.
RIGHT	He came home.

22c. Avoid any omission that forces another word to be used illogically in a double capacity.

WRONG	He never has and never will like his new home.
RIGHT	He never has *liked* and never will like his new home.
RIGHT	He never has *liked* his new home and never will like it.

WRONG	He was pleased, but all the others dissatisfied.
RIGHT	He was pleased, but all the others *were* dissatisfied.

WRONG He is one of the best, if not the best, swimmers in college.

RIGHT He is one of the best swimmers in college, if not the best. [The reader supplies *swimmer*.]

WRONG She was as young, if not younger, than any other girl in camp.

RIGHT She was as young as any girl in camp, if not younger.

22d. In general avoid the use of *so, such, too, etc.,* without the completing clause.

INCOMPLETE I was so tired.

RIGHT I was so tired that I could not sleep.

RIGHT I was exceedingly tired.

INCOMPLETE She has such beautiful eyes.

RIGHT She has such beautiful eyes that they are noticed by everyone who sees her.

RIGHT She has unusually beautiful eyes.

EXERCISE ON MISCELLANEOUS OMISSIONS

Supply all necessary words.

1. They make the resolutions in order to aid themselves lead a happier life.
2. He lived for others as well as himself.
3. I have nearly filled this scrapbook and ready to start on another.
4. He writes about the days he had neither foods nor shelter.
5. I entered University 1940.
6. The men worked on the road, lawn, and garden.
7. Eustacia Vye was of little common sense.
8. I managed to work in a season of track and football my senior year.

9. The phase of electricity which I specialized was wire communication.
10. Their ability to weave and do all sorts of handicrafts is their livelihood.
11. When little Jane is told that her standing in the household is less than a servant, she makes no reply.
12. When I finish University, I plan to enter art school in New York.
13. Romeo was young, and he fell in love with the first girl whom he came in contact.
14. The author writes more about the Barrie country than he does Barrie.
15. He is so different from the others.
16. The parties were enjoyed by John as much if not more than the others.
17. I have not travelled much even though I ride a pass.
18. You may stand any place you wish.
19. The boy is just too smart.
20. The two girls were helpful, but the boy sullen.
21. He assisted his uncle, aunt, and cousin.
22. You must not speak to me that way.
23. I saw Nell was not in the room.
24. The dog is such a nuisance.
25. William tried to go to the house you refer.
26. Please get me a pen, a bottle of ink, and envelope.
27. As soon as the door was opened, the dog wanted out.
28. Here is the hole which the dog escaped.
29. I never have and never can understand why he ran away.
30. The large stadium is filled with people and still coming.

EFFECTIVENESS IN THE SENTENCE

UNITY AND LOGICAL THINKING

23. Avoid bringing into the sentence (a) unrelated ideas or (b) too many details. Complete each thought logically.

Note: For lack of grammatical unity in the sentence consult sections **2, Sentence Fragment,** and **3, Comma Splice.**

23a. Unrelated ideas should be developed in separate sentences. (If the ideas are related, they should be expressed in such a way that the relationship is immediately clear to the reader.)

WRONG   Poetry is difficult to define, but great pleasure can be derived from the reading of nature poetry.

IMPROVED   Poetry is difficult to define. Great pleasure can be derived from the reading of nature poetry.

WRONG   The birds are numerous and the cherries seldom ripen. [Relationship not immediately clear.]

CLEARER   The numerous birds pick most of the cherries before they ripen.

WRONG   Mr. Smith is my teacher and he has a large family.

RIGHT   Mr. Smith is my teacher. He has a large family. [Ideas given equal importance.]

RIGHT   Mr. Smith, my teacher, has a large family. [Unity secured by subordination of one idea.]

WRONG   Ireland has a deep culture, but the country is out of the path of general travel. [Unity thwarted by a gap in the thought.]

IMPROVED   Ireland has a deep culture, but it is insufficiently appreciated because the country is out of the path of general travel.

EXERCISE. Rewrite the following sentences to avoid bringing together unrelated ideas.

1. Mr. Jones has a large family of ten children and has gone to the fair.
2. Mollusks which yield pearls are numerous, and pearl fishing is carried on in many parts of the world.
3. The foreman, speaking in gruff tones and seldom smiling, wore a gray coat.
4. Birds migrate to the warmer countries in the fall and in summer get food by eating worms and insects which are a pest to the farmer.
5. The future of our country is dependent on the thinking of our young people, but we shall always have two political parties.

23b. Excessive detail should not be allowed to obscure the central thought of the sentence.

Such detail, if important, should be developed in separate sentences; otherwise it should be omitted.

OVERLOADED   When I was only four years old, living in a house on Oak Hill, little of which remains today, I could already walk the two miles that separated the house from the railway station.

BETTER   When I was only four years old, I could already walk the two miles between my house and the railway station.

OVERLOADED In 1788, when Andrew Jackson, then a young man of twenty-one years who had been living in the Carolinas, still a virgin country, came into Tennessee, a turbulent place of unknown opportunities, to enforce the law as the new prosecuting attorney, he had the qualities in him which would make him equal to the task.

BETTER   In 1788, when Andrew Jackson came into Tennessee as the new prosecuting attorney, he had the necessary qualifications for the task.

EXERCISE. Recast the following sentences to eliminate excessive detail.

1. The boat, considered seaworthy ten years ago, but now in need of paint and repairs, as is so often true of things that should be discarded, moved out into the bay.

2. Puppies should be fed three times a day, and the food should consist of prepared dog food, milk, and biscuit, and the age of the dogs should be considered.

3. The captain asked for a volunteer and the soldier picked up his pack, which weighed thirty pounds, and asked if he might go.

4. Everybody has a hobby or favorite sport, because there are enough for all to engage in, and we are able to have one that we learn to like.

5. A course in business methods helps the young man to get a job in order that he may prove whether he is fitted for business and thus avoid postponing the test, as so many do, until it is too late.

23c. Comparisons should be complete and logical.

WRONG The scenery is as beautiful as any other place. [Comparison of things not capable of comparison.]

RIGHT The scenery here is as beautiful as it is at any other place.

WRONG I like *Kenilworth* better than any of Scott's novels. [Since *Kenilworth* is one of Scott's novels, the sentence means: "I like *Kenilworth* better than *Kenilworth*."]

RIGHT I like *Kenilworth* better than any other of Scott's novels.

WRONG I like *Kenilworth* best of any other novel by Scott.

RIGHT I like *Kenilworth* best of all the novels by Scott.

WRONG I helped him more than John. [Ambiguous because one term of the comparison is omitted.]

RIGHT I helped him more than I helped John; *or,* I helped him more than John did.

WRONG He is as old, if not older, than his cousin.

RIGHT He is as old as his cousin, if not older.

WRONG He owned a very smart, if not the smartest, dogs I ever saw.

RIGHT He owned one of the smartest dogs I ever saw, if not the smartest.

WRONG Of the two boys he is the oldest. [The comparative, not the superlative, needed with *two.*]

RIGHT Of the two boys he is the older.

WRONG He was so excited. [*So, such,* or *too* usually require a *that*-clause to complete the meaning.]

RIGHT He was so excited that he could not eat.

EXERCISE.   Make comparisons complete and logical.

1. He trusted me more than James.
2. Boston is larger than any city in Massachusetts.

3. The boy was too tired.
4. He is as tall, if not taller, than James.
5. My occupation is more interesting than a clerk.

23d. Avoid awkward, obscure, or confused sentences. Complete every construction logically.

WRONG Because he was sick caused him to stay at home.

RIGHT Because he was sick he stayed at home. [Completing logically the construction with which the sentence begins.]

RIGHT His sickness caused him to stay at home. [Supplying a beginning to fit the ending.]

WRONG A sonnet is when a poem has fourteen lines.

RIGHT A sonnet is a poem of fourteen lines.

WRONG To banish is where a person is driven out of his country.

RIGHT To banish a person is to drive him out of his country.

EXERCISE. Recast the following sentences to eliminate awkwardness or obscurity.

1. I want a resort somewhere I can go to fish.
2. I always have and always will like grand opera.
3. Because she had misplaced her ticket caused her to miss the game.
4. Work has always and always will be unpopular with some people.
5. The first time I saw an automobile was when John took me to town.
6. To succeed is when a person accomplishes his purpose.
7. One hardly knows what to do in the desperate condition he is.

EXERCISE ON UNITY AND LOGICAL THINKING

Revise each sentence as necessary to make it unified, logical, and clear.

1. Our country raises much surplus food and the European countries are suffering from poor crops.
2. The door may be locked and better take a key.
3. One of the most common superstitions is the crossing of the black cat before you.
4. The Quakers believe that justice is the word of the Lord, and the Presbyterians believe in having elders to assist in their government.
5. Alaska is a country for future colonization, and people from the Dust Bowl have gone there to live.
6. The mistake was so awkward.
7. I always have and always will like to play basketball.
8. Cod-liver oil is rich in protein and can be purchased at a drug store.
9. Whole wheat, which is especially nourishing, is being used more and more, especially in some parts of the country, by the leading bakeries to improve the texture and food content of the bread.
10. The present-day farmer must have a knowledge of animals, and the income derived from the sale of these is considerable.
11. He is as strong, if not stronger, than the state champion.
12. I like *David Copperfield* better than any novel by Dickens.
13. Because the grounds were wet caused the postponement of the game.
14. I consider my profession of law better than an engineer.
15. To emigrate is where a person leaves his own country for a new land.

SUBORDINATION

24. Determine the most important idea of the sentence and express it in the main clause. Put lesser ideas in subordinate clauses, phrases, or words. Use co-ordination only for ideas of equal importance.

Note: Can you distinguish readily between phrases and clauses? between main clauses and subordinate clauses? Until you are able to do so you will have difficulty in understanding section **24**. If necessary, master first the fundamentals of the sentence treated under section **2e**, **Sentence Sense**, and then study **Subordination**.

The principle of subordination is of fundamental importance in composition. It is the mark of a writer's maturity. Childish sentences, sadly lacking in subordination, are usually a series (a) of short, choppy sentences or (b) of short main clauses joined by *and*.

Extremely Childish Sentences:

a. Short, Choppy Sentences:

I walked down the road. I saw a bird. It was in a tree. It was singing. [Subordination lacking.]

b. *And* Sentence:

I walked down the road, and I saw a bird, and it was in a tree, and it was singing.   [Subordination lacking.]

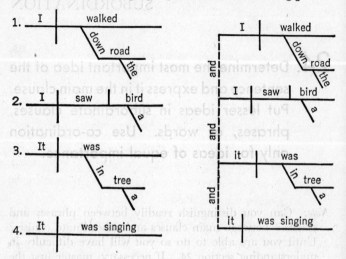

Mature Sentence:

As I walked down the road, I saw a bird singing in a tree.   [Lesser ideas properly subordinated.]

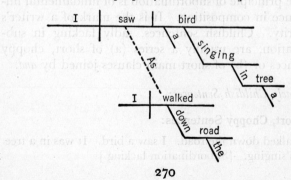

The mature writer, considering the second of the short sentences the most important, has let it stand as the main clause. He has reduced the first sentence to a subordinate clause — an adverbial clause telling when the bird was seen. He has reduced the third sentence to a prepositional phrase and the fourth to a single word — a participle describing *bird*.

It is possible, of course, to desire special emphasis on some idea other than that of *seeing* the bird. If the *singing* of the bird is considered more important, the sentence might read: As I walked down the road, a bird was singing in a tree.

24a. Short, choppy sentences should be combined into longer units in which the lesser ideas are properly subordinated.

CHOPPY   I walked rapidly. I came to a house. It was deserted.

BETTER   I walked rapidly until I came to a deserted house.

CHOPPY   The day was cold. The snow had frozen into a thick sheet of ice. The girl had to be careful as she walked. She walked very slowly. She did not want to slip on the ice. Joe noticed this girl with interest.

BETTER   One cold day after the snow had frozen into a thick sheet of ice, Joe noticed with interest a girl who was walking very slowly. She had to be careful as she walked, for she did not want to slip on the ice.

EXERCISE. Combine the short sentences into longer sentences in which the ideas are properly subordinated.

1. Samuel Houston was an interesting human being. He wished to rise in the world to great power or position.

He wished to help others. He would give his last cent to one in need.

2. A vacation at a boys' camp is next on the list. I never enjoyed myself more than I did there. The World's Fair, in the summer of 1940, was worth while. It was very big and colorful. It was, however, highly commercialized.

3. Hawthorne had a very unhappy boyhood. His father died when Hawthorne was four years old. His mother lived a solitary life. He grew up under unnatural conditions. These conditions probably account for the gloomy stories.

4. Tom had one friend among the servants. This was the gamekeeper. They would go hunting together. One day Tom and the gamekeeper were out hunting. They chased some partridge onto private land. Tom was told never to shoot on that property.

5. We knew that an unusual storm was brewing. The clouds gathered quickly. The winds changed and blew from the east. The little lake became squally. White caps appeared. Masses of floating debris were tossed by the waves on the shore. Then the rain came down in blinding sheets of water. It became dark. We could no longer see the cottages along the lake.

24b. Two or more main clauses should not be carelessly joined by *and, so,* or other co-ordinating words. Less important parts should be carefully subordinated. Use co-ordination only for ideas of equal importance.

INEFFECTIVE   The crowd jammed the stadium, and the noise was clamorous, and the confusion made me nervous.

BETTER   The noisy crowd and the confusion at the
              stadium made me nervous.

INEFFECTIVE   It was a cold afternoon and it was raining, but
              the tennis match was not postponed.
BETTER   Although it was a cold, rainy afternoon, the
              tennis match was not postponed.

EXERCISE. Revise each sentence to subordinate the
less important ideas.

1. I have finished high school and two years in engineering,
   and I should like to have you suggest what steps I should
   take to find a job.
2. The day was hot, and rain threatened to pour down at
   any moment, and the crowd continued to assemble.
3. The chief attraction of the track meet came last, and it
   was the relay.
4. We had just reached the bend in the road on our way
   home, and we saw a truck load of Boy Scouts crowded
   off the highway by an oncoming car.
5. First he collected his specimens, and then he brought
   them to the laboratory, and then he classified them.

24c. Do not place the main thought of the sentence in a subordinate clause (or construction).

FAULTY   William was only a substitute pitcher, winning half
          of his games.
BETTER   Although William was only a substitute pitcher,
          he won half of his games.

FAULTY   The rising water broke the dam, when the town
          was doomed.
BETTER   When the rising water broke the dam, the town
          was doomed.

273

EXERCISE. Revise each sentence to give prominence to the main thought.

1. The insects eat the plant off just below the soil, making growth impossible.
2. All the men and boys worked together to save the house which was too far gone.
3. The author would change from one part of Mark Twain's life to another, causing a lack of interest.
4. He won the Latin scholarship, making the highest average in a class of three hundred.
5. The gasoline tank sprang a leak, when all hope for a record flight was abandoned.

24d. Do not thwart subordination by inserting *and* or *but*.

WRONG Law enforcement is a current problem *and* which is hard to solve.

RIGHT Law enforcement is a current problem which is hard to solve.

WRONG The college needs new dormitories but which cannot be erected until additional funds are provided.

RIGHT The college needs new dormitories which cannot be erected until additional funds are provided.

EXERCISE. Rewrite the sentences to secure proper subordination.

1. The floor should be very smooth and a good linoleum covering it.
2. We need for defense many airplanes, but which cannot be provided until factories can be built to supply them.
3. The burning oil well was roped off and a group of firemen surrounding it.

4. The piping of water from reservoirs to desert places is a problem in engineering, and which requires experience and knowledge.
5. He proposed an experiment, and which could be finished in six months.

EXERCISE ON SUBORDINATION

Give prominence to the main ideas, subordinating less important ones.

1. One night her little boy was sick, and she saw Eustacia's shadow pass the door.
2. I was going home late one afternoon, when I had a serious accident.
3. Staying indoors and looking out the window was no fun; so I put on my raincoat and went outside.
4. Fishing is an art. One must use the right hook. The bait is also important. The weather must be propitious. It must not be too windy.
5. Father Latour was at a friend's house, and he saw two fine horses, and he induced the owner to part with them.
6. I had just started to leave, when I heard a loud noise behind me.
7. The sun was very hot, causing the man to stop work.
8. I graduated from high school, and then I worked in a bank, and so I earned enough to go to college.
9. The lizard is tame, and it will eat flies out of one's hand.
10. We lived in the country, but my father died, and so we moved to the city.
11. The automobile pulled up at the station. It was just noon. The train had already discharged its passengers. The train was about to leave.
12. I was walking down the street, when I found a well-filled purse.

25 coh

COHERENCE IN GENERAL —
DANGLING MODIFIERS

25. Place modifiers as close as possible to the words they modify. Avoid needless separation of related parts of the sentence. Avoid dangling modifiers.

Note: Can you distinguish readily the various modifiers? the several parts of the sentence? Until you are able to do so, you may have difficulty in understanding section **25.** If necessary, master first the fundamentals of the sentence treated in section **2e, Sentence Sense,** and then study **Coherence.** See also **Modifier** and **Modify** in section **1, Grammatical Terms.**

25a. Phrases should be placed near the words they modify.

WRONG The boy says that he means to leave the country *in the first stanza.*

RIGHT The boy says *in the first stanza* that he means to leave the country.

WRONG He played a great part in the war with Mexico *as a statesman.*

RIGHT *As a statesman* he played a great part in the war with Mexico.

276

WRONG   Heated arguments had often occurred *over techni-calities in the middle of a game.*

RIGHT   Heated arguments *over technicalities* had often oc-curred *in the middle of a game.*

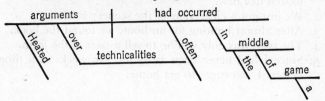

EXERCISE.   Recast the sentences to avoid needless separation of related parts.

1. Romeo received word that Juliet was dead from another messenger.
2. The engineering work was a thing of beauty on all the large buildings.
3. Everybody liked to have Phoebe around except Tom.
4. The high school has a well equipped library for its size.
5. He tells how Lincoln collected fees that his clients did not pay among other things.

25b. Adverbs such as *almost, also, only, just, ever, before, even,* or *merely* should be placed near the words they modify.

AMBIGUOUS   I *only* told her one thing.
CLEAR   I told her *only* one thing.

AMBIGUOUS   He is *just* asking for a trifle.
CLEAR   He is asking for *just* a trifle.

AMBIGUOUS   Anyone who hears Mr. Smith speak, *even* the most sophisticated, will get an inspiration.
CLEAR   Anyone, *even* the most sophisticated, who hears Mr. Smith speak will get an inspiration.

EXERCISE. Place the adverbs near the words they modify.

1. He took the penny home and polished it almost until it looked like new.
2. We just got a clear view of the scenery in time.
3. After almost hunting for an hour, we found the book.
4. The man was only willing to sell a part of the farm.
5. Since I had never been away for five weeks at a time before, I was eager to get home.

25c. Clauses, especially relative clauses, should be placed near the words they modify.

AMBIGUOUS The man will have prosperity *that rises early*.

CLEAR The man *that rises early* will have prosperity.

AMBIGUOUS I saw the deer stop at the edge of the precipice *that was startled*.

CLEAR I saw the deer *that was startled* stop at the edge of the precipice.

25d. Avoid "squinting" constructions — modifiers that may refer either to a preceding or to a following word.

SQUINTING I agreed *on the next day* to help him.

CLEAR I agreed to help him *on the next day*.

CLEAR *On the next day* I agreed to help him.

SQUINTING The tug which was whistling *noisily* chugged up the river.

CLEAR The whistling tug chugged *noisily* up the river.

CLEAR The tug whistled *noisily* as it chugged up the river.

25e. Avoid awkward splitting of infinitives or needless separation of related parts of the sentence.

AWKWARD   You should now begin *to*, if you wish to succeed, *find* a helper.

IMPROVED   If you wish to succeed, you should now begin *to find* a helper.

AWKWARD   There stood the wagon which we *had* early last autumn *left* by the barn.

IMPROVED   There stood the wagon which we *had left* by the barn early last autumn.

AWKWARD   *I*, knowing all the facts, *want* to be excused.

IMPROVED   Knowing all the facts, *I want* to be excused.

25f. Avoid dangling modifiers.

A participle, a gerund, an infinitive, or an elliptical clause or phrase should have in the same sentence a word to which it is clearly and logically related. Otherwise it is said to "dangle." Eliminate such errors (1) by recasting the sentence to make the dangling element agree with the subject of the main clause or (2) by expanding the phrase or elliptical clause into a subordinate clause.

(1) Avoid dangling participles.

DANGLING   *Having grown* weaker and weaker, the struggle ended with his death. [*Having grown* modifies nothing in the sentence. The reader expects it to modify *struggle*, the subject of the main clause.]

RIGHT   *Having grown* weaker and weaker, *he* ended the struggle in death. [*Having grown* modifies *he*, the subject of the main clause in the revised sentence. See the diagram on the next page.]

279

RIGHT *After he had grown weaker and weaker,* he ended the struggle in death. [Participial phrase expanded into a subordinate clause.]

DANGLING The evening passed very pleasantly, *eating* candy and *playing* the radio. [*Eating* and *playing* modify nothing in the sentence.]

RIGHT *We* passed the evening very pleasantly, *eating* candy and *playing* the radio. [*Eating* and *playing* modify *we*, the subject of the main clause. See the diagram below.]

RIGHT The evening passed very pleasantly, *for we were eating candy and playing the radio.* [Participial phrase expanded into a clause.]

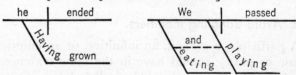

Note: The incorrect sentences cannot be diagrammed, for the dangling participles (*having grown, eating,* and *playing*) have nothing to modify.

EXERCISE. Correct each dangling participle (1) by recasting the sentence to make the dangling participle agree with the subject of the main clause and (2) by expanding the participial phrase into a subordinate clause.

1. Looking toward North Carolina, only the tops of the mountains were visible.
2. Having been very successful in the venture, we find John next in America.
3. Knowing that the winner will be the champions of the state, it is a thrilling moment in the lives of the players.
4. Entering the campus from the west, the first thing a person sees is a grove of elms.
5. Having taken his seat, we began to ask questions of the teacher.

(2) Avoid dangling gerunds.

DANGLING   Before *going* on a long trip, the car must be completely overhauled.

BETTER   Before *you go* on a long trip, the car must be completely overhauled.

BETTER   Before *going* on a long trip, *you* must overhaul the car completely.

DANGLING   On *entering* the stadium, the size of the crowd surprises one.

BETTER   On *entering* the stadium, *one* is surprised by the size of the crowd.

BETTER   When *one enters* the stadium, *one* is surprised by the size of the crowd.

EXERCISE.   Correct each dangling gerund (1) by recasting the sentence to make the dangling gerund agree with the subject of the main clause and (2) by expanding the gerund phrase into a subordinate clause.

1. After sitting there a while, it began to snow.
2. In drawing up any system of classification, it is likely that there will be some overlapping.
3. Before hitching a goat to a wagon, he should be taught several commands.
4. Before driving a colt in the city, he should be accustomed to the sound of cars.
5. By selecting the design according to the standards of beauty and form, an interesting effect can be obtained.

(3) Avoid dangling infinitives.

DANGLING   *To grow* fine sweet peas, strings should support the plants.

BETTER   *To grow* fine sweet peas, support the plant by strings.

DANGLING *To run* efficiently, the mechanic should oil the machine well.

BETTER *To run* efficiently, the machine should be well oiled by the mechanic.

Exceptions: Participles, gerunds, and infinitives designating general action rather than that of a special agent may be correctly used without relation to the subject of the main clause.

RIGHT Taking everything into consideration, the campaign was successful.

(4) Avoid dangling elliptical clauses or phrases.

DANGLING Never take your eye off the ball until knocked from the tee. [You? the eye? the ball?]

BETTER Never take your eye off the ball until you knock it from the tee.

DANGLING While away visiting, the house caught on fire. [Was the house away visiting?]

BETTER While she was away visiting, the house caught on fire.

EXERCISE ON COHERENCE

Make the following sentences coherent.

1. He was only able to go a short distance.
2. Being a bit nervous, his speech was not convincing.
3. The slaves were unwilling to submit to his plans, thinking they could free themselves.
4. While wondering about this phenomenon, the sun sank from view.
5. John and Robert had ridden several days without sleep in the rain.
6. Having a broken arm and nose, I thought the statue was very ugly.

7. He only works when someone is around.
8. The evening passed pleasantly, talking about current events.
9. Corkey always waited for me to come home on the front porch.
10. Feeling keenly about football, relations between the two schools became strained.
11. He gives an account of his life, which is very interesting.
12. Born of peasant stock, one wonders how Mandel achieved greatness.
13. There is little of the arrogance attributed to his nephews about him.
14. It was a June evening returning from the office, when the message came.
15. I had only taken a few steps when someone ran into me.
16. Looking down into the valley, the stream could be seen winding its way.
17. She wanted to really do something worth while.
18. He was completely carried away by the proposal, causing him to forget an important business meeting.
19. You are, considering the whole affair, very fortunate.
20. The problem that bothered me was the selection of my courses upon entering college.
21. There stood, just as grandfather had built it fifty years ago, the clock.
22. Located on a mountaintop, this made it an ideal place for a summer resort.
23. We sat for hours watching the game, shivering.
24. By picking up a colt's leg every day while he is young, he will become accustomed to standing on only three legs.
25. Clym realized the mistake he had made too late.

PARALLELISM

26. Parallel ideas should be expressed in parallel structure. Misleading parallels should be avoided.

Note: Can you distinguish readily the parts of speech? phrases and clauses? main clauses and subordinate clauses? Until you are able to do so you will have difficulty in understanding section 26. If necessary, master first the fundamentals of the sentence treated in section **2e, Sentence Sense,** and then study **Parallelism.**

26a. For the expression of co-ordinate ideas a noun should be paralleled with a noun, an active verb with an active verb, an infinitive with an infinitive, a subordinate clause with a subordinate clause, and so forth.

WRONG Let us consider the *origin* of engineering and *how engineering has progressed.*
[Noun paralleled with a subordinate clause.]

RIGHT Let us consider the ‖ *origin* and
                            ‖ *progress* of engineering.
[Noun paralleled with noun.]

WRONG *Walking* and *to swim* are good exercise.
[Gerund paralleled with infinitive.]

RIGHT ‖ *Walking* and
‖ *swimming* are good exercise.
[Gerund paralleled with gerund.]

WRONG As a young man he *had been* in Africa, *fighting* in Greece, and *following* his general to India.
[Verb paralleled with participles.]

RIGHT As a young man he ‖ *had been* in Africa,
‖ *had fought* in Greece, and
‖ *had followed* his general to India.
[Verb paralleled with verbs.]

WRONG He was told *to report* at the office and *that he would find* instructions there.
[Infinitive paralleled with subordinate clause.]

RIGHT He was told ‖ *to report* at the office and
‖ *to find* instructions there.
[Infinitive paralleled with infinitive.]

WRONG He was *respected* by his associates, *admired* by his friends, and *his employees loved him.*
[Participles paralleled with a main clause.]

RIGHT He was ‖ *respected* by his associates,
‖ *admired* by his friends, and
‖ *loved* by his employees.
[Participle paralleled with participles.]

EXERCISE. Give parallel structure to co-ordinate ideas.

1. His work is calling meetings and to appoint committees.
2. James disliked the plan, refusing to help in any way.
3. The story is vivid, interesting, and one that appeals to every person.

4. The boy wants to earn his living by tutoring, and also success as a writer.

5. She spends all her time shopping and on her studies.

26b. Whenever necessary to make the parallel clear, repeat a preposition, an article, an auxiliary verb, the sign of the infinitive, or the introductory word of a long phrase or clause.

DIFFICULT I admire Tennyson *for the ideals* in his poems and *his style*.

IMPROVED I admire Tennyson ‖ *for the ideals* in his poems and ‖ *for his style*.

DIFFICULT In the wreck the circus lost *a camel* and *elephant*.

IMPROVED In the wreck the circus lost ‖ *a camel* and ‖ *an elephant*.

DIFFICULT He explained *that* the advertising campaign had been successful, business had increased more than fifty per cent, and additional capital was sorely needed.

IMPROVED He explained ‖ *that* the advertising campaign had been successful, ‖ *that* business had increased more than fifty per cent, and ‖ *that* additional capital was sorely needed.

EXERCISE. Repeat the words needed to show the parallel.

1. They would lie on the battlefield for hours and sometimes days.

2. We Americans think that we cannot enjoy life without a radio, an automobile, and summer home.

286

3. The child learns in nursery school to take his turn, to respect the rights of others, and take care of his materials.
4. The airplane can be used for commercial purposes or defense.
5. Failure is due either to lack of preparation or inability to master the subject.

26c. Correlatives (*either . . . or, neither . . . nor, both . . . and, not only . . . but also, whether . . . or*) should be followed by elements that are parallel in form.

WRONG   He was not only *kind* but also *knew* when to help people in trouble.
[Adjective paralleled with verb.]

RIGHT   He was ‖ *not only kind* ‖ *but also helpful* to people in trouble.

WRONG   I debated whether *I should give* the beggar money or *to offer* him food.
[Subordinate clause paralleled with infinitive.]

RIGHT   I debated ‖ *whether to give* the beggar money ‖ *or to offer* him food.

Caution: Do not use parallel structure for sentence elements not parallel in thought. Never use an awkward or unidiomatic expression for the sake of a parallel. Lack of parallel structure is preferable.

EXERCISE ON PARALLELISM

Express parallel ideas in parallel structure.

1. He was quiet and in a serious mood after the talk.
2. The dictionary shows how and the right place to use a word.
3. She told me to go to town and that I would find him there.

4. There was a difference in the way Andrew ran the farm and Robert's way.

5. The sentences are not hard to classify because they are so difficult, but because they are so entirely different.

6. Mr. Jones is considerate in his system of grading but never giving anyone any more than he has earned.

7. Imagine whizzing down a snow-covered mountain at express-train speed, or leap hundreds of feet and land unhurt.

8. He took up drinking, gambling, and killed several people.

9. I find the college to be a pleasant place and offers many advantages for a liberal education.

10. His smoking and the fact that he uses bad language make him an unsuitable candidate.

11. I predict rain or at least it will be a cloudy day.

12. When you have mastered the fundamentals of writing, and after much practice you will become a good writer.

13. Bok began to help by selling papers and other extra jobs.

14. The real creed of a person should be living rather than in words.

15. She learned the method of home management, how to cook and sew, and about the care of children.

16. To send a package by air mail is much faster than if you send it by express.

17. I like teaching better than to be a stenographer.

18. He told me to study and that I should improve my writing.

19. She liked to play golf and tennis, and swimming was also enjoyed.

20. Tom was undecided whether he should go or to stay and help.

POINT OF VIEW

27. Avoid needless shifts in point of view.

27a. Avoid needless shifting of tense or mood.

WRONG   When he *found* the purse, he *hurries* down town to notify the owner. [A shift from past tense to present tense.]

RIGHT   When he *found* the purse, he *hurried* down town to notify the owner.

WRONG   Ruth soon *discovered* her mistake and *thinks* she *is* in love with Andrew.

RIGHT   Ruth soon *discovers* her mistake and *thinks* that she *is* in love with Andrew.

WRONG   First *rise* to your feet and then you *should address* the chairman. [A shift from imperative to indicative mood.]

RIGHT   First *rise* to your feet and then *address* the chairman.

27b. Avoid needless shifting of subject or voice.

A shift in subject often involves a shift in voice. A shift in voice nearly always involves a shift in subject.

WRONG   James liked fishing, but hunting was also enjoyed by him. [The subject shifts from *James* to *hunting*.]

RIGHT   James liked fishing, but he also enjoyed hunting.

WRONG Mary took courses during the summer, and her leisure hours were devoted to tennis. [The subject shifts from *Mary* to *hours*. The voice shifts from active to passive.]

RIGHT Mary took courses during the summer and devoted her leisure hours to tennis.

WRONG Paul hurried up the mountain path and soon the laurel came in sight. [The subject shifts from *Paul* to *laurel*.]

RIGHT Paul hurried up the mountain path and soon came in sight of the laurel.

27c. Avoid needless shifting of person or number.

WRONG Washington welcomed *us* and the police enjoyed showing *one* where to go. [A shift from first to third person.]

RIGHT Washington welcomed *us* and the police enjoyed showing *us* where to go.

WRONG Go to Florida and there one can find many kinds of palms. [A shift from second to third person.]

RIGHT Go to Florida and there you can find many kinds of palms.

WRONG Take your *raincoat* with you. *They* will be needed today. [A shift from singular to plural.]

RIGHT Take your *raincoat* with you. *It* will be needed today.

EXERCISE ON POINT OF VIEW

Correct all needless shifts in tense, mood, subject, voice, person, or number.

1. When we met with an accident, the car was stopped by the brakes instantly.

2. He composed nature poems as he walked along and later would write them down.

3. I smoothed the chair with fine sandpaper. Always rub with the grain.

4. Later he attended a feast given by the Capulets, and there he meets Juliet.

5. Much time is devoted to art. Music was also taught.

6. I find this hobby very enjoyable, and it gives you something to do in your leisure time.

7. Wherever they went they took their language, and it has been mixed with many other languages.

8. While they are in the midst of the preparation, Ernest came to visit them.

9. The story has a very mysterious plot, but there were too many horrible things that happened.

10. He told his aunt that there is someone in the room.

11. It is a book everyone should read, for you can derive much good from it.

12. Everyone was doing their duty.

13. He shows his kindness in his tender care of her when she was ill.

14. If he is devoted to anyone, he would make any sacrifice for him.

15. When she saw him by her bedside, she thinks that she is dreaming.

16. Each person has some peculiar mannerism of their own.

17. No one could carry on the business until they were willing to take a loss.

18. Pick the roses in the morning, and then they should be placed in water.

19. Mary spent the summer in Boston, and the winter was passed in Florida.

20. Every man in the front line did their duty as they saw it.

21. One should listen to the radio, for over it they hear all the latest news.

28 ref

REFERENCE OF PRONOUNS

28. Make every pronoun refer unmistakably to a definite antecedent.[1]

A pronoun can have meaning only as the reader understands the antecedent (usually a noun or another pronoun) to which it refers. The writer should place all pronouns as close as possible to their antecedents. If the reference is not immediately clear to the reader, or if there is any possibility of confusion, the sentence should be recast.

28a. Avoid ambiguous reference. Construct the sentence in such a way that the reader will not hesitate between two antecedents.

WRONG John told William that he had made a mistake. [Who made the mistake?]

RIGHT John said to William, "You have made a mistake."

RIGHT John said to William, "I have made a mistake."

RIGHT In talking to William, John admitted that he had made a mistake.

WRONG He threw the fish into the lake which his brother had caught.

RIGHT He threw into the lake the fish which his brother had caught.

[1] Complete mastery of section **28** will eliminate the sixth most common error in the average student theme.

WRONG He gave the horses several buckets of water. Soon they were running down the lane.

RIGHT He gave the horses several buckets of water. Soon the refreshed horses were running down the lane.

WRONG It is hard for men to like many people who enjoy solitude.

RIGHT It is hard for men who enjoy solitude to like many people.

28b. Avoid remote reference — reference to an antecedent (1) too far removed from the pronoun or (2) so placed in a subordinate construction that it is not central in the mind of the reader.

Make your meaning immediately clear to the reader. Save him the annoyance of searching about for your antecedent.

REMOTE The *lake* covers many acres. Near the shore water lilies grow in profusion, spreading out their green leaves and sending up white blossoms on slender stems. *It* is well stocked with fish. [The pronoun *it* is too far removed from the antecedent *lake*.]

IMPROVED . . . The *lake* is well stocked with fish. [Repetition of the noun.]

IMPROVED . . . The *water* is well stocked with fish. [A synonym is frequently desirable to avoid repetition.]

WRONG Mr. Green acted the part of Hamlet for Miss Murray's benefit. The proceeds allowed *her* to take a long vacation.

IMPROVED Mr. Green acted the part of Hamlet for Miss Murray's benefit. The proceeds allowed Miss Murray to take a long vacation.

IMPROVED Mr. Green acted the part of Hamlet in a benefit play for Miss Murray, who was thus enabled to take a long vacation.

28c. As a rule avoid broad reference (1) to the general idea of a preceding clause or sentence, (2) to a noun not expressed but merely inferred from some word, or (3) to an indefinite antecedent by the use of *it, you, they.*

Note: Informal English allows much latitude in the use of antecedents that must be inferred from the context. Even formal English sometimes accepts the general idea of a clause as an antecedent when the reference is unmistakable. But it is probably wise for the immature writer to make each of his pronouns refer to a specific substantive.

(1) **As a rule do not refer to the general idea of a preceding clause or sentence.**

WRONG Bernard spent many evenings at the theatre, which influenced him to write a comedy. [*Which* has no antecedent.]

RIGHT Bernard spent many evenings at the theatre and was thus influenced to write a comedy. [Pronoun eliminated].

RIGHT Bernard was influenced by his close association with the theatre to write a comedy. [Pronoun eliminated.]

WRONG One should always salute the flag of the United States. This is a sign of loyalty.

RIGHT One should always salute the flag of the United States. This act is a sign of loyalty.

RIGHT One should always salute the flag of the United States as a means of showing loyalty.

(2) As a rule do not refer to a noun not expressed but merely inferred from some word.

WRONG My mother is a music teacher. It is a profession I know nothing about.

RIGHT My mother is a music teacher, but the teaching of music is a profession I know nothing about.

(3) In formal writing avoid the use of the indefinite *it, you,* or *they.*

WRONG If a person displeased or provoked the authorities, *you* soon were killed.

RIGHT If a person displeased or provoked the authorities, he soon was killed.

RIGHT Anyone displeasing or provoking the authorities was soon killed.

WRONG In France *they* could not understand William.

RIGHT In France William could not be understood.

WRONG In the book *it* says that many mushrooms are edible.

RIGHT The book says that many mushrooms are edible.

Note: The indefinite *it* is correct in such idiomatic expressions as *it seems, it is cold, it is raining.*

28d. Avoid the confusion arising from the repetition in the same sentence of a pronoun referring to different antecedents.

CONFUSING Although *it* is very hot by the lake, *it* furnishes a good place for a good plunge. [The first *it* is the indefinite pronoun; the second *it* refers to *lake.*]

RIGHT Although it is very hot by the lake, the water furnishes a good place for a cool plunge.

EXERCISE ON REFERENCE OF PRONOUNS

Reconstruct the sentences as necessary to correct faults in reference.

1. This story happened in an old abandoned lumber camp on Harton's Bay. It was once a prosperous lumber town, but that had been several years ago.
2. Our language is rich in connectives that exactly express our ideas if they are correctly chosen.
3. Many small boys expect to become policemen because of the daring tasks they have to perform.
4. If a person really loves a horse, he believes that his brain is built similar to a human brain, and that he has the ability to act like any human being.
5. I was asked to keep a little girl while her mother went to the store. As soon as the mother left, she began to cry just as hard as she could.
6. His early life was spent in Bonn, on the Rhine, where he learned during childhood to resent the fact that his family lacked aristocracy. He showed this quite often among his aristocratic friends.
7. His description of the cellar of the castle is very good. He speaks of the piles of bones that were in the cellar. This shows some of the savageness that was in people of that long-ago day.
8. I want a clear understanding of human nature, which can be acquired partly by associating with all classes of people. Is there a better place to do this than in college?
9. The smoke problem needs to be studied in order to do away with it altogether.
10. My worst fault is the inability to express myself clearly in the presence of other people. But this is not true when I am with close friends.
11. The designers seem to use their imagination rather than their intellect in creating the new millinery. Some

look like vegetables, others like fruits, and some even look like stove pipes.

12. Package wrapping has always been my job, because they say that I can do it better than anyone else.

13. I left home and hitchhiked to Miami, Florida. This is not the best means of travel, for I had to walk in the rain and sleep in barns.

14. When building roads, the Romans tried to detour around valleys as much as possible for fear that flood waters might cover them and make them useless.

15. One summer while visiting my grandparents I was attracted by three pigeons that decided to settle in their barn loft.

16. The speaker of the evening was a very good one, but it was not enjoyed by the audience because of the weather.

17. They have a banquet each term for members only.

18. If all the impurities are not removed from the iron, it will deprive steel of its ductility and prevent it from being rolled into bars or drawn into wire.

19. When the termite eggs are hatched they grow wings and fly about the country in swarms.

20. The book makes you sorrowful and then glad. This keeps you aroused through the entire book.

21. Mary told Ann that she would be accepted as a member of the club.

22. The fishermen dumped the fish on the dock that had been caught that day.

23. The story awakens your interest in radium, which continues to the end of the book.

24. The sale of his book was successful. His short stories, too, were well received. This gave him a feeling of accomplishment.

25. There is a notice on the outside of the office door that visitors should heed.

29 emp

29. Select words and arrange the parts of the sentence to give emphasis to important ideas.

Ideas vary in importance and should be stressed accordingly. Emphasis may be gained through choice of concrete, vivid words (see section **20**), through elimination of needless words (see section **21**), and through subordination of less important ideas (see section **24**). Emphasis may also be gained:

a. By placing important words at the beginning or end of the sentence — especially at the end.
b. By changing loose sentences into periodic sentences.
c. By arranging ideas in the order of climax.
d. By using the active instead of the passive voice.
e. By repeating important words.
f. By putting words out of their usual order.

29a. Gain emphasis by placing important words at the beginning or end of the sentence — especially at the end. Whenever possible tuck away in the middle of the sentence parenthetical expressions and other elements of minor importance.

WEAK The colonel will bluntly refuse, in all probability.
[The weakest part of the sentence is given the most
emphatic position — the end.]

BETTER The colonel, in all probability, will bluntly refuse.

POSSIBLE In all probability the colonel will bluntly refuse.

WEAK He became an archbishop in his later years, however.

BETTER In his later years, however, he became an archbishop.

EXERCISE. Gain emphasis by rearranging the parts
of the sentences.

1. He had little success, but he was a tireless worker, if
we may believe the reports.
2. The old man withdrew into his cabin for some good
reason we must suppose.
3. He may become an expert accountant by a study of
business methods at home.
4. A trailer saves hotel expense and can be moved about
from place to place readily.
5. However, he could never redeem himself, in my opinion.

29b. Gain emphasis by changing loose sentences into periodic sentences.

A sentence that holds the reader in suspense until
the end is called *periodic*; one that makes a complete
statement and then adds details is called *loose*. Both
types of sentences are good. The loose sentence, more
commonly used, makes for easy and informal writing.
But the periodic sentence, by reserving the main idea
until the end, is more emphatic. Note the difference
between the following sentences (all of which are good).

LOOSE   We shall have the decision of the judge after the last declamation has been given. [A good sentence.]

PERIODIC   After the last declamation has been given, we shall have the decision of the judges. [More emphatic.]

LOOSE   Practice daily if you want to become a good pianist.

PERIODIC   If you want to become a good pianist, practice daily.

Caution: Do not overuse the periodic sentence to the point of making your style unnatural. Variety is desirable.

EXERCISE. Change the following loose sentences into periodic sentences. Note the gain in emphasis.

1. I attended his wedding, many years ago, on a beautiful June afternoon, in a little village near Cincinnati.
2. He returned to the camp when he found that he could be of no further assistance.
3. It was no concern of mine that he neglected his studies.
4. It is of course easy to stand on the side lines and tell others what to do.
5. The workers were afraid to return until the dam had been repaired.

29c. Gain emphasis by arranging ideas in the order of climax.

UNEMPHATIC   We could hear the roar of cannon, the shrieks of the wounded, and the crash of falling timbers.

EMPHATIC   We could hear the roar of cannon, the crash of falling timbers, and the shrieks of the wounded.

UNEMPHATIC His death was expected at any time. He had
           been in poor health for several months.
EMPHATIC   He had long been in poor health. Almost
            hourly his death was expected.

EXERCISE. Arrange the ideas of each sentence in
order of climax.

1. He left the city because of ill health, failure in business,
   and the loss of his club membership.
2. His confident manner, his knowledge of men, and his
   friendliness made him the logical man for the office.
3. Something must be done at once. The commission is
   faced with a deficit.
4. The boy put into his bag the picture of his best girl,
   his new sweater, and a box of candy.
5. Give me death or give me liberty!

29d. Gain emphasis by using the strong active voice instead of the weak passive voice.

WEAK   Under her arm a long, old-fashioned umbrella
         was carried.
STRONGER Under her arm she carried a long, old-fashioned
         umbrella.

WEAK   Honey was gathered by the bee as it flitted from
         flower to flower.
STRONGER The bee, flitting from flower to flower, gathered
         honey.

Exception: If the receiver of the action is more important
   than the doer, the passive voice is more effective.

   EMPHATIC Wheat is grown in Kansas.
   EMPHATIC Any person who attempts to escape will
            be shot.

EXERCISE. Substitute the active voice for the passive voice.

1. As the station is reached, the train is seen coming around a curve.
2. On her head was worn a beautiful green hat.
3. Paul hesitated to enter the room, for he saw that a poster was being made of Jane.
4. On Sunday afternoon many fishermen may be seen trying their luck.
5. The meetings were decided to be held at the home of the girls.

29e. Gain emphasis by repeating important words.

EMPHATIC If it were *done* when 't is *done*, then 't were well
It were *done* quickly: . . . — SHAKESPEARE

EMPHATIC . . . *wet* roads, *wet* fields, *wet* housetops; not a *beautiful*, scarcely a *picturesque* object met my eyes along the whole route; yet to me, *all* was *beautiful*, *all* was more than *picturesque*.

— CHARLOTTE BRONTË

EMPHATIC There is *no mistake*; there has been *no mistake*; and there shall be *no mistake*.

— DUKE OF WELLINGTON

EMPHATIC . . . that government of the *people*, by the *people*, for the *people*, shall not perish from the earth.

— ABRAHAM LINCOLN

EXERCISE. From your reading copy three passages in which emphasis is gained by the repetition of an important word or phrase.

29f. Gain emphasis by putting a word or phrase out of its natural order.

EMPHATIC Trust her I dare not.
EMPHATIC Never did I think that I should be drafted as a
          private.
EMPHATIC Dampen her enthusiasm you cannot.

Caution: This method of securing emphasis, if overused,
          will make the style distinctly artificial.

EXERCISE ON EMPHASIS

Make the changes necessary to give greater emphasis to
the following sentences.

1. At any time, I shall be ready, no matter how late the
   hour is.
2. Extension courses may be taken for credit during any
   period of the year and, of course, at any place of residence.
3. The girl withdrew from school for some very good
   reason, I hear.
4. The soldiers were outnumbered two to one, as you
   may have heard.
5. Scouting develops a boy morally, mentally, and
   physically.
6. It was no fault of hers that the program was a failure.
7. He saw much to interest him: the Statue of Liberty, the
   Metropolitan Art Museum, the tall buildings, and the
   crowds on the street.
8. As the house is approached, faces are seen at the windows, and the lights are turned on.
9. I met her in Boston, many years ago, in a shop on
   Tremont street, late in the fall.
10. It was evident that some mistake had occurred, as
    everyone had left the house before we came.
11. Around her shoulders was draped a gorgeous Spanish
    shawl.

12. I understood from her answer that she knew where I lived, naturally.

13. He walked quickly away after he had examined the wreck.

14. The garage specializes in the washing and greasing of cars and in minor repairs, according to the advertisement.

15. The opening day was anything but encouraging, however.

16. The art of the Indians was crude, but a great deal of originality was shown by some of them.

17. I shall get bread, meat, sugar, and perhaps some extra articles, along with the order.

18. Her charm, her friendliness, her generosity, and her neat appearance made her a favorite with the girls.

19. We shall appreciate the order for roses, if, as you say, you decide to plant them.

20. Home, friends, a job, and a good hobby are necessary to every man.

21. I want the work to be well done in the first place.

22. Your gift is greatly appreciated by me.

23. The boat sailed from New York to Liverpool, late in October.

24. On the other hand, he had done the best he could, according to his story.

25. The people rushed from the building when the fire alarm sounded.

26. Honesty is the best policy, we are often told.

27. The zero hour had come. Already the armies were marching.

28. Make the most of it if this be treason.

29. The car overturned when we struck a rut in the road.

30. Over his gown was worn a blue hood.

VARIETY

30. Vary the length and the structure of your sentences to make your whole composition pleasing and effective.

Note: Can you distinguish readily between main clauses and subordinate clauses? clauses and phrases? compound sentences and compound predicates? Until you are able to do so you will have little success in learning how to vary your sentences. If necessary, master first the fundamentals of the sentence treated in section **2e, Sentence Sense,** and then study **Variety.**

This section deals only with *good* sentences. The types of sentences which you are cautioned not to overuse are just as good as the types which are called to your attention for the first time. But any type of sentence becomes bad if used so frequently that it bores the reader. The ideal is to have at your command many sentence patterns with which to express your ideas in a varied and pleasing manner. Unless your writing is pleasing, it cannot be effective. Compare the two passages below. Both use good sentences. Both employ the same diction. But the first is made up entirely of simple or compound sentences, each of which begins with the subject followed immediately by the verb. The second varies the sentences.

NOT VARIED:	VARIED:
I had not time to be of help. The wrestler dropped at last, and Alan leaped back to get his distance. He ran upon the others like a bull, and he roared, and he went along. They broke before him like water, and they turned, and they ran. One fell against another in their haste.	But I had not time to be of help. The wrestler dropped at last; and Alan, leaping back to get his distance, ran upon the others like a bull, roaring as he went. They broke before him like water, turning, and running, and falling one against another in their haste. — ROBERT LOUIS STEVENSON

30a. Avoid a series of short, simple sentences. Vary the length.

CHOPPY   I settled back to my place. I recharged the pistols. I had fired them earlier. I kept watch with both eye and ear.

IMPROVED   I settled back to my place, recharging the three pistols I had fired, and keeping watch with both eye and ear.   — ROBERT LOUIS STEVENSON

CHOPPY   Our enemies were disputing. They were upon the deck not far off. They were talking loudly. I could hear a word or two above the washing of the seas.

IMPROVED   Our enemies were disputing not far off upon the deck, and that so loudly that I could hear a word or two above the washing of the seas.

— ROBERT LOUIS STEVENSON

30b. Avoid a series of sentences that begin with the subject.

This type of sentence, like all others discussed in section 30, is good. It should be at the command of every writer. But most freshmen use almost nothing else. To avoid overuse of sentences beginning with the subject the writer may:

(1) Begin with a prepositional phrase.

OVERUSED The lame beggar crouched in the doorway, carefully hiding his box of pennies.

VARIED In the doorway crouched the lame beggar, carefully hiding his box of pennies.

(2) Begin with an adverbial clause.

VARIED While the lame beggar crouched in the doorway, he carefully hid his box of pennies.

(3) Begin with an adverb.

VARIED Carefully hiding his box of pennies, the lame beggar crouched in the doorway.

(4) Begin with an infinitive phrase.

VARIED To hide his box of pennies carefully, the lame beggar crouched in the doorway.

(5) Begin with a participial phrase.

VARIED Hiding carefully his box of pennies, the lame beggar crouched in the doorway.

Caution: Many students already overuse this type of sentence.

(6) Begin with a nominative absolute.

VARIED The box of pennies having been carefully hidden, the lame beggar crouched in the doorway.

(7) Begin with a co-ordinating conjunction.

VARIED And the lame beggar crouched in the doorway, carefully hiding his box of pennies.

EXERCISE. Compose a good sentence that begins with the subject. Then vary it in each of the seven ways indicated on the preceding page.

30c. Avoid a series of aimlessly compound sentences, especially those formed with *and*.

(1) Avoid the compound sentence by using a subordinate clause.

AIMLESSLY COMPOUND   The Mississippi river is the longest river in the world, and in the springtime it often overflows its banks, and many people are endangered.

IMPROVED   The Mississippi River, which is the longest river in the world, often endangers many people during the springtime by overflowing its banks.

(2) Avoid the compound sentence by using a compound predicate.

CHILDISH   He put on his coat, and then he picked up his hat and cane, and then he hurried from the house.

MATURE   He put on his coat, picked up his hat and cane, and then hurried from the house.

(3) Avoid the compound sentence by using an appositive noun or modifiers.

COMPOUND   The town had a population of three thousand, and a tornado struck it, and it was practically demolished.

IMPROVED   The town, a place of three thousand people, was struck by a tornado and practically demolished.

(4) Avoid the compound sentence by using phrases.

COMPOUND   The streets were icy and we could not drive the car.

IMPROVED   On account of the icy streets we could not drive the car.

COMPOUND   He was the mayor of the town, and he was a genial fellow, and he invited the four young boys into his study.

IMPROVED   The mayor of the town, a genial fellow, invited the four young boys into his study.

30d. Learn to vary the subject-verb sequence by inserting words or phrases.

SUBJECT–VERB   The auditorium is across from the park and is a gift of the alumni.

VARIED   The auditorium, across from the park, is a gift of the alumni.

SUBJECT–VERB   The crowd sympathized with the visitors and applauded every good play.

VARIED   The crowd, sympathizing with the visitors, applauded every good play.

30e. Learn how, occasionally, to use a question, an exclamation, or a command instead of the usual statement.

STATEMENT   Even foodstuffs are to be taxed to meet the deficit.

QUESTION   Must we tax even foodstuffs to meet the deficit?

COMMAND   Tax even foodstuffs to meet the deficit.

EXCLAMATION   Imagine taxing even foodstuffs to meet a deficit!

EXERCISE ON VARIETY

Point out the sentence variety in the following paragraphs.

Be sure then to read no mean books. Shun the spawn of the press on the gossip of the hour. Do not read what you shall learn, without asking, in the street and the train. Dr. Johnson said "he always went into stately shops;" and good travellers stop at the best hotels; for though they cost more, they do not cost much more, and there is the good company and the best information. In like manner the scholar knows that the famed books contain, first and last, the best thoughts and facts. Now and then, by rarest luck, in some foolish Grub Street is the gem we want. But in the best circles is the best information. If you should transfer the amount of your reading day by day from the newspaper to the standard authors — But who dare speak of such a thing?

— RALPH WALDO EMERSON

If you have the consciousness of genius, do something to show it. The world is pretty quick, nowadays, to catch the flavor of true originality; if you write anything remarkable, the magazines and newspapers will find you out, as the schoolboys find out where the ripe apples and pears are. Produce anything really good, and an intelligent editor will jump at it. Don't flatter yourself that any article of yours is rejected because you are unknown to fame. Nothing pleases an editor more than to get anything worth having from a new hand. There is always a dearth of really fine articles for the first-rate journal; for, of a hundred pieces received, ninety are at or below the sea-level; some have water enough, but no head; some head enough, but no water; only two or three are from full reservoirs, high up that hill which is so hard to climb.

— OLIVER WENDELL HOLMES

LARGER ELEMENTS

THE PARAGRAPH

Except in dialogue and other special types of writing, paragraphs are usually from one to three hundred words in length. Just as chapters mark the chief divisions of books, paragraphs mark the chief divisions of chapters. The paragraph break gives the reader a breathing spell. It serves notice that he is passing to a new topic or to another part of the topic; to a new place or time in the story, or to a new character.

31. Make paragraphs effective by giving to them unity, coherence, and adequate development.

31a. Give unity to the paragraph by making each sentence contribute to the central thought or topic sentence.

The **topic sentence** gives the gist of the paragraph. Often it is the first sentence, but it may be any sentence in the paragraph; and sometimes it is not expressed at all but merely implied. The topic sentence, whether the writer states it in so many words or not, is the central thought around which he builds his paragraph. Any sentence, any part of a sentence, which does not contribute to this central thought should be stricken out. If the unrelated idea is important, it should be developed in a separate paragraph.

In each of the following unified paragraphs the topic sentence is indicated by italics.

GOOD PARAGRAPH — TOPIC STATED FIRST

A corn-field in July is a sultry place. The soil is hot and dry; the wind comes across the lazily murmuring leaves laden with a warm, sickening smell drawn from the rapidly growing, broad-flung banners of the corn. The sun, nearly vertical, drops a flood of dazzling light upon the field over which the cool shadows run, only to make the heat seem the more intense.[1]   [3 sentences.   66 words.]

— HAMLIN GARLAND

GOOD PARAGRAPH — TOPIC STATED FIRST AND REPEATED AT THE END OF THE PARAGRAPH

A man's fate lies in his own hands. Many of the greatest men the world has ever seen have become great, only after overcoming many obstacles. Abraham Lincoln did not allow poverty to stand in his way. Theodore Roosevelt, although handicapped by a weak physique in his youth, acquired an iron constitution. If these men had not had the will power and determination to overcome their handicaps, they would never have attained success. These men practically decided their own fate. They did nothing miraculous. *Any man who is determined to overcome the obstacles facing him can make of his life what he will.*

[8 sentences.   103 words.]   — STUDENT PARAGRAPH

GOOD PARAGRAPH — TOPIC STATED WITHIN THE PARAGRAPH

His habits were as regular as his person. He daily took his four stated meals, appropriating an hour to each;

[1] From *Main-Travelled Roads*. Reprinted by permission.

he smoked and doubted eight hours, and he slept the remaining twelve of the four-and-twenty. *Such was the renowned Wouter Van Twiller, — a true philosopher, for his mind was either elevated above, or tranquilly settled below, the cares and perplexities of this world.* He had lived in it for years, without feeling the least curiosity to know whether the sun revolved round it, or it round the sun; and he had watched, for at least half a century, the smoke curling from his pipe to the ceiling, without once troubling his head with any of those numerous theories by which a philosopher would have perplexed his brain, in accounting for its rising above the surrounding atmosphere. [4 sentences. 136 words.]

— WASHINGTON IRVING

GOOD PARAGRAPH — TOPIC STATED AT THE END OF THE PARAGRAPH

He is a swarthy man of fifty; well-made and good-looking; with crisp dark hair, bright eyes, and a broad chest. His sinewy and powerful hands, as sunburnt as his face, have evidently been used to a pretty rough life. What is curious about him is, that he sits forward in his chair as if he were, from long habit, allowing space for some dress or accoutrements that he has altogether laid aside. His step too is measured and heavy, and would go well with a weighty clash and jingle of spurs. He is close-shaved now, but his mouth is set as if his upper lip had been for years familiar with a great mustache; and his manner of occasionally laying the open palm of his brown hand upon it, is to the same effect. *Altogether one might guess Mr. George to have been a trooper once upon a time.* [6 sentences. 149 words.]

— CHARLES DICKENS

GOOD PARAGRAPH — WITH THE IMPLIED TOPIC, "SUCH WERE THE ACTIVITIES IN MAIN STREET"

A man in cuffless shirt-sleeves with pink arm-garters, wearing a linen collar but no tie, yawned his way from Dyer's Drug Store across to the hotel. He leaned against the wall, scratched a while, sighed, and in a bored way gossiped with a man tilted back in a chair. A lumber-wagon, its long green box filled with large spools of barbed-wire fencing, creaked down the block. A Ford, in reverse, sounded as though it were shaking to pieces, then recovered and rattled away. In the Greek candy-store was the whine of a peanut-roaster, and the oily smell of nuts.[1]

[4 sentences. 99 words.]   — SINCLAIR LEWIS

Note: The topic sentence, when stated, is most commonly placed first in the paragraph. But some variety is desirable. The uniform beginning of paragraphs with the topic sentence soon becomes monotonous.

FAULTY PARAGRAPH — NO CENTRAL TOPIC

Michigan is a hunter's paradise. Deer, quail, and other kinds of wild game abound in the piney woods of the upper peninsula. Michigan has perhaps more coast line than any other state in the Union, being practically surrounded by Lake Superior, Lake Michigan, and Lake Huron. Along the coast almost every cove affords an ideal location for vacation camps. The lakes that fashion the state into two peninsulas, the upper and the lower, abound in fish which are eagerly sought by fishermen for pleasure or profit.

[The topic shifts from (1) *hunter's paradise* to (2) *coast line* providing sites for *vacation camps* and then to (3) *fishermen.* Each of these ideas might well be developed in a separate paragraph. Another remedy would be to supply a topic sentence, such as *Michigan is a paradise for the lover of the out-of-doors,* to which each of the ideas might be made to contribute.]

IMPROVED — CENTRAL TOPIC SUPPLIED

Michigan is a paradise for the lover of the out-of-doors. Made up of two peninsulas, the upper and the lower, it probably

[1] From *Main Street.* Reprinted by permission of Harcourt, Brace and Company.

314

has more coastline than any other state in the Union. In the waters of Lake Superior, Lake Huron, and Lake Michigan, which practically surround the state, teem fish, eagerly sought by fishermen for pleasure or profit. Here every cove affords an ideal location for vacation camps. Anyone who prefers hunting to fishing can find deer, quail, and other kinds of game in the piney woods of the upper peninsula. Surely Nature was in an extravagant mood when she created Michigan.

FAULTY PARAGRAPH: NEW TOPIC INTRODUCED

An examination is not always a fair test of a student's knowledge. Not infrequently students get nervous and worried while taking examinations. At such times they cannot think clearly and may even forget all they know. On the other hand, some students who study little throughout the year make good grades by cramming just before examinations. In less than a week, however, they will know much less than the faithful student who may be too nervous to set down his ideas in writing. Examinations may also be unfair tests whenever the questions cover only unimportant parts of the course. Teachers who make out such examinations are heartily and justly disliked.

[The last sentence, which introduces a new topic, violates the unity of the paragraph. The sentence should be stricken out; or, if the topic is of sufficient interest to the writer, it may be developed in a second paragraph.]

EXERCISE. Read carefully six paragraphs from some essay, underscoring (or supplying) the topic sentence for each paragraph. Point out any violation of unity.

31b. Give coherence to the paragraph by so interlinking the sentences that the thought may flow smoothly from one sentence to the next.

Rely first of all on (1) arrangement of the sentences in a clear order and then on the use of (2) pronouns referring to the preceding sentence, (3) repeated words or ideas, (4) transitional expressions, and (5) parallel structure.

(1) Arrange the sentences of the paragraph in a clear, logical order.

POOR ARRANGEMENT OF SENTENCES

After the death of Saul, David ruled Israel for forty years. Once he incurred the king's anger and was driven ignominiously from court. As a shepherd lad he had lived in the hills of Judea. He had vanquished the mighty Philistine with his slingshot. The sad-faced Saul was charmed with his songs. He was the sweetest singer in all Israel.

ORDERLY SEQUENCE OF SENTENCES

David, the shepherd lad who lived in the hills of Judea, was the sweetest singer in all Israel. It was he who charmed the sad-faced Saul with his songs. It was he, too, who vanquished the mighty Philistine with his slingshot. Later he incurred the anger of Saul and was driven from court. But upon Saul's death David came back and ruled Israel for forty years.

This paragraph about David is made clearer by re-arrangement in "time order," one of the simplest and best of the ways in which sentences may be arranged. At times sentences that do not lend themselves naturally to chronological order may be grouped in "space order," according to which the paragraph moves from the near to the distant, from the distant to the near, from the left to the right, etc.; or in "order of climax," according to which the movement is from the least to the most important. Any clear and logical order is satisfactory.

(2) Link sentences by means of pronouns referring to antecedents in the preceding sentences.

EXAMPLES

Keimer made verses too, but very indifferently. *He* could not be said to write them, for his manner was to compose them in the types directly out of his head.

— BENJAMIN FRANKLIN

The excessive airs which those people give themselves, founded on the ignorance of us unmarried people, would be more offensive if they were less irrational. We will allow *them* to understand the mysteries belonging to their own craft better than we, who have not had the happiness to be made free of the company: but their arrogance is not content within these limits. — CHARLES LAMB

The word itself (taboo) is used in more than one signification. *It* is sometimes used by a parent to his child. . . .

— HERMAN MELVILLE

The crew are divided into two divisions, as equally as may be, called the watches. Of *these* the chief mate commands the larboard, and the second mate the starboard. *They* divide the time between them. . . .

— RICHARD HENRY DANA, JR.

EXERCISE. In one of your books read carefully several pages of English prose, underlining each pronoun used to link sentences. Check the antecedent (in a preceding sentence) to which each pronoun refers.

(3) Link sentences by repeating words or ideas used in the preceding sentence.

EXAMPLES

But, in a larger sense, we cannot dedicate — we cannot *consecrate* — we cannot hallow this ground. The brave men,

living and dead, who struggled here, have *consecrated* it, far above our poor power to add or detract.
— ABRAHAM LINCOLN

The wind seemed to be *heaving* and *heaving*, with multitudinous little howling devils. They were *heaving* up and *heaving* under. — JOHN MASEFIELD

You found upon that a general *law*, that all hard and green apples are sour; and that, so far as it goes, is a perfect induction. Well, having got your natural *law* in this way. . . . — THOMAS HENRY HUXLEY

The steward is the captain's servant, and has charge of the pantry, from which every one, even the mate himself, is excluded. These *distinctions* usually find him an enemy in the mate. . . . — RICHARD HENRY DANA, JR.
[*Distinctions* repeats an idea rather than a word.]

EXERCISE. Examine again the pages read for the exercise under **31b** (2), underlining each repeated word used to link sentences within the paragraph.

(4) Link sentences by using such transitional expressions as the following:

Addition: moreover, further, furthermore, besides, and, and then, likewise, also, nor, too, again, in addition, equally important, next, first, secondly, thirdly, *etc.*, finally, lastly.

Contrast: but, yet, and yet, however, still, nevertheless, however, on the other hand, on the contrary, after all, notwithstanding, for all that, in contrast to this, at the same time, although this may be true.

Comparison: similarly, likewise, in like manner.

Purpose: to this end, for this purpose, with this object.

Result: hence, therefore, accordingly, consequently, thus, thereupon, wherefore.

Time: meanwhile, at length, immediately, soon, after a few days, in the meantime, afterwards.

Place: here, beyond, near by, opposite to, adjacent to, on the opposite side.

Summary, repetition, exemplification, intensification: to sum up, in brief, on the whole, in sum, in short, as I have said, in other words, to be sure, as has been noted, for example, for instance, in fact, indeed, in any event.

EXAMPLES

It is the unpunctual who are the slaves of time, which constantly rushes them to and fro with whips and scourges. *Further*, unpunctual persons are unmannerly.

— ARNOLD BENNETT

[Note also the repetition of the word *unpunctual* as an aid in coherence.]

It was also in the great hall of the palace of the Olympian king that the gods feasted each day on ambrosia and nectar, their food and drink, the latter being handed round by the lovely goddess Hebe.   *Here* they conversed of the affairs of heaven and earth. . . .   — THOMAS BULFINCH

[Note also the use of the pronoun *they* as an aid in coherence.]

They fought with more pertinacity than bulldogs. . . . *In the meanwhile* there came along a single red ant. . . .

— HENRY DAVID THOREAU

EXERCISE.   Examine again the pages read for the exercise under **31b** (2), underlining all transitional expressions used to link sentences within the paragraph.

(5) Link sentences by means of parallel structure — that is, by repetition of the sentence pattern.

EXAMPLES

Water was gurgling in the ground beneath him. Water was running up his sleeves, and down his neck. Water spouted on him as he beat away the folds to get air.

— JOHN MASEFIELD

[Note also the repetition of the word *water* as an aid in coherence.]

He stood up hurriedly, and the water rose above his boots. He looked up, and an opening in the clouds showed him the moon. . . .   — JOHN MASEFIELD

[Note also the use of the pronoun *he* as an aid in coherence.]

31c. Develop the paragraph adequately. Supply enough information to satisfy the reader, but do not make the paragraph overlong.

(1) Avoid overlong paragraphs.

In modern prose, paragraphs seldom run to more than three or four hundred words, and the average is much shorter. Whenever a writer finds that he needs more than three hundred words to develop his central thought, he should, if possible, divide his material into two or more paragraphs.

EXERCISE. The two following paragraphs were written by Richard Steele more than two hundred years ago. Indicate the two or three paragraphs into which a writer of the present century would probably divide each of Steele's paragraphs.

It is a most vexatious thing to an old man who endeavors to square his notions by reason, and to talk from reflection and experience, to fall in with a circle of young ladies at their afternoon tea-table. This happened very lately to be my fate. The conversation, for the first half-hour, was so very rambling that it is hard to say what was talked of, or who spoke least to the purpose. The various motions of the fan, the tossings of the head, intermixed with all the pretty kinds of laughter, made up the greatest part of the discourse. At last this modish way of shining, and being witty, settled into something like conversation, and the talk ran upon fine gentlemen. From the several characters that were given, and the exceptions that were made, as this or that gentleman happened to be named, I found that a lady is not difficult to be pleased, and that the town swarms with fine gentlemen. A nimble pair of heels, a smooth complexion, a full-bottom wig, a laced shirt, an embroidered suit, a pair of fringed gloves, a hat and feather; any one or more of these and the like accomplishments ennoble a man, and raise him above the vulgar, in a female imagination. On the contrary, a modest, serious behavior, a plain dress, a thick pair of shoes, a leathern belt, a waistcoat not lined with silk, and such like imperfections, degrade a man, and are so many blots in his escutcheon. I could not forbear smiling at one of the prettiest and liveliest of this gay assembly, who excepted to the gentility of Sir William Hearty, because he wore a frieze coat, and breakfasted upon toast and ale. I pretended to admire the fineness of her taste, and to strike in with her in ridiculing those awkward healthy gentlemen that seem to make nourishment the chief end of eating. I gave her an account of an honest Yorkshire gentleman, who (when I was a traveler) used to invite his acquaintance at Paris to break their fast with him upon cold roast beef and mum. There was, I remember, a little French marquis, who was often pleased to rally him unmercifully upon beef and pudding, of which our countrymen would despatch a pound or two with great alacrity, while this antagonist was piddling at a mushroom, or the haunch of a frog. I could perceive the lady was pleased with what I said, and we parted very good friends, by virtue of a maxim I always observe, never to contradict or reason with a sprightly female. I went home, however, full of a great many serious reflections upon what had passed, and though, in complaisance, I disguised my sentiments, to keep up the good humor of my fair companions, and to avoid being looked upon as a testy old fellow, yet out of the good-will I bear to the sex, and to prevent for the future their being imposed upon by counterfeits, I shall give them the distinguishing marks of a true fine gentleman.

[14 sentences. 513 words.]

When a good artist would express any remarkable character in sculpture, he endeavors to work up his figure into all the perfections his imagination can form, and to imitate not so much what is, as what may or ought to be. I shall follow their example, in the idea I am going to trade out of a fine gentleman, by assembling together such qualifications as seem requisite to make the character complete. In order to do this I shall premise in general, that by a fine gentleman I mean a man completely qualified as well for the service and good as for the ornament and delight of society. When I consider the frame of mind peculiar to a gentleman, I supposed it graced with all the dignity and elevation of spirit that human nature is capable of. To this I would have joined a clear understanding, a reason free from prejudice, a steady judgment, and an extensive knowledge. When I think of the heart of a gentleman, I imagine it firm and intrepid, void of all inordinate passions, and full of tenderness, compassion, and benevolence. When I view the fine gentleman with regard to his manners, methinks I see him modest without bashfulness, frank and affable without impertinence, obliging and complaisant without servility, cheerful and in good humor without noise. These amiable qualities are not easily obtained; neither are there many men that have a genius to excel this way. A finished gentleman is perhaps the most uncommon of all the great characters in life. Besides the natural endowments with which this distinguished man is to be born, he must run through a long series of education.

Before he makes his appearance and shines in the world, he must be principled in religion, instructed in all the moral virtues, and led through the whole course of the polite arts and sciences. He should be no stranger to courts and to camps; he must travel to open his mind, to enlarge his views, to learn the policies and interest of foreign states, as well as to fashion and polish himself, and to get clear of national prejudices, of which every country has its share. To all these more essential improvements he must not forget to add the fashionable ornaments of life, such as are the languages and the bodily exercises most in vogue; neither would I have him think even dress itself beneath his notice. [13 sentences. 403 words.]

(2) Avoid short, inadequately developed paragraphs.

In dialogue paragraphs are normally short since a break comes with each speaker. In ordinary writing a very short paragraph is sometimes used for emphasis or for a transition between longer paragraphs. But a series of paragraphs less than fifty words in length (except in dialogue) suggests inadequate development of the thought. If such choppy paragraphs form a unit, they should be combined to develop one topic. If not, each paragraph should be given adequate development.

PARAGRAPHS THAT SHOULD BE COMBINED

A republic is not the best form of government for every nation. Those who advocate a republican form of government for every nation overlook the fact that all nations may not be able to govern themselves.

[2 sentences. 36 words.]

Mexico is an example of such a nation. The inability of the Mexican people to govern themselves has been shown by the repeated revolutions throughout that country.

[2 sentences. 27 words.]

The Mexican people are, as a whole, an illiterate and untrained race. They freely follow the leadership of the most daring man. Because of their ignorance they need a strong leader to guide them until they are capable of governing themselves. [3 sentences. 41 words.]

The American government, after acquiring the Philippine Islands, did not immediately change them into a republic because of their incapability for adopting and understanding the republican form of government. But after the people have been sufficiently educated and fitted to manage a republic, they will be given their freedom. Those who advocate a republican form of government for any nation should first stop and consider the ability of that nation to govern itself. [3 sentences. 73 words.]

[The four paragraphs should be joined to make a unified whole developing the topic, *A republic is not the best form of government for every nation.*]

PARAGRAPHS THAT SHOULD BE EXPANDED

On board a ship the chief mate is a sort of first lieutenant. His duties are numerous and important.

[The reader wants to know more about the duties of the first mate.]

The second mate has a hard life. He does manual labor with the crew, and yet he must expect obedience from his fellow workers.

[Other details should be given to show the hard life of the second mate.]

The cook is more popular than the second mate. His favor is sought by every sailor.

[Something more about the cook is needed — perhaps the reason, or reasons, for his popularity and an incident to illustrate it. Each of the three fragmentary paragraphs given above should be expanded into a paragraph of a hundred words or more.]

(3) Develop the paragraph by any method (or by any combination of methods) that fits your needs.

Analysis shows that good paragraphs may be developed by many methods and by innumerable combinations of methods. Indeed, some good paragraphs almost defy analysis. No one method, or combination of methods, is superior to another. Knowledge of different methods of paragraph development is helpful in that it calls to mind various possibilities for adequate treatment of a topic. A few of the many possible methods of development are illustrated by the following paragraphs.

PARAGRAPHS DEVELOPED BY INSTANCES OR EXAMPLES

The Typee language is one very difficult to be acquired; it bears a close resemblance to the other Polynesian dialects, all of which show a common origin. The duplication of words, as "lumee lumee," "poee poee," "muee muee," is one of their peculiar features. But another, and a more annoying one, is the different senses in which one and the same word is employed; its various meanings all have a certain connection, which only makes the matter more puzzling. So one brisk, lively little word is obliged, like a servant in a poor family, to perform all sorts of duties; for instance, one particular combination of syllables expresses the ideas of sleep, rest, reclining, sitting, leaning, and all other things anywise analogous thereto, the particular meaning being shown chiefly by a variety of gestures and the eloquent expression of the countenance.

[4 sentences. 141 words.]　　　— HERMAN MELVILLE

A nickname can not be manufactured. It just happens. It is something which is taken for granted before anyone realizes that it is a nickname. No amount of thinking could produce a nickname which would stick. In fact, this very thing was tried out during the first World War. When the first division of the A.E.F. was three days out from New York, someone awoke to the fact that our soldiers had no nickname. This was a grave omission on our part, for our Allies had such names as "Tommy" and "Poilu." Suggestions were asked for, but many, such as "Ginga" and "Red Avengers," were pure inventions, while the term "Doughboy" seemed too common. Finally, it was decided that the decision should be left to the French. In France our soldiers were hailed with, "Vive les Lessies," and so for a space of time it was "Leddies." General Pershing did not seem satisfied, and he asked for suggestions from the newspaper men. One paper asked, "How about 'Sammies,' from 'Uncle Sam'?" We thought surely this would stick, but our soldiers objected to it. No one knows who started calling the soldiers "Yanks." No one knows when it was started. It just happened, and it sticks!

[16 sentences. 206 words.] — STUDENT PARAGRAPH

Chivalry is becoming a thing of the past. Men are seldom courteous to women or concerned about their welfare. Take, for example, an incident which occurred in a street car of our city. The car was crowded with clerks who were going home, tired and worn out after a hard day's work; as usual, most of the men had found seats, and many weary women were striving to maintain their balance by hanging onto the jerking, swaying straps overhead. One impertinent old gentleman, evidently priding himself on his good fortune in getting a seat, gazed up into the face of a woman standing near him and inquired if she had voted at the last election. On being answered in the affirmative, he informed her that since she voted like a man, she could stand up like a man, and immediately began a calm perusal of the evening paper. One sees such evidence every day of the disappearance of chivalry, and one is not surprised that women long for "ye good old days when knighthood was in flower."

[7 sentences. 177 words.] — STUDENT PARAGRAPH

A man can make of himself what he will. One of the greatest orators in history became an effective speaker only after he had overcome many obstacles. At the age of seven he was a poor, fatherless boy, severely handicapped by a serious impediment in his speech. But he was ambitious and persevering. He was undaunted by difficulties. He decided to become a statesman, and that he became. But he did not accomplish his purpose without many long, discouraging hours of practice. It is a well known story how, with pebbles in his mouth, he worked to overcome his defect in speech, how he shut himself up in a cell, and how he was derided by the Assembly. But in the end he won out. Such is the story of Demosthenes, the Attic orator and statesman. It was a long way from the awkward, stammering boy on the Grecian seashore to the most skillful, finished speaker of Athens, but his will power and determination carried him along the way, and brought him at last to the coveted goal. [11 sentences. 177 words.]

— STUDENT PARAGRAPH

PARAGRAPHS DEVELOPED BY COMPARISON OR CONTRAST

It is because of this universality of athletic sports that English training is briefer and less severe. The American makes, and is forced to make, a long and tedious business of getting fit, whereas an Englishman has merely to exercise and sleep a trifle more than usual, and this only for a brief period. Our oarsmen work daily from January to July, about six months, or did so before Mr. Lehmann brought English ideas among us; the English 'varsity crews row together nine or ten weeks; Our football players slog daily for six or seven weeks; English teams seldom or never "practice," and play at most two matches a week. Our track athletes are in training at frequent intervals throughout the college year, and are often at the training-table six weeks; in England six weeks is the maximum period of training, and the men as a rule are given only three days a week of exercise on the cinder-track. To an

American training is an abnormal condition; to an Englishman it is the consummation of the normal.[1]

[6 sentences.   177 words.]   — JOHN CORBIN

Stage coaches were fast enough for our grandfathers. But the era in which they lived has given way to an entirely different one, in which rapid transportation plays an all-important part. The growth of the large cities necessitates swift communication and transportation. In the days in which our grandfathers conducted their affairs, small villages and many farms were the rule. The inhabitants of the villages and the independent farmers could obtain all that was needed for their living at home or near at hand, and commerce with outside communities was not necessary. In these days, however, the inhabitants of the large cities and towns, which have to a large extent taken the places of the villages and individual farms, are dependent on others for the necessities of life. Forces often far removed from the place of consumption furnish these necessities, which must be transported with great speed to the consumers. Formerly all that was needed for a community could be produced within itself or within easy traveling distance, but now all the necessities of a community must be transported great distances. [8 sentences.   181 words.]

                              — STUDENT PARAGRAPH

There is perhaps no better place in the world in which to study people than in New York City. It is a city of contrasts, of lights and shadows. One need ride only a mile or two in the great metropolis to find as strong contrasts in types of people as one would find in riding thousands of miles in other parts of the world. There is, first of all, the wealthy, fashionable society class. The families of such live on Fifth Avenue, in handsome old residences with coats of arms over the door. They arrive in luxurious limousines, and once in a while they even deign to glance over the heads of their fluffy, white poodle-dogs at the plebeian pedestrians. They are haughty, proud, superior;

[1] Reprinted from *An American at Oxford*, by permission of the author.

but have they not a right to be? they seem to say. He has an office in Wall Street, and she had the most elaborate debutante party in years. They are aristocrats, and they are well aware of their superiority. Then there are the immigrants — poor, ignorant foreigners, who live on the East Side in damp, cold, dark cellars. The foul odor, the filth, the noise from the elevated railroads — all this is maddening to the outsider. The children play in the dirty, narrow, winding streets. Their faces, although haggard and wizened, show traces of life and intelligence, while those of their parents are hard, and show signs of oppression, misery, and hunger. The steps of these older ones, as they go about their tiny shops, are slow from drudgery and poverty. Poor, unhappy wretches! They have so little, and the rich have so much. [15 sentences. 270 words.]

— STUDENT PARAGRAPH

A tree or a bush — which is the better for a man to pattern his life after? The life of a man may indeed closely resemble the life of a tree or a bush. A tree is tall and stately, growing ever upwards as if it had but one purpose, and that — to reach the skies. A bush is just the opposite. It spreads itself out and sends its branches here and there and everywhere as if it can never make up its mind what its purpose of existence is. Cannot the life of a man be like this? One man, like unto the tree, has a set goal and a firm purpose towards which he constantly struggles. He overcomes the obstacles that confront him and goes straight forward, never faltering, never swerving. Another, like the bush, never comes to any conclusion as to what is his ideal, his aim in life. He has no goal that is a constant inspiration to him. He aims towards nothing, but is first swayed this way and then that by his changing moods. He follows every whim, and with a new one, changes for the hundredth time. The first man achieves great success and rises high as does the tree; the other is at the end a failure, living in the shadow of the tree. And now — which is the better? Let each speak for itself.

[15 sentences. 232 words.]   — STUDENT PARAGRAPH

PARAGRAPHS DEVELOPED BY DEFINITION

Well, what I mean by Education is learning the rules of this mighty game. In other words, education is the instruction of the intellect in the laws of Nature, under which name I include not merely things and their forces, but men and their ways; and the fashioning of the affections and of the will into an earnest and loving desire to move in harmony with those laws. For me, education means neither more nor less than this. Anything which professes to call itself education must be tried by this standard, and if it fails to stand the test, I will not call it education, whatever may be the force of authority or of numbers upon the other side. [4 sentences. 119 words.]

— THOMAS HENRY HUXLEY

An explanation of the "dog watches" may, perhaps, be of use to one who has never been at sea. They are to shift the watches each night, so that the same watch need not be on deck at the same hours. In order to effect this, the watch from four to eight P.M. is divided into two half, or dog, watches, one from four to six, and the other from six to eight. By this means they divide the twenty-four hours into *seven* watches instead of *six*, and thus shift the hours every night. As the dog watches come during twilight, after the day's work is done, and before the night watch is set, they are the watches in which everybody is on deck. The captain is up, walking on the weather side of the quarter-deck, the chief mate on the lee side, and the second mate about the weather gangway. The steward has finished his work in the cabin, and has come up to smoke his pipe with the cook in the galley. The crew are sitting on the windlass or lying on the forecastle, smoking, singing. or telling long yarns. At eight o'clock, eight bells are struck, the log is hove, the watch set, the wheel relieved, the galley shut up, and the other watch goes below. [8 sentences. 219 words.] — RICHARD HENRY DANA, JR.

PARAGRAPHS DEVELOPED BY ENUMERATION OF DETAILS
OR REASONS

My aunt was a tall, hard-featured lady, but by no means ill-looking. There was an inflexibility in her face, in her voice, in her gait and carriage, amply sufficient to account for the effect she had made upon a gentle creature like my mother; but her features were rather handsome than otherwise, though unbending and austere. I particularly noticed that she had a very quick, bright eye. Her hair, which was gray, was arranged in two plain divisions, under what I believe would be called a mobcap; I mean a cap, much more common then than now, with sidepieces fastening under the chin. Her dress was of a lavender color, and perfectly neat, but scantily made, as if she desired to be as little encumbered as possible. I remember that I thought it, in form, more like a riding-habit with the superfluous skirt cut off, than anything else. She wore at her side a gentleman's gold watch, if I might judge from its size and make, with an appropriate chain and seals; she had some linen at her throat not unlike a shirt collar, and things at her wrists like little shirt wristbands.

[7 sentences. 193 words.]   — CHARLES DICKENS

The captain, in the first place, is lord paramount. He stands no watch, comes and goes when he pleases, and is accountable to no one, and must be obeyed in everything, without a question, even from his chief officer. He has the power to turn his officers off duty, and even to break them and make them do duty as sailors in the forecastle. Where there are no passengers and no supercargo, as in our vessel, he has no companion but his own dignity, and no pleasures, unless he differs from most of his kind, but the consciousness of possessing supreme power, and, occasionally, the exercise of it.   [4 sentences. 108 words.]

— RICHARD HENRY DANA, JR.

The second mate's is proverbially a dog's berth. He is neither officer nor man. The men do not respect him as an officer, and he is obliged to go aloft to reef and furl the topsails, and to put his hands into the tar and slush, with the rest. The crew call him the "sailor's waiter," as he has to furnish them with spun-yarn, marline, and all the other stuffs that they need in their work, and has charge of the boatswain's locker, which includes serving-boards, marline-spikes, et cetera. He is expected by the captain to maintain his dignity and to enforce obedience, and still is kept at a great distance from the mate, and obliged to work with the crew. He is one to whom little is given and of whom much is required. His wages are usually double those of a common sailor, and he eats and sleeps in the cabin; but he is obliged to be on deck nearly all his time, and eats at the second table, that is, makes a meal out of what the captain and the chief mate leave.

[7 sentences. 186 words.]   — RICHARD HENRY DANA, JR.

PARAGRAPHS DEVELOPED BY COMBINATIONS OF METHODS

It is to the newer countries — that is, to the countries where material progress is yet in its earlier stages — that laborers emigrate in search of higher wages, and capital flows in search of higher interest. It is in the older countries — that is to say, the countries where material progress has reached later stages — that widespread destitution is found in the midst of the greatest abundance. Go into one of the new communities where Anglo-Saxon vigor is just beginning the race of progress; where the machinery of production and exchange is yet rude and inefficient; where the increment of wealth is not yet great enough to enable any class to live in ease and luxury; where the best house is but a cabin of logs or a cloth and paper shanty, and the richest man is forced to daily work — and though you will find an absence of wealth and all its concomitants, you will find no beggars. There is no luxury, but there is no destitution. No one makes an easy living, nor a very good living; but every one *can* make a living, and no one able and willing to work is oppressed by the fear of want.

[5 sentences. 200 words.]   — HENRY GEORGE

[Developed chiefly by comparison and details.]

I have never understood why a good fake should not be as valuable as an original. If a man can reproduce an article so that not one man in ten thousand can tell the difference between the model and the copy, what element is it in the model which gives it its value? I can understand its having a special value, if it is an object of peculiar historical interest. For instance, the actual sword which Cromwell wore at Naseby would be amusing, and one would be annoyed to find that one had been palmed off with a copy. But when it comes to reproducing a Chippendale chair, or an old frame, what does it matter whether you have the form as it was first put forth, or its exact double? [1]   [5 sentences.   131 words.]

— HILAIRE BELLOC

[Developed chiefly by comparison and examples.]

EXERCISES.   A. Indicate the method of development that seems most appropriate for each of the following topic sentences.

1. Life in a big city has its disadvantages as well as its advantages.
2. Sometimes we fail to sense the true meaning of patriotism.
3. Americans dislike walking.
4. Students should acquire the habit of thinking for themselves.
5. A man is not always master of his fate.
6. The study of birds is a fascinating avocation.
7. There is no such thing as an uneducated man.
8. We need (do not need) a larger stadium.
9. The snowstorm created a new world.
10. Life moves at a faster pace in the North than in the South.

[1] Reprinted from *Short Talks with the Dead and Others*, by permission of Harper & Brothers.

11. Dams are valuable in the defense program.
12. A columnist should have an open mind.
13. It is more fun to swim in the ocean than in a lake.
14. Two states claim the distinction of being the birth-place of Andrew Jackson.
15. The youth of today needs a practical education.
16. Football players on college teams should (should not) be paid for their services.
17. The TVA has brought prosperity to the South.
18. There is gold in the Kentucky hills.
19. The center of population has shifted.
20. The cheering section is an important factor at a football game.

B. From one of the topic sentences develop a paragraph by giving instances or examples.

C. From one of the topic sentences develop a paragraph by comparison or contrast.

D. From one of the topic sentences develop a paragraph by definition.

E. From one of the topic sentences develop a paragraph by giving details or reasons.

F. From one of the topic sentences develop a paragraph by a combination of methods.

plan 32

PLANNING THE WHOLE COMPOSITION

32. Select an appropriate subject and arrange your ideas effectively.

32a. Select an appropriate subject.

(1) Select a subject that appeals to you.

Below are listed, not titles for papers, but suggestions which may be helpful in finding a suitable title. Some of the suggestions will meet, without change in wording, the needs of a proposed paper. In that case only proper capitalization (see section 9c) will be needed to make the suggestion into a title. More frequently, perhaps, a suggestion will need limitation or sharpening of wording before it is suitable as a title.

SUGGESTIONS FOR WRITTEN WORK
Home and the Individual

1. Being an elder brother
2. Being a younger sister
3. The first money I ever earned
4. My first date
5. How I plan my budget
6. What makes a gentleman?
7. Stamp collecting as a hobby
8. Keeping a scrap book
9. My pet ambition
10. My pet aversion
11. People who have influenced my thinking
12. Apron strings

335

13. Am I a good citizen?
14. A vivid childhood memory
15. Letter writing as an art
16. An unusual hobby
17. My hobby and why I like it
18. The appeal of bargains
19. Speaking on the radio
20. The duties of a social secretary
21. Forms of stinginess
22. Who is the average person?
23. Getting out of a rut
24. How I spent my first dime
25. My first long trousers
26. Robbing a wasp's nest
27. My first picture
28. Living from one pay day to the next
29. Why I dislike my name
30. How to choose neckties
31. A character from fiction I should like to meet
32. The only child
33. What old people have taught me
34. Every boy should have a dog
35. How to tame a chipmunk
36. My home town
37. Rice and old shoes
38. The nuisance of the radio
39. The radio and adult education
40. My first vacation

School and College

1. Thoughts upon entering college
2. Freshman Week
3. Homesickness
4. Earning one's way through college
5. The night before the big game
6. College slang
7. Sadie Hawkins' Day
8. Why I am going to college
9. My English (history, Spanish) teacher
10. The value of convocation
11. NYA and the colleges
12. Life in a fraternity (sorority) house
13. The fraternity initiation
14. Waiting on the table in a cafeteria
15. Freshmen should wear green caps
16. The chaperone, then and now
17. Peculiarities of the college team
18. Are examinations fair?
19. The writing laboratory
20. The cheering section in action

plan 32

Health, Recreation, and Sports

1. The coon hunt
2. A summer camp in the mountains
3. Horseback trails
4. Walking in the snow
5. Suitable swimming places
6. The value of social dancing
7. Duties of a camp counselor
8. Is play a waste of time?
9. Learning to bowl
10. The value of good posture
11. Origin and development of tennis
12. How to hike and enjoy it
13. Youth hostels
14. Interesting trails in the Smokies
15. Folk dancing for fun
16. Lifesaving as a vocation
17. Are athletes dumb?
18. Pitching a tent
19. Golf, a sport for the young and the old
20. Badminton
21. Sport with bow and arrow
22. Athletics in ancient Greece
23. Can the average length of life be increased?
24. What is jazz?
25. Learning to swim
26. The art of tap dancing
27. The future of professional football
28. What is a good sport?
29. Collecting old glass
30. Shooting with the camera
31. Around the country in a trailer
32. America likes baseball
33. What is sportsmanship?
34. Football is a spectacle
35. Tying trout flies
36. Directing a campfire group
37. Fishing for mountain trout
38. Making a campfire
39. Sailing a boat
40. Duties of the quarterback

Economics and Sociology

1. How to buy a used car
2. What is the freight differential?
3. Should medicine be socialized?
4. Visible results of the TVA
5. The war and the American tourist
6. The National Park Service
7. Soil conservation
8. Share croppers in the South

32 plan

9. CCC camps
10. Racketeering and racketeers
11. The South, the nation's number one problem (hope)
12. Causes of juvenile delinquency
13. What is a pacifist?
14. What constitutes national wealth?
15. The rich resources of Alaska
16. Unemployment insurance
17. Old-age pensions
18. The used-car problem
19. The government housing projects
20. Advertising over the radio
21. G-man
22. The tobacco auction
23. Where does the tax money go?
24. The purpose of the clearinghouse
25. Good and bad advertising
26. The problem of the Dust Bowl
27. How to apply for a job as a reporter
28. How to sell magazines
29. Securing a Federal farm loan
30. Reciprocal trade agreements
31. Peruvian gold
32. Argentina, the world's granary
33. Cuba, the world's sugar bowl
34. Life in the Amazon jungle
35. Production of Panama hats
36. Ranching in the Argentine
37. The parole system
38. Bee keeping
39. The gold hoard in Kentucky
40. The right to strike

History and Political Science

1. The Pony Express
2. The Mugwumps
3. Colonial sports
4. The Stamp Act
5. The Monroe Doctrine applied today
6. The Louisiana Purchase
7. The purchase of Alaska
8. The "Good-neighbor Policy" of F.D.R.
9. The third term for President
10. Maximilian in Mexico
11. The lost state of Franklin
12. The woman's movement in England
13. The Rome-Berlin Axis
14. The mutiny on the *Bounty*

plan 32

15. Palestine, the Zionist movement
16. The fight between the C.I.O. and the A.F. of L.
17. The new agrarian policy in Mexico
18. Expropriation of oil in Mexico
19. The Pan American Union
20. The diplomatic background of the Panama Canal

Biological Sciences

1. Iris in Tennessee
2. Wild plants and their uses in medicine
3. Fire, the enemy of the forests
4. Can the average length of life be increased?
5. Vaccination for smallpox
6. Vitamins from plants
7. Insect pollination
8. Typhoid carriers
9. Plants as soil binders
10. Mushrooms
11. Veneer woods
12. Seed dispersal
13. Loss to crops by chewing insects
14. The history of the Japanese beetle
15. The story of the honey bee
16. Chemical warfare on insects
17. The termite
18. Selection of timber for furniture making
19. Aquarium plants
20. Sea weeds: the kelps and their relatives
21. Mushroom poisoning
22. Yeasts and vitamins
23. Household insects
24. Artificial pollination of corn
25. Migration of birds
26. Canned blood (called *plasma*)
27. The window garden
28. Feeding birds in winter
29. Industrial diseases
30. How to collect butterflies
31. How to estimate standing timber
32. Do animals ever remember?
33. Horses have personalities
34. What to plant in a flower garden
35. Bacteriophage
36. Microbes of Bubonic Plague
37. Pasteur and the serum for hydrophobia
38. Plant respiration
39. Insect pollination
40. Beneficial bacteria

32 plan

Chemistry and Physics

1. Synthetic diamonds
2. Nylon, the new silk
3. Thunder and lightning
4. Amateur photography
5. The atom
6. Perfumes
7. Mirages
8. The properties of rayon
9. The history of table salt
10. Dalton and the atomic theory
11. Hard and soft water
12. Alloys and their uses
13. The making of soap
14. What is food allergy?
15. The work of ultraviolet rays
16. The discovery of insulin
17. The spectroscope
18. Discovery of iodine
19. Why is wood smoke blue?
20. Sulfanilamide
21. Sweet potato starch
22. Coal, the raw material of many products
23. The chemistry of warfare
24. Plastics
25. High octane gasoline
26. Atmospheric fixation of nitrogen
27. Dyestuffs from coal
28. Wood distillation
29. The by-products of copper
30. The dry cell

Agriculture

1. The value of hotbeds and cold frames to the farmer
2. How to grow tomatoes
3. The gross structure of a plant
4. Strawberry growing
5. Chrysanthemums for the home
6. Growing dahlias
7. The electric hotbed
8. The production of turnip seed
9. Soil erosion, a national problem
10. The value of the farm wood lot
11. Wild life on the farm
12. The apple from the tree to the consumer
13. How to make a hot bed
14. How to produce quality cotton
15. The benefits of diversified farming
16. The Federal Farm Loan system
17. How great cities are fed
18. Problems of share cropping
19. Dandelions
20. Good seeds make good crops

21. Filling a silo
22. Wild onions
23. Making a tobacco bed
24. Care of a lawn
25. Work of the 4-H Club
26. The work of the county agent
27. The home demonstration worker
28. Frozen foods
29. Making butter
30. Raising a prize calf

31. Judging cattle
32. Curing tobacco
33. Budding trees
34. Mushroom cultivation
35. Spraying fruit trees
36. A dairy show
37. Growing asparagus
38. Hybrid corn
39. Controlling Johnson grass
40. The value of winter cover crops

Engineering

1. Newsprint from Southern pine
2. Electricity in the modern home
3. The depth bomb
4. The powder plant
5. Mining tin
6. The incandescent lamp
7. Laying out the railroad curve
8. Planning a skyscraper
9. How to read a gas meter
10. Diesel engines
11. The future of television
12. Air conditioning every home
13. Boulder Dam
14. The most wonderful machine I know
15. Construction of the Panama Canal
16. Construction of the Suez Canal
17. Building a warship

18. Assembling an automobile
19. Painting automobiles
20. Operating a tractor
21. Making a short-wave set
22. The cream separator
23. Flying an airplane
24. Hydraulic brakes
25. Electric refrigeration
26. Gas refrigeration
27. The mining of coal
28. Manufacturing paper bags
29. Bridging the Mississippi
30. Concrete highways
31. The electric vacuum cleaner
32. A machine gun
33. The Springfield rifle
34. Spillways
35. Smelting iron ore
36. Gliders
37. Training for aviation
38. The airplane engine

Home Economics

1. How to set a table for two
2. The importance of vegetables in one's diet
3. Table manners and customs
4. The story of bread making
5. Foods in the Bible
6. Government grading of foods
7. Mosaics and their use
8. What the consumer should know about the foods he buys
9. Family life yesterday and today
10. Shoes ancient and modern
11. Diet and dental disease
12. Food fads and fallacies
13. Safety in the home
14. Pellagra in the South
15. Planning a wardrobe
16. The family budget
17. The value of the nursery school
18. The baby in the practice house
19. What is a home?
20. The efficient kitchen
21. The efficient buyer of foods
22. Is cheap food economical?
23. How to test woolen cloth
24. The value of the apple in the diet
25. What we know about vitamin A
26. Milk in the child's diet
27. Symbolism in design
28. Period furniture for dining rooms
29. The soy bean in the human diet
30. Weight reduction

(2) Limit the subject to fit the needs of the proposed paper and sharpen the wording of the title.

Never select a title that is too broad for adequate treatment in the proposed theme. If you wish to write a paper of several thousand words, "Amateur Photography" may be a satisfactory title. But if you plan to write only a few hundred words, you should limit yourself to one phase of the subject, such as "Developing a Film" or "The Growth of My Interest in Photography."

EXERCISE. From the "SUGGESTIONS FOR WRITTEN WORK" select five topics suitable, without limitation, for papers of five hundred words. Select five others suitable as titles for longer papers, or even for books. Suggest phases of these broader topics that might serve as titles for short papers.

32b. Make an outline of the type specified by your instructor. The types most commonly used are:

(1) The complete sentence outline.

(2) The topical outline.

(3) The paragraph outline.

What the blueprint is to the builder the outline is to the writer. On going into a house under construction, one will find the builder erecting every part according to carefully drawn plans. After the house has been completed, one no more expects to see the blueprints lying around than to see an outline printed with an essay. But as long as the house is being built, the plans are most important. And so is the outline of great value to the writer until he has completed his paper.

Many persons prefer the complete sentence outline on the ground that it means more to the person who reads it. To the writer a topical outline may be clear enough and, at the same time, almost meaningless to the reader. The use of complete sentences forces the writer to express himself with greater clarity. Complete sentence outlines and topical outlines have the same parts and the same grouping; they differ only in the fullness of expression. The paragraph outline differs widely. It makes no effort to classify the material into major headings and subheadings but simply gives the topics of paragraphs in the order in which they come.

Let us observe more closely the nature of an outline by reading a short essay and then reconstructing the outline on which the essay was written.

RIVETING A SKYSCRAPER [1]

The most curious fact about a riveter's skill is that he is not one man but four: "heater," "catcher," "bucker-up," and "gun-man." The gang is the unit. Riveters are hired and fired as gangs, work in gangs, and learn in gangs. If one member of a gang is absent on a given morning, the entire gang is replaced. A gang may continue to exist after its original members have all succumbed to slippery girders or the business end of a pneumatic hammer or to a foreman's zeal or merely to the temptations of life on earth. And the skill of the gang will continue with it. Men overlap each other in service and teach each other what they know. The difference between a gang which can drive 525 inch-and-an-eighth rivets in a working day and a gang which can drive 250 is a difference of co-ordination and smoothness. You learn how not to make mistakes and how not to waste time. You learn how to heat a rivet and how not to overheat it, how to throw it accurately but not too hard, how to drive it and when to stop driving it, and precisely how much you can drink in a cold wind or a July sun without losing your sense of width and the balance of a wooden plank. And all these things, or most of them, an older hand can tell you.

The actual process of riveting is simple enough — in description. Rivets are carried to the job by the rivet boy, a riveter's apprentice whose ambition it is to replace one of the members of the gang — which one, he leaves to luck. The rivets are dumped into a keg beside a small coke furnace. The furnace stands on a platform of loose

[1] From "Skyscrapers: Builders and Their Tools," *Fortune*, II (October, 1930), 85–94. Copyright *Time, Inc.* Reprinted by permission.

boards roped to steel girders which may or may not have been riveted. If they have not been riveted there will be a certain amount of play in the temporary bolts. The furnace is tended by the heater or passer. He wears heavy clothes and gloves to protect him from the flying sparks and intense heat of his work, and he holds a pair of tongs about a foot-and-a-half long in his right hand. When a rivet is needed, he whirls the furnace blower until the coke is white hot, picks up a rivet with his tongs, and drives it into the coals. His skill as a heater appears in his knowledge of the exact time necessary to heat the steel. If he over-heats it, it will flake, and the flakes will permit the rivet to turn in its hole. And a rivet which gives in its hole is condemned by the inspectors.

When the heater judges that his rivet is right, he turns to face the catcher, who may be above or below him or fifty or sixty or eighty feet away on the same floor level with the naked girders between. There is no means of handing the rivet over. It must be thrown. And it must be accurately thrown. And if the floor beams of the floor above have been laid so that a flat trajectory is essential, it must be thrown with considerable force. The catcher is therefore armed with a smallish, battered tin can, called a "cup," with which to catch the red-hot steel. Various patented cups have been put upon the market from time to time, but they have made little headway. Catchers prefer the ancient can.

The catcher's position is not exactly one which a sports-man catching rivets for pleasure would choose. He stands upon a narrow platform of loose planks laid over needle beams and roped to a girder near the connection upon which the gang is at work. There are live coils of pneumatic tubing for a rivet gun around his feet. If he moves more than a step or two in any direction, he is gone; and if he loses his balance backward he is apt to end up at street level without time to walk. And the object is to catch a red-hot iron rivet weighing anywhere from a quarter of a pound to a pound and a half and capable, if he lets it pass, of drilling an automobile radiator or a man's skull 500 feet below as neatly as a shank of shrapnel. Why more rivets do not fall is the great mystery of skyscraper construction. The only reasonable explanation offered to date is the reply of an erector's foreman who was asked what would happen if a catcher on the Forty Wall Street job let a rivet go by him around lunch hour. "Well," said the foreman, "he's not supposed to."

There is practically no exchange of words among riveters. Not only are they averse to conversation, which would be reasonable enough in view of the effect they have on the conversation of others, but they are averse to speech in any form. The catcher faces the heater. He holds his tin can up. The heater swings his tongs, releasing one handle. The red iron arcs through the air in one of those parabolas so much admired by the stenographers in the neighboring windows. And the tin can clanks.

Meantime the gun-man and the bucker-up have prepared the connection — aligning the two holes, if necessary, with a drift pin driven by a sledge or by a pneumatic hammer — and removed the temporary bolts. They, too, stand on loose-roped boards with a column or the beam between them. When the rivet strikes the catcher's can, he picks it out with a pair of tongs held in his right hand, knocks it sharply against the steel to shake off the glowing flakes, and rams it into the hole, an operation which is responsible for his alternative title of sticker. Once the rivet is in place, the bucker-up braces himself with his dolly bar, a short heavy bar of steel, against the capped end of the rivet. On outside wall work he is sometimes obliged to hold on by one elbow with his weight out over the street and the jar of the riveting shaking his precarious balance. And the gunman lifts his pneumatic hammer to the rivet's other end.

The gun-man's work is the hardest work, physically, done by the gang. The hammers in use for steel construction work are supposed to weigh around thirty pounds and actually weigh about thirty-five. They must not only be held against the rivet end, but held there with the gunman's entire strength, and for a period of forty to sixty seconds. (A rivet driven too long will develop a collar inside the new head.) And the concussion to the ears and to the arms during that period is very great. The whole platform shakes, and the vibration can be felt down the column thirty stories below. It is common practice for the catcher to push with the gun-man, and for the gun-man and the bucker-up to pass the gun back and forth between them when the angle is difficult. Also on a heavy rivet job the catcher and the bucker-up may relieve the gun-man at the gun.

(1) For a complete sentence outline express each heading in the form of a sentence according to the following model:

RIVETING A SKYSCRAPER

CENTRAL IDEA Riveting requires skillful work under dangerous conditions.

I. Riveters work in well co-ordinated, skillful gangs of four.

    A. The gang works as a unit.

    B. Replacements are made by an overlapping of service.

    C. Skill, judgment, and experience are required.

II. The rivets must be prepared.

    A. The rivets are brought to the furnace by the rivet boy.

    B. The furnace stands in a precarious position.

    C. The heater must have specialized equipment and skill.

        1. He must have special clothing and tongs.

        2. He must have skill in order to heat the rivets properly.

III. Passing the rivets from the furnace to the place where they are used is an exacting and dangerous process.

 A. Rivets must be thrown, sometimes under difficult conditions.

 B. The catcher receives them in a battered tin "cup."

 C. He stands in a dangerous position.

 D. Only his skill in catching red-hot rivets insures the safety of the persons below.

 E. The whole process of passing rivets is conducted silently and methodically.

IV. Securing the rivets in place requires the exercise of great strength, dexterity, and co-operation.

 A. The gun-man and the bucker-up align the holes from dangerous positions.

 B. The catcher inserts the red-hot rivet.

 C. The bucker-up braces himself with his dolly bar against the end of the rivet.

 D. The gun-man has the heaviest work.

  1. He must handle the heavy gun.

  2. He must endure great concussion and vibration.

  3. He usually is assisted by the catcher.

  4. He sometimes passes the gun to the bucker-up.

(2) For a topical outline express each heading in the form of a noun or phrase according to the following model:

RIVETING A SKYSCRAPER

I. Skillful co-ordination of a riveting gang of four.

 A. Unity of the gang.

 B. Replacements of members.

 C. Necessity for skill, judgment, and experience.

II. Preparation of the rivets.

    A. Delivery to the furnace.

    B. Precarious position of the furnace.

    C. Work of the heater.

        1. His equipment.

        2. His skill.

III. Passing of the red-hot rivets.

    A. Need for throwing.

    B. Receptacle used by the catcher.

    C. Dangerous position of the catcher.

    D. Skill of the catcher.

    E. Silence during the whole process.

IV. Securing the rivets in place.

    A. Alignment of the holes.

    B. Insertion of the rivet.

    C. Precarious work of the bucker-up.

    D. Hard work of the gun-man.

        1. Use of the heavy gun.

        2. Concussion and vibration.

        3. Assistance from the catcher.

        4. Interchange with the bucker-up.

(3) In a paragraph outline express the gist of each paragraph in a sentence according to the following model:

RIVETING A SKYSCRAPER

1. Riveters work in well co-ordinated, skillful gangs of four men.

2. Rivets must be heated with care.

3. The red-hot rivets must be thrown to the place where the riveting is being done.

4. The catcher, standing in a dangerous position, must have great skill.

5. The whole process of throwing and catching the rivets is carried on in silence.

6. The catcher, the gun-man, and the bucker-up co-operate in securing the rivet in place.
7. The work of the gun-man is the hardest.

32c. Develop the outline as necessary during the preparation of the paper.

The outline given above for "Riveting a Skyscraper" represents the author's finished work, the most perfect organization he has been able to achieve. No doubt the outline was repeatedly changed from the time the author began to assemble his first disorganized ideas about riveters until he had the article finally ready for press. And some of the changes, perhaps, were made as late as the final revision. For the outline is a developing, growing plan which the writer does not hesitate to change at any stage of his composition whenever he hits upon a way to improve it. He naturally tries to perfect his plan before starting the writing, but the actual writing will almost certainly suggest a few further changes in organization.

The first step toward an outline is the jotting down of ideas on the subject. The student may find that he needs to supplement his knowledge by observation and by reading. He should not hesitate to jot down a long list of ideas. Classification of ideas and rejection of needless ones will be easier than the finding of something worth including. Anyone starting an outline on "Riveting a Skyscraper" might set down a list somewhat as follows:

1. Throwing the rivets.
2. The gun.
3. Noise of the gun.
4. The catcher and his can.

5. The bucker-up and his dolly bar.
6. Work of the gun-man.
7. The furnace.
8. Skill required in heating.
9. The rivet boy's duties.
10. Danger from dropped rivets.
11. Danger to the riveters.
12. Co-operation of the gang.
13. Replacements.
14. The actual process of inserting the rivets.
15. Insurance rates for riveters.

The next step is the grouping of the topics according to their relationships and the arrangement of the groups in some effective order. Topics that do not fit into the plan will be rejected, and new topics will be added as they are thought of. Usually the student will find it helpful to write at the head of his rough outline his central idea or guiding purpose. Such a statement of the scope and purpose of the paper will suggest topics to be discarded and others to be added.

EXERCISE. Make a list of ideas suggested by one of the topics given below. Then group the ideas and arrange them in (1) a topical outline, (2) a complete sentence outline, and (3) a paragraph outline.

Scrapbooks	Swimming
Deep-sea Fishing	Camping
My Home Town	Gardening

32d. In the outline use consistently one system of notation, and indent headings to indicate degrees of subordination.

Any system of notation will do, but the one used for the complete sentence outline and the topical outline under section **32b** is in very common use and may well be adopted. This system, it will be noted, is as follows:

I. .... [Used for major headings.]

  A. .... [Used for subheadings of the first

  B. .... degree.]

    1. .... [Used for subheadings of the sec-

    2. .... ond degree.]

Seldom will a short outline (or even a longer one) need subordination beyond the first or second degree. If it does, it may use *a*, *b*, *c*, etc., for the third degree and (*1*), (*2*), (*3*), etc., for the fourth degree.

The indention, as well as the notation, should indicate the degree of subordination. Major headings (*I, II, III*, etc.) should be indented equally, subheadings of the first degree (*A, B, C*, etc.) should be indented more, and subheads of the second degree (*1, 2, 3*, etc.) should be indented still more.

CONFUSING LACK OF INDENTION

II. The rivets must be prepared.

A. The rivets are brought to the furnace by the rivet boy.

B. The furnace stands in a precarious position.

C. The heater must have specialized equipment and skill.

1. He must have special clothing and tongs.

2. He must have skill in order to heat the rivets properly.

IMPROVED

II. The rivets must be prepared.

    A. The rivets are brought to the furnace by the rivet boy.

    B. The furnace stands in a precarious position.

C. The heater must have specialized equipment and skill.

    1. He must have special clothing and tongs.

    2. He must have skill in order to heat the rivets properly.

32e. Give parallel structure to parallel parts of the outline.

(See the full discussion of parallel structure under section 26.)

WRONG

II. Preparation of the rivets.

    A. Delivering to the furnace. [Participle or gerund as the core of the topic.]

    B. Precarious position of the furnace. [Noun.]

    C. The heater works hard. [Sentence.]

        1. His equipment. [Noun]

        2. Skillful. [Adjective.]

RIGHT

II. Preparation of the rivets.

    A. Delivery to the furnace.   [Noun.]

    B. Precarious position of the furnace. [Noun.]

    C. The work of the heater.   [Noun.]

        1. His equipment.   [Noun.]

        2. His skill.   [Noun.]

The major headings (*I, II, III*, etc.) should be expressed in parallel structure, as should each group of subheadings. But it is unnecessary to strive for parallel structure between different groups of subheadings; for example, between "A, B, C" under "I" and "A, B, C" under "II." Parallel structure is no problem in the complete sentence outline, for parallelism is insured by the requirement of complete sentences.

32f. Make sure that the outline covers the subject, that it treats of everything promised by the title.

The adequacy of the outline is the most vital consideration. The notation, the indention, and the parallel structure are all helpful matters of form. But the adequacy of the outline is fundamental. The major headings (*I, II, III*, etc.) must be sufficient in number and in scope to satisfy the expectation aroused by the title. And each of these major headings must, in turn, be covered by its subheadings just as the title is covered by the major headings. These subheadings, however, should not be unduly detailed. If one of the major headings is to cover no more than a paragraph of the paper, it may not need any subheadings whatever.

WRONG (titles not covered by the major headings)

Geology of the United States
  I. States east of the Mississippi.
 II. Texas.

History of the United States
  I. Period before 1800.
 II. Period from 1800 till 1860.

RIGHT (titles properly covered)

Geology of the United States
  I. States east of the Mississippi.
 II. States west of the Mississippi.

History of the United States
  I. Period before 1800.
 II. Period from 1800 till 1860.
III. Period since 1860.

It would also be proper to leave the main headings unchanged and to alter the titles to agree, thus: "Geology of Texas and the States East of the Mississippi" and "History of the United States before the Civil War." The title and the major headings must have the same scope. The student will often find, on coming to outline his subject adequately, that he has more material than he can develop properly in the allotted number of words. He should promptly limit his subject and reword his title accordingly.

32g. Make sure that the parts of the outline are logically arranged.

Logical arrangement is second in importance only to adequacy. If the outline is disorganized and ineffective, the paper that follows it will also be disorganized and ineffective.

(1) Do not scatter your ideas.

Related ideas should be brought together. As the student begins his outline he is happy to have as many ideas as possible on the subject and jots them down hastily without regard to order. Then he must group these under two or more major headings. Compare the first hasty jotting down of ideas on "Riveting a Skyscraper" with the grouping in the finished outline (section 32b).

(2) Arrange the parts in a natural, easy order.

The problem of arrangement within the paper as a whole is much the same as that within each separate paragraph. (See section 31b(1)). The nature of the subject will suggest an appropriate arrangement, usually "time order," or "space order," or "order of climax."

(3) Do not allow headings to overlap.

Overlapping often occurs when a writer attempts a division according to more than one principle.

WRONG (overlapping)

History of the United States

I. Period before 1800.	[Time.]
II. The South.	[Space.]
III. Negroes.	[Group.]

RIGHT (division according to a single principle)

History of the United States

I. Period before 1800.	I. The North	I. Whites
II. Period from 1800 till 1860.	II. The South	II. Negroes
	III. The West	
III. Period since 1860.		

(4) Do not co-ordinate any heading that should be sub-ordinated. Do not subordinate any heading that should be co-ordinated.

WRONG

History of the United States

I. Period before 1800.
  A. Period from 1800 till 1860.
II. The War of 1812.
III. The Monroe Doctrine.

RIGHT

History of the United States

I. Period before 1800.
II. Period from 1800 till 1860.
  A. The War of 1812.
  B. The Monroe Doctrine.

32h. Do not make a single subhead anywhere in the outline.

The outline must have at least two main headings, *I* and *II*. If it has a subheading marked *A*, it must also have a *B*. If it has a subheading marked *1*, it must also have a *2*.

ILLOGICAL

History of the United States

I. Period before 1800.

If the history continues after 1800 the outline should indicate it by another major heading. Otherwise the title should read, "History of the United States before 1800."

32i. In general let the outline provide for a prompt beginning and end. Avoid such meaningless headings as " Introduction," " Body," and " Conclusion."

Seldom does a paper need a formal introduction or conclusion. Usually it is wise to begin promptly and to end as soon as the last topic has been adequately treated. Even when some part of the outline is to serve as an introduction or conclusion it should not be called "Introduction" or "Conclusion." It should be given a more informative title.

EXERCISE ON OUTLINING

Examine carefully the outline written for the exercise under section 32c to make sure that it does not violate section 32d, 32e, 32f, 32g, 32h, or 32i.

33 lib

33. Learn how to use the library and how to prepare a term paper.

33a. Learn how to find needed material in the library by

(1) Using the card catalogue.
(2) Using reference books.
(3) Using indexes to periodicals.
(4) Preparing a bibliography in an acceptable form.

(1) Learn how to use the card catalogue.

The card catalogue is the index to the whole library. It lists every book and every magazine, whether it is housed back in the stacks, on the open shelves of the reference room, or in any other part of the building. In many libraries one general card catalogue lists all books owned by the university and indicates whether the book is kept in the general library or with some special collection in another building.

Usually the card catalogue consists of cards three by five inches in size arranged alphabetically in drawers.

These may be "author" cards, "title" cards, or "sub-ject" cards; for in most libraries each book is listed once according to its author, again according to its title, and yet again according to its subject or subjects. Let us take, for example, *Microbe Hunters*, by Paul Henry De Kruif. If the student wishes to determine whether his library has this book, he may look under the name of the author: De Kruif, Paul Henry. The author card is as follows:

925
D33m

    De Kruif, Paul Henry, 1890–

      Microbe hunters, by Paul de Kruif ...　New York, Harcourt, Brace and company [c1926]

    6 p. l., 3–363 p.　ports.　22½ᶜᵐ.

    CONTENTS.—Leeuwenhoek.—Spallanzani.—Pasteur.—Koch.—Roux and Behring.—Metchnikoff.—Theobald Smith.—Bruce. — Ross vs. Grassi. — Walter Reed.—Paul Ehrlich.

    1. Scientists.　2. Bacteriology—Hist.　3. Micro-organisms.　I. Title.

                                        26—5317

    Library of Congress　　◯　　QR31.A1D4　1926

    Copyright A 883455　　　　[40x37]

But the student may also look for the same book under the title: *Microbe Hunters*. If he does not know the author's given name, he will probably save time by looking for the title card, which repeats all the information found on the author card. Compare the author card reproduced above with the title card shown on the following page.

This card, it will be noted, is exactly the same as the author card except for the typewritten title at the top.

In the upper left-hand corner is the call number,[1] indicating where the book is shelved. Immediately after
the typewritten title come the author's name, surname
first, and the date of his birth.   Then follow the printed
title, with the author's name in normal order, the place

[1] The top line of this number is from the Dewey Decimal classification
of books.   In the United States most libraries use either this system or
the Library of Congress system. The Dewey Decimal system has the
following main classes:

000	General Works	500	Natural Science
100	Philosophy	600	Useful Arts
200	Religion	700	Fine Arts
300	Sociology	800	Literature
400	Philology	900	History

The Library of Congress system has the following main classes:

A	General Works	M	Music
B	Philosophy, Religion	N	Fine Arts
C	History	P	Language and Literature
D	Foreign History	Q	Science
E, F	American History	R	Medicine
G	Geography, Anthropology	S	Agriculture
H	Social Sciences	T	Technology
J	Political Science	U	Military Science
K	Law	V	Naval Science
L	Education	Z	Library Science, Bibliography

of publication, the publisher, and the date. The next line tells the number of pages in the book, shows that it contains portraits, and gives the height as $22\frac{1}{2}$ centimeters. After a brief list of contents, very helpful in showing the reader whether the book contains what he wants, appear the three subject headings under which the book is listed in the card catalogue. The next line indicates that the card was printed by the Library of Congress (where it was given the call number QR31.A1D4) in 1926 as No. 5317.

The first of the three subject cards will appear under the typewritten heading "Scientists" as follows:

```
925        SCIENTISTS.
D33m
        De Kruif, Paul Henry, 1890–
            Microbe hunters, by Paul de Kruif ...  New York, Harcourt,
        Brace and company [1926]

            6 p. l., 3–363 p.  ports.  22½ᶜᵐ.

            CONTENTS.—Leeuwenhoek.—Spallanzani.—Pasteur.—Koch.—Roux and
        Behring.—Metchnikoff.—Theobald Smith.—Bruce. — Ross vs. Grassi. —
        Walter Reed.—Paul Ehrlich.


            1. Scientists. 2. Bacteriology—Hist. 3. Micro-organisms.    I. Title.
                                                                26—5317
            Library of Congress       ◯       QR31.A1D4  1926
            Copyright  A 883455                [40x37]
```

The two other subject cards are identical except that they are catalogued under the typewritten headings "Bacteriology — History" and "Micro-organisms." Subject headings are often written in red.

In addition to the regular subject cards, some libraries provide "analytical" cards to point out important sections of a book that might otherwise be overlooked. De Kruif's *Microbe Hunters*, for example, has a section on Pasteur which may be called to the reader's attention by the following analytical card:

```
925        PASTEUR, LOUIS, 1822-1895.
D33m
        De Kruif, Paul Henry, 1890–
            Microbe hunters, by Paul de Kruif ...  New York, Harcourt,
        Brace and company ₍ᶜ1926₎

            6 p. l., 3-363 p.  ports.  22½ᶜᵐ

            CONTENTS.—Leeuwenhoek.—Spallanzani.—Pasteur.—Koch.—Roux and
        Behring.—Metchnikoff.—Theobald Smith.—Bruce.— Ross vs. Grassi. —
        Walter Reed.—Paul Ehrlich.


            1. Scientists.  2. Bacteriology—Hist.  3. Micro-organisms.    I. Title.

                                                              26—5317
        Library of Congress       ◯      QR31.A1D4 1926
        Copyright  A 883455               ₍40x5⁷₎
```

Since books are catalogued in so many different ways, the student should not give up too quickly the search for what he wants. If he does not find all that he wants under the first subject consulted, he should look under related subjects. Works not listed under "Agriculture" may appear under "Farming," or "Gardening," or "Soils." Especially helpful are the cards giving cross references to other subjects under which the reader should look. Under "Agriculture," for example, might appear a card reading "Agriculture, see also Agronomy."

THE ORDER OF THE CARDS [1]

It is not enough, especially in a large library, to know that the cards are arranged alphabetically. Hundreds

[1] The order used in the card catalogue is much like that generally found in indexes for books or periodicals, in encyclopedias, and in other reference books.

of cards may be listed under a single heading such as "England," "Lincoln," or "Washington." The reader who knows the principle of arrangement will save much time in finding what he wants.

(*1*) *Person*, (*2*) *place*, (*3*) *title*. When the same word names a person or place or begins a title, the order is: person, place, title.

EXAMPLE Lincoln, Abraham [Person.]
Lincoln, Nebraska [Place.]
Lincoln and Seward, by Gideon Welles [Title.]

(*1*) *Books by a person*, (*2*) *books about a person*. Books written by a person come first; books written about a person follow.

EXAMPLE Shakespeare, William. Hamlet
Shakespeare, William. Macbeth
Shakespeare, William. A life of William Shakespeare, by Sidney Lee

(*1*) *Saints*, (*2*) *popes*, (*3*) *kings*, (*4*) *others*. Saints, popes, and kings are listed in this order by their first names, followed by the surnames of other persons. Kings are grouped according to their countries.

EXAMPLE George, Saint
George I, king of Great Britain
George II, king of Great Britain
George V, king of Hanover
George, king of Saxony
George, Henry
George, William

Cards for subjects. Cards on a single subject are arranged alphabetically according to the name of the author, which appears on the line immediately below. Subdivisions of a subject are usually arranged alphabetically.

EXAMPLE Michigan
   Michigan — Agriculture
   Michigan — Biography
   Michigan — Constitutional convention
   Michigan — University

But subdivisions of history are arranged chronological

EXAMPLE Mexico — History — Conquest, 1519–1540
   Mexico — History — Spanish colony, 1540–1810
   Mexico — History — Wars of Independence, 1810–1821
   Mexico — History — European intervention, 1861–1867

Names or titles beginning with abbreviations. Abbreviations are usually filed as if they were spelled out. Instead of *Mc* look for *Mac*; instead of *Dr.* look for *Doctor*; instead of *St.* look for *Saint*; etc.

"Short before long." In the catalogue a short word followed by other words always comes before a longer word of which the short word is a part. *Short poems* comes before *Shortage of power*.

EXAMPLE Short and long
   Short poems
   Shortage of power
   Shorthorn

SECURING A BOOK FOR EXAMINATION

When a student wishes to consult a book in the library, he should look in the card catalogue to find any one of the cards for the book — author card, title card, or subject card. From the upper left-hand corner of this card he should write the full call number on a "call slip," a small slip of paper provided by the library. He should also write on this call slip any other information required, but the full and exact call number (with the number of the volume if the book is one of a series) is the essential thing. He should then give the call slip to the attendant at the loan desk in order that the book may be brought from the stacks.

EXERCISES. Use the card catalogue of the library to do the following exercises.

1. Does the library have a copy of *Microbe Hunters*, by Paul Henry De Kruif? [You should answer this question by looking in the card catalogue either under the author or under the title. You should look under both before deciding that the book is not in the library, for sometimes a card may be misplaced or temporarily removed. Note that librarians do not italicize titles and capitalize only the words that would be capitalized in ordinary writing.]

2. How many books by Paul Henry De Kruif does the library have? [Look for the author cards. Distinguish between author and subject cards. Do not count the same book twice.]

3. Find the card for *Microbe Hunters* under the subject "Scientists." How many cards does the library have under this heading? Are there subheadings? [If the cards are very numerous, estimate the number instead of counting them. If your library does not have *Microbe Hunters*, use some other title.]

4. Find the card for *Microbe Hunters* under the subject "Bacteriology — Hist." How many cards does the library have under this subheading? What other subheadings do you find under "Bacteriology"?

5. Find the card for *Microbe Hunters* under the subject "Micro-organisms." Are there any subheadings? Are there any cross references to other subjects?

6. List the subheadings under "Education." In what order are they arranged? List the subheadings under "U.S. — History." In what order are they arranged?

7. Does your library classify its books according to the Dewey Decimal system or the Library of Congress system? Under what subject does the card catalogue list works dealing with the classification of books?

(2) Learn how to find and use reference books.

Dictionaries, encyclopedias, atlases, and other books especially helpful for reference are usually kept on the open shelves of the reference room, where students may use them directly without the trouble of having them brought from the stacks. Each of these books is listed in the card catalogue, and the call number will often aid in finding the book. The student should learn the general location of the chief classes of reference books in order that he may turn to them without loss of time. For a detailed list of such books, with a short description and evaluation of each, he should consult Mudge's *Guide to Reference Books.* A few of the more important reference books are listed below.

DICTIONARIES (UNABRIDGED)

Dictionary of American English (Craigie). 1936—.

New Century Dictionary. 1927–1933. 2 vols.

New Standard Dictionary. 1913, 1938.

Oxford English Dictionary (also called *A New English Dictionary,* or *Murray's Dictionary*). 1888–1933. 10 vols. and supplements.

Webster's New International Dictionary. 1934.

SPECIAL DICTIONARIES

Allen's Synonyms and Antonyms. 1921.
Crabb's English Synonyms. 1917.
Fernald's *English Synonyms and Antonyms.* 1931.
Fowler's *Dictionary of Modern English Usage.* 1926.
Johnson's *New Rhyming Dictionary and Poet's Handbook.* 1931.
Partridge's *Dictionary of Slang and Unconventional English.* 1937.
Roget's *Thesaurus of English Words and Phrases.* 1932.

GENERAL ENCYCLOPEDIAS

Columbia Encyclopedia. 1935. Supplement, 1938.
Encyclopaedia Britannica. 24 vols. 1929.
Encyclopedia Americana. 30 vols. 1918–1920.
New International Encyclopaedia. 24 vols. 1914–1916.

SPECIAL ENCYCLOPEDIAS

Adams' *Dictionary of American History.* 1940. 6 vols.
Bailey's *Cyclopedia of American Agriculture.* 1908–1909. 4 vols.
Bryan's *Dictionary of Painters and Engravers.* 1903–1905. 5 vols.
Catholic Encyclopedia. 1907–1922. 17 vols.
Encyclopedia of Social Sciences. 1930–1935. 15 vols.
Grove's *Dictionary of Music and Musicians.* 1927–1928. 5 vols. and supplements.
Harper's Encyclopedia of Art. 1937. 2 vols.
Hastings' *Dictionary of the Bible.* 1898–1902. 5 vols.
Hastings' *Encyclopaedia of Religion and Ethics.* 1908–1927. 13 vols.
Hutchinson's Technical and Scientific Encyclopedia. 1936. 4 vols.
Jewish Encyclopedia. 1901–1906. 12 vols.
McLaughlin and Hart's *Cyclopedia of American Government.* 1914. 3 vols.

Monroe's *Cyclopedia of Education.* 1911–1913. 5 vols.
Munn's *Encyclopedia of Banking and Finance.* 1937. 2 vols.
Van Nostrand's Scientific Encyclopedia. 1938.
Thorpe's *Dictionary of Applied Chemistry.* 1937—.

ATLASES AND GAZETTEERS

Hammond's *New-World Loose Leaf Atlas.* 1936.
Lippincott's *New Gazetteer.* 1931.
Rand-McNally Commercial Atlas. 1939.
The Times Survey Atlas of the World. 1920–1922.

YEARBOOKS — CURRENT EVENTS

American Year Book. 1910–1919. 1925—.
Americana Annual. 1923—.
Annual Register. 1758—.
Britannica Book of the Year. 1938—.
New International Year Book. 1907—.
Statesman's Year-Book. 1864—.
University Debaters' Annual. 1915—.
World Almanac. 1868—.

BIOGRAPHY

Chambers's Biographical Dictionary. 1935.
Current Biography. 1940—.
Dictionary of American Biography. 1928–1937. 20 vols.
Dictionary of National Biography. 1885–1937. 63 vols. and
  supplements.
Europa. 1930—.
Thomas' *Universal Pronouncing Dictionary of Biography and
  Mythology.* 1930.
Kunitz's *American Authors, 1600–1900.* 1938.
Kunitz's *Authors Today and Yesterday.* 1934.
Kunitz's *British Authors of the Nineteenth Century.* 1936.

Kunitz's *Living Authors*. 1931.
Who's Who. 1848—.
Who's Who in America. 1899—.

LITERATURE

Apperson's *English Proverbs and Proverbial Phrases*. 1929.
Bartlett's *Familiar Quotations*. 1937.
Cambridge Bibliography of English Literature. 1940. 3 vols.
Harper's Dictionary of Classical Literature and Antiquities. 1897.
Harvey's *Oxford Companion to Classical Literature*. 1937.
Harvey's *Oxford Companion to English Literature*. 1937.
Manly and Rickert's *Contemporary British Literature*. 1935.
Millett's *Contemporary American Authors*. 1940.
Modern Humanities Research Association, *Annual Bibliography of English Language and Literature*. 1920—.
Stevenson's *Home Book of Quotations*. 1937.

EXERCISES. Do the following exercises as a means of locating the more important works of reference and of acquainting yourself with them.

A. Draw the floor plan of the reference room of your library, indicating the location of the more important books of reference. Indicate, for example, the locations of (1) unabridged dictionaries, (2) general encyclopedias, (3) atlases, and (4) the *Dictionary of National Biography* or some other collection of short biographies.

B. Trace the history of the word *sanguine* and quote several passages to illustrate the various uses of the word. [Consult the *Oxford English Dictionary*.]

C. Distinguish between *pattern*, *model*, *exemplar*, and *ideal*. Write sentences to illustrate the use of each word. [Consult *Webster's New International Dictionary*, with attention to the special paragraphs on synonyms.]

D. What was the value of all exports of the United States during 1938? What was the value of imports from Chili during 1939? [Consult one of the yearbooks.]

E. Locate a good map of Abyssinia and state where you find it. [Use an atlas, of course.]

F. Look up in a general encyclopedia the articles on the "Organ," "Marriage," and "Wheat." Then look up each of the articles in the appropriate special encyclopedia. State where you find each article.

(3) Learn how to use indexes to periodicals.

The typical periodical is a magazine issued weekly, monthly, or quarterly. Newspapers usually appear daily or weekly. For the convenience of those who wish to consult the current issues, these periodicals are kept for a few months or possibly a year on open shelves or racks; then bound into volumes, each of which commonly includes the issues of six months or a year. These bound volumes may be kept on the open shelves in the reference room, in a special periodical room, or back in the stacks. The card catalogue shows whether the library has a given periodical and often indicates where it may be consulted. But a more convenient special catalogue to periodicals is often kept in the reference room or periodical room.

To make the contents of periodicals available to readers without detailed examination of each issue, indexes are being constantly worked up and printed in book form. These printed indexes do for articles in periodicals what the card catalogue does for books in the library. The card catalogue lists each book, and consequently it lists each periodical in the library. But it does not list each article in the periodicals. This important work is left to the periodical indexes, the chief of which are mentioned below, with the year in which each was begun.

INDEXES TO PERIODICALS

GENERAL

Reader's Guide. 1900—.
   (Preceded by *Poole's Index.* 1802–1906.)
International Index. 1907—.
New York Times Index. 1913—.
Book Review Digest. 1905—.

SPECIAL

Agricultural Index. 1916—.
Art Index. 1929—.
Dramatic Index. 1909—.
Education Index. 1929—.
Engineering Index. 1884—.
Experiment Station Record. 1889—.
Index Medicus. 1879–1926; *Quarterly Cumulative Index Medicus.* 1927—.
Index to Legal Periodicals. 1908—.
Industrial Arts Index. 1913—.
Psychological Index. 1894–1936.
Subject-Index to Periodicals. 1919–1922; 1926—.
Technical Book Review Index. 1917–1929; 1935—.

These indexes are compiled as rapidly as possible after the periodicals appear. In the case of the *Reader's Guide* (an index to over one hundred magazines of general interest) the index is only a few weeks behind the appearance of the articles. From time to time the issues for single months or for short periods of a few months are combined into longer units, and finally into a volume covering two years. The earlier volumes cover as many as five years, as will be seen from the following list.

Reader's Guide

I	1900–1904	VII	1925–1928
II	1905–1909	VIII	1929–June, 1932
III	1910–1914	IX	July, 1932–June, 1935
IV	1915–1918	X	July, 1935–June, 1937
V	1919–1921	XI	July, 1937–June, 1939
VI	1922–1924	XII	July, 1939–June, 1941

Any student wishing to find all references to a given subject listed by the *Reader's Guide* would have to look through each of the larger volumes and the smaller ones covering the most recent months or month. Usually he is concerned only with articles that have appeared during a certain period, and he looks accordingly in the volumes covering that period.

EXERCISES. Do the following exercises as a means of learning how to use indexes to periodicals.

1. On your drawing of the floor plan of the reference room (or periodical room) indicate where the indexes to periodicals may be found. Indicate also the locations of any special list or catalogue of periodicals and any unbound or bound periodicals that may be kept in the room.

2. How many articles on the League of Nations are listed by the *Reader's Guide* for the period 1905–1909? Are more listed for the period 1919–1921 or for the period July, 1937– June, 1939?

3. How many articles on "Goats" are listed by the *Reader's Guide* for July, 1937–June, 1939? Are more listed by the

Agricultural Index for the same period? Do these indexes list the same articles?

4. How many articles on "Diesel engines" are listed by the *Reader's Guide* for the period July, 1937–June, 1939? Are more listed by the *Engineering Index* for the same period? Do these indexes list the same articles?

5. Consult the *New York Times Index* to determine the date of the marriage of the Duke of Windsor. [Since all important newspapers report events on the same day, the *New York Times Index* is a useful guide to other newspapers.]

(4) Learn how to prepare a bibliography in an acceptable form.

A bibliography is a list of books, pamphlets, or articles dealing with any given subject. A bibliographical entry usually falls into three divisions: (1) the author's name (if it is given); (2) the title; (3) the facts of publication — place, publisher, date.

1. Author's name (surname first for alphabetizing)

EXAMPLES De Kruif, Paul Henry.
Parker, William R.

2. The title (in italics for books; in quotation marks for parts of books or for articles in periodicals).

EXAMPLES *Microbe Hunters.* [Title of a book.]
"On Milton's Early Literary Program." [Title of an article from a periodical.]

3. Facts of publication — place, publisher, date.

EXAMPLES New York: Harcourt, Brace, 1926. [For a book.]
Modern Philology, XXXIII (August, 1935), 49–53. [For a magazine article. Here the place of publication is on pages 49–53 of the thirty-third

volume of a magazine entitled *Modern Philology*.
The date of publication is given as August, 1935.
In the case of periodicals the publisher and the
city of publication are usually omitted.]

An acceptable form for the two entries is as follows:

De Kruif, Paul Henry. *Microbe Hunters*. New York: Harcourt, Brace, 1926.

Parker, William R. "On Milton's Early Literary Program." *Modern Philology*, XXXIII (August, 1935),
49–53.

This bibliographical form (sometimes slightly varied)
is commonly used by books and periodicals in the fields
of the languages and the social sciences. Scientific
periodicals tend to use boldface Arabic numerals for
the volume number and to place the date at the end.
Indexes to periodicals employ a compact form, but one
not commonly used in books or periodicals and consequently not suitable as a model.

Whatever bibliographical form a writer adopts, he
should give due heed to the three divisions of each entry: the author's name (if it is given), the title, and the
facts of publication. He should take great pains to be
consistent, using commas, periods, italics (underscoring), and quotation marks exactly as they are called
for by his model. This model will usually be suggested
by the periodical, the organization, or the department
for which the paper is being written. If the instructor
does not specify some other form, the student may
well adopt the commonly used form illustrated by the
following bibliography. The items may be arranged
in a single alphabetical list or classified in some logical
way, such as "Books" and "Periodicals."

BIBLIOGRAPHY

"Architecture." *Encyclopaedia Britannica,* 14th edition, II, 274–287.

Balcom, H. G. "New York's Tallest Skyscraper, the Empire State Building." *Civil Engineering,* I (March, 1931), 467–471.

Binger, Walter D. *What Engineers Do.* New York: W. W. Norton, 1938.

Fleming, R. "Half Century of the Skyscraper." *Civil Engineering,* IV (December, 1934), 634–638.

Gillett, H. W. *High Silicon Structural Steel.* Technological Papers, Bureau of Standards, No. 331, Washington: Government Printing Office, 1926.

Hool, George A., and Nathan C. Johnson. *Handbook of Building Construction.* 2 vols. New York: McGraw-Hill, 1920.

Naumburg, Elsa (Herzfeld), Clara Lambert, and Lucy Sprague Mitchell. *Skyscraper.* New York: John Day, 1933.

New York *Times,* March 31, 1937.

"Skyscraper Steel Erection in the RCA Building." *Engineering News-Record,* CIX (November 24, 1932), 618–619.

"Skyscrapers: Builders and Their Tools." *Fortune,* II (October, 1930), 85–94.

Spurr, H. V. "Bank of Manhattan Company Building." *Civil Engineering,* I (March, 1931), 471–477.

Stang, Ambrose H., Martin Greenspan, and William R. Osgood. *Strength of a Riveted Steel Rigid Frame Having a Curved Inner Flange.* U. S. Department of Commerce, National Bureau of Standards, No. 1161, Washington: Government Printing Office, 1938.

EXERCISE. Prepare a bibliography of at least ten items on one of the subjects listed below. Include at least

two books, two general reference works, and two articles
from periodicals.

> American Negro Poetry
> Development of Jersey Cattle
> Federal Housing Administration
> Interpretation of Rembrandt's Painting
> Preparation of Cheeses
> Religious Ceremonies and Rites of the Hopi Indians
> Sulfanilamide
> Television

33b. Learn how to prepare a term paper by taking the following steps:

(1) Selecting and limiting the subject.

(2) Making a preliminary bibliography and a tentative outline.

(3) Spotting (and evaluating) useful passages and taking notes.

(4) Writing the paper and using footnotes.

(5) Making the final bibliography and the final outline.

(1) Select a subject that appeals to you, is adequately treated in your library, and is not too broad.

Nothing can take the place of a proper interest in the
subject of the investigation. The term paper gives the
student an opportunity to follow up his special interest,
to go to the library and find what has been written
about it. Almost any subject that he may think of is
adequately treated in a good library. He should not
expect, of course, to find much about events of too recent occurrence. Usually several months pass before

magazines can treat events properly, and a longer period is needed for books.

The chief danger, however, is that a student will select a subject too general for a term paper, which usually runs from one or two thousand words to four or five thousand. Let us suppose that a student is interested in the general field of engineering. From the field of engineering — or from that of literature, of science, of law, of agriculture, of medicine — he may draw many excellent topics. But clearly he cannot use for his term paper such a general topic as "Engineering." Nothing less than an encyclopedia could do justice to the subject. He might think of electrical engineering, chemical engineering, mechanical engineering, civil engineering — still much too broad. Civil engineering might suggest construction, and then construction of highways, of bridges, of railroads, of skyscrapers. Even these separate phases of construction are, perhaps, more suitable for books than for articles. Skyscrapers, for instance, require months for planning, checking, financing. "Planning the Skyscraper" would be broad enough — perhaps too broad — for the term paper. Or one may start after the construction is already under way, using some such title as *Skyscrapers: Getting Up the Steel Framework*.

EXERCISE. From the general fields of literature, science, law, agriculture, or medicine suggest titles that might be broad enough for books and others suitable for term papers.

(2) Make a preliminary bibliography and a tentative outline.

Once you have determined the subject, find in the library books and articles that give information you need. Look under the subject, and also under related subjects, in the card catalogue. Use reference books of various kinds and the indexes to periodicals. Do not overlook the short bibliographies at the end of articles in the encyclopedias, or in textbooks, or in miscellaneous works of reference.

Write down about a dozen of the most promising titles on cards three by five inches in size ("bibliography cards"), putting only one title on each card and following exactly the bibliographical form that you have decided to use. Some students add the library call number for convenience in consulting the book or periodical later. Use a fountain pen and make a record that will not need to be copied until you write out your final bibliography on completion of the term paper. To make incomplete entries that must be supplemented later, or to make a typewritten copy on another card, is a serious waste of time. If you use the form illustrated in section **33a(4)**, the bibliography card will appear as on the following page.

Next read one or two brief treatments of your subject, perhaps in encyclopedias or other reference works. Then outline as well as you can the paper you propose to write. This outline, of course, will not be complete. No doubt you will need to change it in many ways as you learn more of your subject. But you must have some plan for your term paper before you can profitably undertake the next step. If you have taken for your

subject *Skyscrapers: Getting Up the Steel Framework*, you
will probably learn by reading a brief general article
that your outline should include:

I. Supervisors and directors
II. Transportation problems
III. Derrick gangs
IV. Riveters

At least such a skeleton outline as this is essential before you begin your search for useful material. Only
material that will fit into some part of the outline is
really useful. Therefore the outline should be improved and expanded as rapidly as possible, though it
will be subject to change throughout the whole process
of writing the term paper.

(3) Learn how to spot (and evaluate) useful passages and
    take notes.

Seldom will a whole book, or even a whole article,
be of use as subject matter for any given term paper.
To find what the student needs for his particular paper
he must turn to many books and articles, rejecting most

of them altogether and using from others a section here and there. He cannot take the time to read each book carefully. He must use the table of contents and the index, and he must learn to scan the pages rapidly until he spots the passages he needs.

One important consideration always is the reliability of the source. Does the author seem to know his subject? Do others speak of him as an authority? Is he prejudiced? Is the work recent enough to give the information needed?

The universally approved system for the taking of notes employs cards or paper sheets of uniform size, usually four by six inches. Each card contains a single note with a heading to indicate just where it will fit into the outline. If the term paper is to use the customary footnotes, each card must also show the source of the note, and the exact page or pages of the source.

Let us suppose that a student, in preparing a term paper on *Skyscrapers: Getting Up the Steel Framework*, has spotted the following passage as one that will be of use.

Actual erection is done altogether by the derrick gangs. It is they who raise the steel from the trucks to the working level, who assort it by number with reference to the erector's plan, who swing it into place and bolt it there. They are clever and hardened men. An assistant foreman, like a profane orchestra conductor, directs the derrick, yelling at the bull-stick man who turns the boom, signaling with his arms and his hands to the man who yanks the engineer's bell, jerking his head at the tag line pair whose line guides the dangling column. The sluggish load swings over. The fall line eases an inch, a half inch, till the rivet holes coincide.[1]

[1] "Skyscrapers: Builders and Their Tools," *Fortune*, II (October, 1930), 89. Copyright *Time*, Inc. Reprinted by permission.

On a card four by six inches in size the student will write the following note.

Derrick Gangs

The derrick gangs, under the direction of an assistant foreman, arrange the steel according to specifications. With the aid of the derrick they raise the parts to the proper level, swing them into place, and bolt them securely.

"Skyscrapers: Builders and Their Tools," p. 89.

A précis note

(An original of 117 words is reduced to 38 words of the student's phraseology.)

The heading "Derrick Gangs" refers to the section of the outline to which the note belongs. The reference at the bottom gives the exact page from which the note is taken. The student saves time by abbreviating this reference, for he can supply the complete form whenever he needs it by consulting his bibliography card. See the full reference in the bibliography in section **33a(4)**. Another satisfactory abbreviation would be: "*Fortune*, p. 89." The note itself summarizes in the student's own phraseology the ideas in the source. The summary may, according to need, be shorter or longer. A carefully written abbreviation of a source, expressed in the note-taker's own phraseology, is called a "précis."

But at times the student may wish to use the subject matter of a passage in full. If so, he will take the substance down in his own words, paraphrasing the source somewhat as follows:

Derrick Gangs

The derrick gangs are entirely responsible for the erection of the steel structure. They arrange the pieces according to the architect's plan and raise them from the trucks to the level on which the work is being done. With utmost precision they fit the swinging beams into their proper slots and securely bolt them down. The versatile assistant foreman is "like a profane orchestra conductor." In directing the raising of the girders, he signals one man when to ring the engineer's bell, calls

---

out to the bull-stick man when to turn the boom; and in addition, with a jerk of his head, shows the tag line pair how to guide and where to stay the swaying column.

"Skyscrapers: Builders and Their Tools," p. 89.

In this paraphrase the student wishes to include one of the phrases of the original. Therefore he inserts the phrase in quotation marks. Unusual care must be taken to use one's own phraseology — to get entirely away from the original so far as arrangement of words is concerned — or else to enclose in quotation marks the borrowed sentences or phrases.

Very seldom should the student take a note that is merely a quotation. Too many quotations in the ordinary term paper suggest a lack of mastery of the subject. And besides, the more a student quotes the less practice he gets in composition. When he does find a passage which he wishes to quote in his paper, he should do justice to the author by copying the passage very carefully, putting in every word, every capital letter, every comma exactly as in the original. Then he should enclose the whole in quotation marks. Otherwise he may later forget that the passage is quoted and may be guilty of plagiarism — of using another's phraseology as if it were his own.

EXERCISES.

A. Use the fourth paragraph of "Riveting a Skyscraper" (reprinted in section **32b**) to write a short précis note of less than twenty-five words. [Be careful to avoid the phraseology of the source. Write one or two effective sentences in which you express the gist of the paragraph.]

B. Use the same paragraph to write a longer précis note, perhaps one third the length of the source. [Avoid entirely the phraseology of the source. Include more details than the shorter précis of Exercise A permitted. Write the sentences so carefully that the note might be used in a term paper without further revision.]

C. Make a paraphrase of the first four sentences of the same paragraph. [Avoid entirely the phraseology of the source. Use synonyms freely, but do not hesitate to use some of the words of the original. A paraphrase is approximately the same length as the source and should be expressed in equally effective sentences.]

D. Read carefully the paragraph from Herman Melville reprinted on page 325. First write a précis of the paragraph consisting of a single sentence. Then write another précis half as long as the paragraph. Finally write a paraphrase fully as long as your source. [Avoid entirely the phraseology of the source. Choose your words carefully. Give variety to your sentences.]

(4) Learn how to use footnotes in the writing of the term paper.

After a large number of notes have been taken — notes covering every major section of the outline and every subsection — the student is ready to begin writing. He will arrange his notes in the order of the outline and will write them down, section by section. Naturally he will have to expand some parts, to cut others; and especially will he need to provide transitional sentences and even transitional paragraphs. He must write the material in the best way he can — in his own style, in his own words.

Since the bulk of the material consists of notes which the student has taken down from others, he naturally should give credit. To do so, he makes use of footnotes. When he copies down, for example, the note on "Derrick Gangs," he will put at the end a number (^{1}, or ^{2}, or ^{3}, etc.) referring to the same number at the bottom

of the page, where the reader will be told the exact
source of the material thus:

[1] "Skyscrapers: Builders and Their Tools," *Fortune*, II (October, 1930), 89.

If the student uses another note from the same source,
he should shorten the footnote thus:

[1] "Skyscrapers: Builders and Their Tools," p. 90.[1]

In this note he uses p. (the plural is pp.) for "page."
He omits the p. (or pp.) only when the page is preceded
by the volume number in Roman numerals.   If the

[1] It would perhaps be sufficient to use " 'Skyscrapers,' p. 90." When
the author's name is known, secondary references are frequently made
by use of the name followed by *op. cit.*, an abbreviation of the Latin
opere citato, meaning "in the work cited."   The first reference would
appear thus:

[1] Walter D. Binger, *What Engineers Do* (New York, 1938), p. 63.

A later reference to the same book might appear thus:

[1] Binger, *op. cit.*, p. 68.

But some writers prefer the following:

[1] Binger, *What Engineers Do*, p. 68.   (A long title would be shortened.)

The abbreviations most commonly used in footnotes are as follows:

cf.	compare
ed.	edited, edition, editor
f., ff.	and the following page or pages
ibid.	in the same place
l., ll.	line, lines
loc. cit.	in the place cited
MS.	manuscript
n.	note
n.d.	no date given
n.p.	no publisher given
n.s.	new series
op. cit.	in the work cited
p., pp.	page, pages
sic	thus (inserted in brackets to call attention to some irregularity in the original)
tr.	translated, translator
vol., vols.	volume, volumes

second reference to the article in *Fortune* happens to come immediately after the first (that is, without any intervening reference), the second footnote should be further shortened by use of *Ibid.*, an abbreviation of the Latin *ibidem*, meaning "in the same place." The footnote will read thus:

¹ *Ibid.*, p. 90.

If the second footnote chances to refer to the same page as the first ("p. 89"), the footnote will read simply thus:

¹ *Ibid.*

Any reader who may wish to check the source needs only to look back to the first footnote for the detailed reference.

The general principle to be followed in using footnotes is to make the first reference to each source detailed and to abbreviate as much as clarity will permit all following references. The student term paper printed at the end of this section illustrates the correct use of footnotes. These may start with ¹ on each page or may be numbered consecutively throughout the paper.

(5) Learn how to make out a final bibliography and a final outline.

Almost from the start of the work on the term paper, the student has a preliminary bibliography. As he works up his paper he eliminates some items and adds others. Not until he has completed his paper can he know the items that should make up his final bibliography. Now, with his writing completed, he may look through his footnotes. Every book or article listed even once belongs in his bibliography. His instructor may ask him to include everything that he has examined, whether he has actually used it for a footnote or not. In that case his bibliography may have, instead of a dozen items, as many as fifty or a hundred. Once he has determined the items that should be included, he can easily arrange the bibliography cards and copy them, either in one alphabetical list or in a classified list.

The tentative outline usually undergoes even more change than the preliminary bibliography. It develops steadily during the course of the note-taking and the writing. Perhaps even after the paper is half written the student may hit upon some better plan of organization. If so, let us hope that he does not hesitate to change his outline. The outline was never intended as anything but a guide. Certainly it should never chain the student to any one plan after he has thought of a better one.

Since outline and paper have developed together, the outline may serve as guide to the contents of the theme. It should be copied carefully along with the other parts of the term paper and placed at the beginning. The bibliography regularly comes at the end. Thus the order of the completed term paper should be:

1. The Outline (Table of Contents)
2. The Term Paper, with Footnotes
3. The Bibliography.

A Specimen Term Paper

BOULDER DAM

by Shelton Douglas

OUTLINE

I. History.
   A. Colorado River Commission.
   B. Geological survey.
   C. Choice of site.
   D. Swing-Johnson Bill.
   E. Choice of name.

II. Preliminary construction.
   A. Boulder City.
      1. Location, cost, population, and government.
      2. Types of business.
   B. Diversion tunnels.
   C. Cofferdams.

III. Construction of the dam proper.
   A. Location.
   B. Bids.
   C. Type.
   D. Architecture.
   E. Obstacles.
   F. Size.
   G. Materials.
   H. Workmen.

IV. Lake Mead.
   A. Location.
   B. Size.
   C. Purpose.
   D. Cost of water storage.
   E. Loss of water.

V. Hydro-electric power.

388

lib 33

BOULDER DAM

When the idea of an immense dam across the Colorado River to control the flood waters first became a dream, there was much dispute among the states through which the river flowed as to whom the river belonged. To settle the dispute, the Colorado River Commission was organized in 1921. This commission held a conference in Santa Fe, New Mexico, in 1922. There were representatives from Colorado, Arizona, California, Utah, Nevada, New Mexico, Wyoming, and the United States Government. The representative of the government was Herbert Hoover. After a lengthy discussion, a compact was adopted and signed on November 24, 1922.[1] Six of the states approved the compact, but Arizona refused because she "objected to the inclusion of the Gila, and while the prior appropriation doctrine would thereby be destroyed between the two basins by the allocation of waters to each of them, yet it would remain in full force and effect as between California and Arizona, and that while the upper basin states had escaped the danger which they had feared by California appropriating a great amount of water through the all-American canal that it intended to build, yet the same danger would still confront Arizona." [2] Several years passed before the compact was declared valid, without Arizona ever having approved it. The compact was so worded, however, that Arizona could enter if she saw fit, but her entrance was not necessary to make it valid.

The United States Geological Department then sent out a party to survey the Colorado River and to locate a site for the dam. Prior to this time, however, the Bureau of Reclamation had spent twenty years studying the Colorado River and had investigated over seventy different sites for a dam.[3] From the hydrographic and geologic

[1] Ralph B. Simmons, *Boulder Dam and the Great Southwest* (Los Angeles, 1936), p. 58.

[2] Elwood Mead and Raymond F. Walter, *Boulder Dam Today.* (Reprinted from *Engineering News-Record*, CIV (February 6, 1930), 244.)

[3] *Ibid.*, p. 38.

information gathered by the geological survey, the Colorado River was divided into three parts. The upper section consisted of the river basin formed by Colorado, Utah, New Mexico, and Wyoming. This section was about equally divided between irrigation and potential water-power. The middle section consisted of about five hundred miles of canyons into which little or no water drained, but where the river fell three thousand feet. The lower section contained the southern half of Arizona and the southeastern part of California. This section was chiefly agricultural. As soon as complete information was learned concerning the Colorado River, the Colorado River Board, formed by Congress in 1928, made a report on the "economy, engineering feasibility, safety, and practical soundness"[1] of the proposed Boulder Canyon Project, which consisted of a dam, reservoir, power plant, and the all-American canal.

Two sites were considered for the dam. One was in the upper part of Black Canyon, and the other in Boulder Canyon. Black Canyon was chosen by Frank E. Weymouth,[2] civil engineer appointed by Congress to choose the dam site, because it was "more accessible, the canyon narrower . . . the reservoir capacity greater, and the entire project less expensive to construct"[3] than in Boulder Canyon. The four purposes of the dam were divided into two parts, agricultural and economic. In the eyes of the government the agricultural purposes, control of the flood waters of the Colorado and regulation of the flow or irrigational waters, were the most important because of the vast amount of rich land that would become productive. If there had not been economic purposes, however, the dam would probably still be a dream because of the huge cost of such a structure.

On December 21, 1928, President Coolidge approved the Swing-Johnson Bill.[4] This bill authorized, subject to

[1] Simmons, *Boulder Dam*, pp. 61, 62.
[2] *Ibid.*, p. 75.
[3] *Ibid.*, p. 63.
[4] "Boulder Dam is taken over by the Government," Knoxville *News-Sentinel*, Feb. 29, 1936, p. B-8.

lib 33

future appropriations, the construction of a dam in Black Canyon, and a reservoir to contain not less than 20,000,000 acre-feet.[1] To begin with, the dam was called "Boulder Dam," but on September 17, 1930, the name was changed to "Hoover Dam," because of the work of Herbert Hoover. When the Republican administration was overthrown, the name was changed back to the original "Boulder Dam" by Secretary of the Interior, Harold L. Ickes.[2]

Before construction on the dam could be started, there were many things to be done. As the nearest city, Las Vegas, Nevada, was nearly thirty miles from the dam site, the government built a city which we know as Boulder City. The entire city — including streets, buildings, sewerage, water, and electrical power systems — was planned on paper before the earth was removed for the construction of the streets. Located about seven miles from the dam in the heart of the desert, it is probably the most peaceful, most modern, and most sanitary city ever built.[3] The Federal Government spent $2,000,000 on the construction of the sewerage, water, and electric distribution systems, and on buildings. The Six Companies, Inc. spent nearly $1,000,000 on the construction of air-conditioned dormitories for the men employed on the construction of the dam.[4] During the construction of the dam, the population of Boulder City was nearly 6,000.[5] It is governed by the city manager plan of government. The city manager is responsible, however, to the construction engineer. The police force is made up of one chief and eight assistant rangers. The only court is a Federal Court, and it does not have many cases to try. The most common punishment for breaking a law was expulsion from the city, which meant immediate discharge from work.[6]

When the public learned that the government was to construct Boulder City, approximately 4,100 applications

[1] Simmons, *Boulder Dam*, p. 79.
[2] *Ibid.*, p. 96.
[3] *Ibid.*, p. 143.
[4] *Ibid.*, p. 146.
[5] *Ibid.*, p. 148.
[6] *Ibid.*, p. 149.

to set up private businesses were received by the government. Out of this number about sixty were approved. Those approved included practically every known type of legitimate business. To create competition, at least two permits were issued for each type of business. The permits were issued only to American citizens.[1]

Four diversion tunnels and two cofferdams were also constructed before work on the dam proper was started. The diversion tunnels were used to divert the Colorado River around the site of the dam. Each of the four tunnels was driven through solid rock. The diameter of the tunnels when lined with three feet of concrete is fifty feet. The total length of the tunnels is three miles.[2] In laying the concrete lining, the cross-section of the tunnel was divided into three parts. The lower 74° was poured first, then the side-wall portions of 88° each, and finally the roof of 110° was poured. The concreting was started at the upstream openings, and was poured in consecutive forty-foot sections.[3] Over 300,000 cubic yards of concrete were used in the tunnels.[4] Each of the cofferdams is composed of a layer of sand, gravel, cobbles, and boulders surmounted by a curved mound of rolled earth and gravel. The entire structure was covered by a six-inch reinforced concrete pavement. The upper cofferdam was 98 feet high, 480 feet long, 750 feet thick at the base, and 70 feet thick at the top, while the lower cofferdam was 66 feet high, 360 feet long, 500 feet thick at the base, and 50 feet thick at the top.[5]

The dam proper is located about one and one-half miles below the upper end of Black Canyon.[6] Bids for its con-

---

[1] Simmons, *Boulder Dam*, p. 144.
[2] Elwood Mead, *Boulder Canyon Project — Questions and Answers* (U. S. Department of the Interior, Bureau of Reclamation, Washington, 1936), p. 3.
[3] C. H. Vivian, "Construction of the Hoover Dam," *Compressed Air Magazine*, XXXVII (December, 1932), 4010.
[4] Mead, *Boulder Canyon Project*, p. 1.
[5] Wesley R. Nelson, "Construction of the Hoover Dam," *Compressed Air Magazine*, XXXVIII (March, 1933), 4071.
[6] Mead-Walter, *Boulder Dam Today*, p. 10.

struction were opened on March 4, 1931.[1] The lowest
of the three bids submitted was that of the Six Companies,
Inc., of San Francisco. Their bid was $48,890,995.50.[2]
The construction contract, which stated that the government would furnish almost all the materials and would
assume all loss and damage from flood after the diversion
tunnels and cofferdams had been built, was signed on
April 20, 1931.[3] The dam is of the arch-gravity type;
i.e., it is a curved structure depending upon its weight to
hold it in place.[4] The architecture of the dam is very
simple. The only pure ornament comprises two sculptured
panels, monolithically cast in concrete, emphasizing the
entrances to the passenger elevators. Oskar Hansen made
the models. Irrigation, Navigation, Power Development,
Flood Control, and Water Supply will be represented in
one location, and the seals of the seven states through which
the Colorado River flows in the other location.[5] The main
obstacle in the construction was the intense heat. In the
summer the temperature was anywhere from 100° to 130°
in the shade, but at the dam site there was no shade.[6]

The dam itself rises 727 feet above bed-rock, the same
height as the observation platform on the Woolworth
Building in New York City.[7] It is 660 feet thick at the
base and 45 feet thick at the crest. The length along the
crest is 1,282 feet.[8] The maximum water pressure against
the base of the dam is 45,000 pounds per square foot.[9]
The total weight of the dam is nearly 6,600,000 tons.[10]
Every state in the Union furnished at least one of the ma-

[1] Simmons, *Boulder Dam*, p. 95.

[2] *Ibid.*, p. 102.

[3] *Ibid.*, p. 80.

[4] Frederic Majer, "Many Uses for Monster Dams," *Young America*,
January 28, 1938, p. 9.

[5] Gordon B. Kaufmann, "The Architecture of Boulder Dam,"
Architectural Concrete, II (1936), 4.

[6] Simmons, *Boulder Dam*, p. 98.

[7] Ivan E. Houk, "High Masonry Dams in the West," *Du Pont Magazine*, XXVI ("Holiday," 1932), 11.

[8] Majer, "Many Uses for Monster Dams," p. 8.

[9] Mead, *Boulder Canyon Project*, p. 1.

[10] *Ibid.*, p. 2.

terials which were used in the dam or its construction.[1] The sand and gravel used in the concrete was gotten from government-owned gravel pits eight miles above the dam site on the Arizona side of the river. Enough concrete was used in the construction of the dam to build a paved highway 16 feet wide from Miami, Florida, to Seattle, Washington,[2] or a highway 20 feet wide from San Francisco to Chicago.[3] The concrete was mixed in huge plants, and transported to the site of the dam by trains and cableways. More than 5,000,000 barrels of cement were used in making the concrete. The pouring of the concrete was a slow process because of the great amount of heat which was liberated while the concrete was setting. Over 582 miles of steel tubing, through which cold water circulated, was used to cool the concrete. Fifty-one million pounds of steel was used to reinforce the concrete.[4]

Every man engaged in the actual construction work was American-born, and was given a thorough examination when employed to assure healthy physique, stamina, and courage. Ralph Lowry was the construction engineer in charge of the dam.[5] Over sixty per cent of all the men employed were ex-service men.[6] They worked in shifts of eight hours, twenty-fours hours out of the day, seven days a week. There was no overtime except in emergencies. The minimum wage paid per eight-hour day was $4.00. Some workers, however, were paid as high as $10.00 per day.[7]

Immediately back of the dam is the huge reservoir known as Lake Mead. Covering 146,000 acres, it is the largest reservoir in the world. When it is full, it will have a volume of 30,500,000 acre-feet. This is enough water to cover the state of Connecticut to a depth of ten feet, or

[1] Simmons, *Boulder Dam*, p. 177.
[2] Mead, *Boulder Canyon Project*, p. 1.
[3] Simmons, *Boulder Dam*, p. 123.
[4] *Ibid.*, p. 108.
[5] "Colorado River's Flow Equals That of the Mississippi," *Memphis Commercial Appeal*, September 27, 1936.
[6] Simmons, *Boulder Dam*, p. 148.
[7] *Ibid.*, p. 169.

the state of New York to a depth of one foot. Ten years
will be required to fill the reservoir. If the dam were
closed down, the reservoir would hold the entire average
flow of the Colorado River for two years.[1] The reservoir
extends from Black Canyon to Bridge Canyon, a distance
of one hundred and fifteen miles. It has a maximum depth
of 600 feet and a maximum width of eight miles. The
shore line is over 550 miles long.[2]

The main purpose of the reservoir is to catch the water
so that it may be saved during rainy seasons and released
during dry seasons. Another purpose is to catch the silt
which comes down with the water. The silt will act as a
purifier, and thus be very beneficial to the cities which
get their water supply from the Colorado River below the
dam. It is estimated that 137,000 acre-feet of silt will
enter the reservoir each year. At this rate 222 years will
be required to fill the reservoir with silt.[3] Twenty-five
cents an acre-foot will be charged for storing water in the
reservoir. This does not seem very much, but will involve
a payment of $250,000 a year by the Metropolitan Water
District.[4] There will be very little loss of water from
leakage, because the major portion of Lake Mead is a hilly
basin of hard rock. The greatest loss will be from evapora-
tion.

The power plant at the base of the dam contains seventeen generators, capable of generating about 1,835,000
horsepower.[5] Fifteen of the generators are 82,500 kilovolt-
ampere generators. The other equipment consists of fifteen 115,000 horsepower hydraulic turbines, and a number
of transformers. The power is divided as follows: State
of Arizona 18%, State of Nevada 18%, Metropolitan
Water District 36%, smaller municipalities 6%, City of
Los Angeles 13%, and the Southern California Edison
Company 9%.[6] The cost of power at the dam is 1.63 mills

---

[1] *Ibid.*, p. 123.
[2] *Ibid.*, p. 123.
[3] *Ibid.*, p. 72.
[4] Mead-Walter, *Boulder Dam Today*, p. 7.
[5] Majer, "Many Uses for Monster Dams," p. 9.
[6] *Boulder Dam* (Union Pacific Railway, 1934), p. 9.

per kilowatt-hour.[1] President Roosevelt started the first generator, 3,500 horsepower, turning on September 11, 1936, two years before the scheduled time.[2]

BIBLIOGRAPHY

Boulder Dam. Union Pacific Railway, 1934.

Houk, Ivan E. "High Masonry Dams in the West." *Du Pont Magazine*, XXVI ("Holiday," 1932), 11–14.

Kaufmann, Gordon B. "The Architecture of Boulder Dam." *Architectural Concrete*, II (1936), 3, 4.

Knoxville *News-Sentinel*, February 29, 1936.

Majer, Frederic. "Many Uses for Monster Dams." *Young America*, January 28, 1938.

Mead, Elwood. *Boulder Canyon Project — Questions and Answers.* U. S. Department of the Interior, Bureau of Reclamation, Washington: Government Printing Office, 1931.

Mead, Elwood, and Raymond F. Walter. *Boulder Dam Today.* Reprinted from *Engineering News-Record*, CIV (February 6, 1930), 240–253.

Memphis *Commercial Appeal*, September 27, 1936.

Memphis *Press Scimitar*, September 11, 1936.

Nelson, Wesley R. "Construction of the Hoover Dam." *Compressed Air Magazine*, XXXVIII (March, 1933), 4069–4074.

Simmons, Ralph B. *Boulder Dam and the Great Southwest.* Los Angeles: Pacific Publishers, 1936.

Vivian, C. H. "Construction of the Hoover Dam." *Compressed Air Magazine*, XXXVII (December, 1932), 4010–4017.

[1] Mead-Walter, *Boulder Dam Today*, p. 6.
[2] "Boulder Dam Releases its Pent-up Forces at Last; Roosevelt Presses Electric Key and Valves Open," Memphis *Press Scimitar*, September 11, 1936, p. 2.

LETTERS

34. Business letters and formal social notes should follow carefully the forms prescribed by usage.[1]

34a. Give due attention to each of the six parts of a business letter:

(1) The heading.
(2) The inside address.
(3) The salutation (or greeting).
(4) The body of the letter.
(5) The complimentary close.
(6) The signature.

Business letters are preferably typewritten on one side only of sheets $8\frac{1}{2}$ by 11 inches in size. These sheets are folded either (1) once horizontally and twice in the other direction to fit the regular commercial envelope about $3\frac{1}{2}$ by $6\frac{1}{2}$ inches in size or (2) twice horizontally to fit the official envelope about 4 by 10 inches in size.

Personal letters and social notes are commonly

[1] Personal and informal social notes (more common than formal social notes) allow greater freedom. The inside address is usually omitted.

written by hand on note paper — a four-page sheet to be folded once horizontally for insertion in an envelope specially prepared to match. Both sides of the sheets may be used.

Personal letters vary greatly with the occasion and the personality of the writer. Business letters and formal social notes are more definitely limited by usage.

Model Business Letter

24 Main Street Selma, Alabama March 30, 1941	*Heading*
The Texas Company Road Map Division 135 East 42nd Street New York, New York	*Inside address*
Gentlemen:	*Salutation*
From the Melrose Service Station, where I am a regular purchaser of Texaco gasoline, I have learned that you give road information at your New York office.	
Please map out for me the easiest route from Selma to Boston. On past trips I have followed Route 11 as far as Winchester, Virginia, and I suppose that route is still the best if there are not too many detours. For the best roads from Winchester to Boston, however, I am in particular need of your suggestions, and I shall greatly appreciate any help you can give me.	*Body*
Yours truly,	*Complimentary close*
James B. Hall	*Signature*
James B. Hall	

Model Addressed Envelope

```
James B. Hall
24 Main Street
Selma, Alabama
```

```
                              The Texas Company
                              Road Map Division
                              135 East 42nd Street
                              New York, New York
```

(1) **The heading must give the full address of the writer
and the date of the letter.**

The heading is usually blocked as in the model, but
it may be indented and either punctuated at the end or
left open.

BLOCKED   24 Main Street   [Open punctuation is
          Selma, Alabama   regularly used with
          March 30, 1941   the blocked heading.]

INDENTED 24 Main Street   [Without end-punctua-
             Selma, Alabama   tion.]
                March 30, 1941

INDENTED 24 Main Street,   [With end-punctua-
             Selma, Alabama,   tion.]
                March 30, 1941.

Any of these three forms may be used.   The important
thing is to be consistent — to adopt one form and to
use it throughout the heading, the inside address, and
the outside address.

If there is a letterhead (which supplies the address), the date may be written either under the letterhead or flush with the right-hand margin.

(2) **The inside address (identical with the address to appear on the envelope) must give the name and the full address of the person to whom the letter is written.**

The inside address must be consistent with the heading. That is, it must be (1) blocked, or (2) indented without end-punctuation, or (3) indented with end-punctuation in accordance with the form adopted for the heading.

(3) **The salutation (or greeting) should be consistent with the tone of the letter and the complimentary close.**

The salutation is written flush with the left-hand margin two or three spaces below the inside address and is followed by a colon. The following salutations are used:

Dear Sir:
Dear Madam:
Gentlemen: (*or* Dear Sirs:)
Mesdames: (*or* Ladies:)
My dear Sir: [More formal.]
My dear Madam: [More formal.]
Sir: [Most formal; seldom used.]
Madam: [Most formal; seldom used.]

Dear Mr. Jones:
My dear Mr. Jones: [More formal.]
Dear Mrs. Jones:
Dear Dr. Smith:
Dear Major White:
My dear Major White: [More formal.]

In salutations *Mr.*, *Mrs.*, and *Dr.* are the only abbreviations permissible.

(4) The body of the letter should follow the principles of good writing.

Typewritten business letters are usually single-spaced, with double spacing between paragraphs. All paragraphs (1) should be indented equally or (2) should begin flush with the left-hand margin (as in the model). The subject matter should be well organized and paragraphed, but the paragraphs are frequently shorter than in ordinary writing. The style should be clear and direct. Indirect, abbreviated, or overused phrases should be avoided.

INDIRECT	Your kind favor . . . Your esteemed favor . . .
BETTER	Your letter . . .
INDIRECT	I beg to inform you that we have . . . I beg to send . . . Permit us to report that we now supply . . . I wish to apply . . .
BETTER	We have . . . I send . . . We now supply . . . I apply . . .
ABBREVIATED	Yours of the 5th instant . . . Hope to have . . . Enclose check for six dollars.
BETTER	Your letter of May 5 . . . We hope to have . . . I enclose a check for six dollars.
OVERUSED	Hoping to receive . . . Wishing you success . . . Trusting you will be pleased . . . [The participial close.]
BETTER	We hope to receive . . . We wish you success . . . I trust you will be pleased . . .

(5) The complimentary close should be consistent with the tone of the letter and the salutation.

Ordinary business letters beginning with the usual *Dear Sir*, etc., should close with *Yours truly, Yours very*

truly, or *Very truly yours*. A letter introduced by the
formal *Sir* should close with *Yours respectfully*, *Respectfully yours*, or *Very respectfully yours*. Professional letters,
or business letters addressed to acquaintances with such
an opening as *Dear Mr. White*, may well close with the
more friendly *Yours sincerely*, *Sincerely yours*, *Faithfully
yours*, or *Cordially yours*.

(6) The signature should be written by hand directly below the complimentary close.

If the name does not appear in the letterhead, it may
be typed just below the signature. Neither professional
titles nor degrees should be used with the signature, but
the writer's official capacity may be indicated:

WRONG James M. Smith, LL.D.
PERMISSIBLE James M. Smith
President

A married woman or a widow should sign her own
name (*Mary Hughes Black*, not *Mrs. John K. Black*) and
place *Mrs.* in parentheses before it.

CORRECT (Mrs.) Mary Hughes Black
ALSO CORRECT Mary Hughes Black
(Mrs. John K. Black)

EXERCISES ON BUSINESS LETTERS

A. Write to the circulation manager of *Time*, 330 East
22nd Street, Chicago, Illinois, asking him to enter your
subscription to the magazine.

B. Write another letter to the circulation manager of *Time*,
asking to have your address changed for the period of your
summer vacation.

C. Write a letter to Mr. Robert Brown, manager of the Riverside Tennis Club, 346 Elm Street, St. Louis, Missouri, asking permission to use the tennis courts for an exhibition game.

D. Write to some hotel in another city to reserve a room.

34b. Formal social notes should follow definite conventions.

Formal notes are always written in the third person. They have no heading, no inside address, no salutation, no complimentary close, and no signature. Every word (except the street number and the abbreviations *Mr.*, *Mrs.*, and *Dr.*) is spelled out in full. Acceptances and regrets follow the form of the invitation closely, repeating the hour and date to insure understanding. The verb used in the reply is always in the present tense.

Model Formal Invitation

Mr. and Mrs. James Wilson request the pleasure of Mr. William Brown's company at dinner on Monday, June tenth, at seven o'clock.
1241 Elm Street
June third

Model Formal Acceptance

Mr. William Brown accepts with pleasure the kind invitation of Mr. and Mrs. James Wilson to dinner on Monday, June tenth, at seven o'clock.
9 Maple View
June fourth

Model Formal Regret

Mr. William Brown regrets that, because of illness, he is unable to accept Mr. and Mrs. James Wilson's kind invitation to dinner on Monday, June tenth, at seven o'clock.

9 Maple View
June fourth

EXERCISE ON FORMAL NOTES

Write a formal note of invitation to a dinner. Then write an appropriate acceptance and an appropriate regret.

INDEX

Numbers in **boldface** refer to rules; other numbers refer to pages. An *ex* indicates that appropriate drill exercises are included.

405

INDEX

INDEX

testing the value of, 380; titles of, italicized, **10a:** 117, 118

Borrowed phrases, in quotation marks, **16d:** 163

Both . . . and, parallel structure with, **26c:** 287

Brackets, **17g:** 174, 175 *ex;* not to be used for deletions, 106

Breaking words into syllables at the ends of lines, **8c:** 104

Broad reference (antecedent not expressed), **28c:** 294, 295

Bunch, for *group*, **19:** 209

Bursted, bust, busted, for *burst*, **19:** 209

Business letters, **34a:** 397–403 *ex;* body, 401; close, 401, 402; heading, 399, 400; inside address, 400; model addressed envelope, 399; model letter, 398; salutation, 400; signature, 402

But, only, hardly, scarcely, misused with negative, **19:** 209

But what, but that, for *what, that*, **19:** 209

But which construction, **24d:** 274, 275 *ex*

Cacophony, **20d:** 246 *ex*

Calculate, for *think*, **19:** 210

Call number, 360

Can, distinguished from *may*, **19:** 210

Canceling or inserting words, 106

Cannot help but, for *cannot help*, **19:** 210

Can't hardly, double negative, **19:** 210

Can't seem to, illogical, **19:** 210

Capacity, ability, **19:** 204

Capitals, **9:** 110–116 *ex;* after the colon, 171; common-noun elements of proper names, 112; days of the week, months, special days, 110; deity, words pertaining to, 111; family relationships, 112; first word of a line of poetry, a sentence, or a quotation, **9e:** 113, 114; historical periods, events, documents, 111; important words in titles of books, **9c:** 113; in abbreviations, 111; organizations of all kinds, 110; personifications, 111; pronoun *I* and interjection *O*, 113; proper names, **9a:** 110, 111 *ex;* races and languages, 110; specific persons or places, 110; titles preceding a name, **9b:** 112, 113 *ex;* unnecessary capitals, **9b:** 114 *ex*

Card catalogue, **33a:** 358–366 *ex;* order of cards, 362–364; types of cards, 359–362

Case, **5:** 72–80 *ex;* defined, 3, 72; diagrams to test case, 72, 74, 76, 78, 79; following *than*, or *as*, **5a:** 74; in a prepositional phrase, **5f:** 77–79 *ex;* in an appositive, 72; nominative, 73, 74; objective, 77–79; possessive, 75–77; predicate nominative, **5b:** 74; subject of clause used as object, **5a:** 74; *who* or *whom*, 74, 77–79; with infinitives, **5g:** 79

Cause, inaccurate statement of, **19:** 210

Cause of, in incomplete statements, **19:** 210

Caused by or *due to*, **19:** 214

Central idea, stated at head of outline, 147, 151

Change in construction, **23d:** 267 *ex*

Change in mood, **27a:** 289

Change in number or person, **27c:** 290

Change in subject or voice, **27b:** 289, 290

Change in tense, **7d:** 96, **27a:** 289

Changing final *y* to *i*, **18:** 183, 184 *ex*

Choppy sentences: causing lack of subordination, **24a:** 271, 272 *ex;* causing wordiness, **21c:** 254, 255

407

INDEX

143 *ex;* parenthetical expressions, 12d: 139–141 *ex;* parts that might be erroneously read together, 12e: 143; superfluous, 13: 147–150 *ex;* vocatives, 12d: 139–141 *ex*

Common, mutual, 19: 211

Common noun, defined, 13

Company, for *guests,* 19: 211

Compare to, compare with, 19: 211

Comparison of adjectives and adverbs, 4d: 69; defined, 4, 11

Comparison or contrast, as a method of developing a paragraph, 327–329

Comparisons to be completed logically, 23c: 266, 267 *ex*

Complected, for *complexioned,* 19: 211

Complement, defined, 4, 5

Complimentary close: in business letters, 401, 402; omitted in formal social notes, 403

Compound numbers, hyphen in, 18c: 186

Compound predicate: skillfully used, for variety, 30c: 308; wrongly detached, 2d: 26, 27 *ex*

Compound sentence: commas with, 12a: 129–131 *ex;* defined and diagrammed, 18, 19; variety in, 30c: 308, 309

Compound words: hyphen in, 18c: 185, 186; possessive of, 158

Compound-complex sentence, defined and diagrammed, 19

Concession, subjunctive of, 99

Conciseness, 21: 252–258 *ex*

"Conclusion," to be avoided in an outline, 32i: 357

Concrete noun, defined, 14

Concreteness, 20a: 238, 239 *ex*

Condition contrary to fact, subjunctive with, 7e: 98

Conjectural statement, indicated by question mark in parenthesis, 168

Conjugation: defined, 5, 11; conjugation of the verb *to do,* 5, 6

Conjunctions: co-ordinating, 7; correlatives, parallel structure with, 26c: 287; defined, 6, 7, 46; diagrammed, 47 *ex;* listed, 40; omission of, 22b: 259, 260; selection for exact meaning, 20a: 239, 240 *ex;* subordinating, 7

Conjunctive adverbs: defined, 7; distinguished from pure conjunctions, 152, 153; semicolon between clauses joined by, 3c: 61, 14a: 152, 153

Connectives, repeated for clearness, 286

Connotation, 20e: 248, 249 *ex*

Considerable, misused as noun or adverb, 19: 211

Consonants, final (in spelling), 182

Construction: confused or incomplete, 23d: 267 *ex;* defined 7; parallel, 26: 284–288 *ex;* split, 25e: 279; "squinting," 25d: 278

Contact, as a verb, 19: 211

Continual, continuous, 19: 211

Contractions: apostrophe with, 15c: 159; avoided in formal writing, 19f: 203; when proper, 19: 212

Contract from, faulty idiom, 19: 212

Contrary, contrariness, for *stubborn, stubbornness,* 19: 212

Co-ordinate, defined, 7

Co-ordinating conjunction, 7, 40

Co-ordination, 24: 269–275 *ex;* diagram to test, 270; excessive, because of *and* sentences, 24b: 272, 273 *ex;* excessive, because of choppy sentences, 24a: 271, 272 *ex;* false (*and* or *but* joining main and subordinate clauses), 24d: 274, 275 *ex*

Copula, defined, 7

Correction of proof, 8f: 109

Correction of written work, 8e: 106–108

Correlatives, in parallel structure, 26c: 287

INDEX

INDEX

INDEX

413

INDEX

INDEX

INDEX

Note taking, 379–384 *ex*

Notorious, for *noted*, **19**: 224

Noun clause, defined, 14

Nouns: agreement of, **6**: 81–91 *ex;* case of, **5**: 72–80 *ex;* collective, number of, **6a**: 87; compound, hyphen in, **18c**: 185, 186; defined, 13, 14, 40; diagrammed, 41, 42; misused as adjectives, **4e**: 70; plurals of, **18b**: 184, 185 *ex;* proper, capitals for, **9a**: 110, 111 *ex;* uses in general, 13, 40–43 *ex*

Nowhere near, for *not nearly*, **19**: 224

Nowheres, for *nowhere*, **19**: 224

Number: after *there is*, *there are*, **6a**: 84, 85 *ex;* defined, 14; of collective nouns, **6a**: 87; of *each*, *every*, etc., **6a**: 86; of pronouns referring to antecedents, **6b**: 88–91 *ex;* of verbs in agreement with subject, **6a**: 82–88 *ex;* shift in, **27c**: 290; subjects joined by *and*, **6a**: 83, 84 *ex;* subjects joined by *or* or *nor*, **6a**: 83, 84 *ex*

Numbers, **11**: 124–127 *ex;* at the beginning of a sentence, 125; consistency in use of, 125; formation of plural, 159; hyphen in compounds, **18c**: 186; in dates, street numbers, decimals, etc., 125; repetition in parentheses, 124; when to use figures, 125; when to write out, **11f**: 124–126 *ex*

O, *oh*, **19**: 224

O.K., in formal English, **19**: 224

Object, defined and illustrated, 14, 15

Object of a prepositon, defined, 15

Objective case, 77–79 *ex;* in prepositional phrases, **5f**: 77–79 *ex;* with infinitives, **5g**: 79

Objective complement, defined, 5

Obligation, expressed by *should*, **7f**: 101

Obsolete words, **18d**: 202, 203

Off of, redundant, **19**: 224

Oh, *O*, **19**: 224

Omissions, **22**: 259–262; article, conjunction, or preposition, **22b**: 259, 260; double capacity, **22c**: 260, 261; from quotation, indicated by dots, 167; sheer carelessness, **22a**: 259; *so*, *such*, *too*, without completing clauses, **22d**: 261

On, redundant use of, **19**: 224

Only, *alone*, **19**: 206

Only, *but*, etc., not used with negative, **19**: 209

Only, position of, 224, **25b**: 277, 278 *ex*

Or, *nor*, as correlatives, **19**: 225

Order in the paragraph, for coherence, 315, 316

Order in the sentence, for emphasis, **29a**: 298, 299 *ex;* **29f**: 302, 303

Organizing the theme, 343 ff.

Other times, for *at other times*, **19**: 225

Ought to of, for *ought to have*, **19**: 225

Out, redundant use of, **19**: 225

Out loud, for *aloud*, etc., **19**: 225

Outlines, 343–357 *ex;* central idea stated, 347, 351; fullness, **32f**: 354, 355; gradual development of, **32c**: 350, 351 *ex;* logical order, **32g**: 355, 356; notation and indention, **32d**: 351–353; parallel structure, **32e**: 353, 354; single subheads to be avoided, **32h**: 357

Outlines, types of, **32b**: 343–350; complete sentence, 347, 348; paragraph, 349, 350; topical, 348, 349

Outside address, of a letter, 399

Outside of, for *outside*, **19**: 225

Over with, for *over*, **19**: 225

Overfrequent paragraphing, 323, 324

Overlapping topics in outline, 356

Overloaded sentence, **23b**: 264, 265 *ex*

417

INDEX

INDEX

INDEX

gr	1=grt	2=frag	3=cs	4=ad
	Grammatical Terms	Fragment	Comma Splice	Adjectives & Adverbs
GRAMMAR	5=ca	6=agr		7=t
	Case	Agreement		Tense
		a-Sub. & Verb	*b*-Pron. & Ant.	Mood, Shall & Will
m	8=ms	9=cap	10=ital	11=ab
MECHANICS	Manuscript Form & Revision	Capitals	Italics	Abbreviations & Numbers
p	12=,/	13=O	14=;/	15=ap
	Comma	Superfluous Commas	Semicolon	Apostrophe
PUNCTUATION	16=",/	17= ./ ?/ !/ :/ -/ ()/ ()/		
	Quotation Marks	Period and Other Marks		
sp	18=sp			
SPELLING	Spelling			
	a-By Observation	*b*-By Rules	*c*-Hyphenated Words	*d*-Spelling List
d	19=g	20=e	21=w	22=∧
DICTION	Good Use Glossary	Exactness	Wordiness	Omission of Words
ef	23=u	24=sub	25=coh	26=//
EFFECTIVENESS	Unity and Logical Thinking	Subordination *a*-Choppy Sentences *b*-And Sentences	Coherence in general	Parallelism
IN THE SENTENCE	27=pv	28=ref	29=emp	30=var
	Point of View	Reference of Pronouns	Emphasis	Variety

	31=¶		32=plan	
LARGER	Paragraph		Planning the Whole Composition	
	a-Unity	*b*-Coherence	*c*-Fullness	
ELEMENTS	33=lib		34=let	
	Library & Term Paper		Letters	